D0458901

PRAISE FOR *GENERATION IMPACT*

"*Generation Impact* profiles a new generation of philanthropists and demonstrates how they could influence society more than any generation to come before them – making this a book relevant to readers from all walks of life."

Charles Best
Founder, DonorsChoose.org

"Anyone who participates in philanthropy – whether as supporter or recipient – needs to understand the profound changes that are being led by a new generation of donors. The fascinating first-person essays in this book, along with the keen analysis and commentary by authors with deep personal experience in the field, offer new and important insights into the minds of the young donors who will help shape philanthropy's future."

Mark Kramer
Founder and Managing Director, FSG
Visiting Lecturer, Harvard Business School

"This book makes me feel good knowing the rising generation is poised to fix all the things. Yay, young people!"

Nancy Lublin
CEO, Crisis Text Line
Former CEO, DoSomething.org
Founder, Dress for Success

"*Generation Impact: How Next Gen Donors are Revolutionizing Giving*, by Sharna Goldseker and Michael Moody, shines a powerful, inspiring spotlight on today's most significant and promising characteristic of American philanthropy—the energy, innovation, and determined quest for impact of Gen X and Millennial donors. This beautifully-written, long overdue book is peopled with an engaging array of young women and men, often speaking in their own names and voices, who are already doing great good for society and who, if history is any guide, are likely to lead America's philanthropic sector to its most impressive impact-achievement ever! This book is guaranteed to send soaring the spirits of anyone who cares about the present and future of America's civic sector today."

Joel L. Fleishman
Author, The Foundation: A Great American Secret—How Private
Wealth is Changing the World
Professor of Law and Public Policy, Duke University

"Goldseker and Moody pull the curtain back from the broad terms of "Next Gen" and "Millennial" to help us see the real personalities and lives of those who are using their wealth to change the world. While previous generations and mainstream finance think in "either/or" frameworks of making money or giving grants, these new century fiduciaries operate within an understanding of blended value and seek to structure their capital to generate various levels of financial return with social and environmental impact. *Generation Impact* profiles a diverse set of actors seeking their own paths to being responsible asset owners in support of our world's most promising changemakers."

Jed Emerson
Founder, Blended Value Group

"With great abundance comes great responsibility. In Sharna and Michael's stunningly important book we have a deep and learned look into how (with "engagement") and why ("to achieve impact") Gen Xers and Millennials are becoming today's philanthropists. Give yourself the gift of knowing what to expect as you engage with emerging philanthropists from these cohorts. Join these authors as they bring to life the motivations, actions, and philosophies of giving of these remarkable, dedicated philanthropists who expect to help solve the social, economic, political, and cultural issues of the past and present, and who want to lead us toward a magnificent future for our planet and its peoples. I am sure that many of my silent generation cohort will love learning about the feeling of engagement and passion for impact among these young philanthropists."

James (Jay) E. Hughes, Jr.
Author, Family Wealth: Keeping it in the Family, Family and The Compact Among Generations
Co-author, The Cycle of the Gift, The Voice of the Rising Generation, and Family Trusts

"*Generation Impact* is a thoughtful, astute exploration that shows how new and established families can engage with the next generation to regenerate family philanthropy, deepening their legacy and broadening their impact."

Melissa A. Berman
President, Rockefeller Philanthropy Advisors

"This is awesome! A must read. The authors Goldseker and Moody have given voice to a generation of philanthropists who are already beginning to change the face of giving. However, they do much more – they give us access to how this generation thinks about the world, their place in it, and how to create social change. These young people are creating a revolution and the authors – in a cogent and thoughtful manner – enlighten all of us, families and their advisors, about how to further the positive force of their efforts."

Fredda Herz Brown
Founder and Senior Consultant, Relative Solutions
Founding Board Member, Family Firm Institute
Co-author, The Family Wealth Sustainability Toolkit

"Michael and Sharna are <u>the</u> premier leaders on next gen philanthropy. They eloquently demonstrate the stories and strategies to leverage impact, educating readers on the unique value of next gen donors – today and tomorrow."

Emily Davis
Author, Fundraising and the Next Generation

"The new book by Sharna Goldseker and Michael Moody won't be a classic someday. It is. Now. Their book is all about now and giving and this generation that, right before our very eyes, emerged from being the "next generation" to what Goldseker and Moody reveal is the "now generation"—that generation with the intellectual, human, and financial capital needed to tackle the massive challenges confronting the planet, the country, and their own backyards. The Goldseker/Moody approach to telling the stories of these givers and this new age of giving is fresh and creative: at once inspirational and how to, heartening, and instructive. For families, emerging philanthropists, and old pros trying to disrupt themselves, this book is a lantern in dark times, a light in the world we are all trying to fathom – and fix."

Joline Godfrey
Author, Raising Financially Fit Kids

"There is a new generation of donors and the time to get to know them is today! Goldseker and Moody show us how to tap into their philanthropic minds as they transform the world of giving. Filled with fascinating first-person stories as well as insights from years of research, this will be a book you pull off the shelf again and again so you can make the most of the coming philanthropic revolution."

David Stillman
Co-author, Gen Z @ Work

"Goldseker and Moody's research makes it clear that the Millennial Generation of philanthropists prioritizes impact as a core value. Drawing on the extraordinary voices of this rising cohort of donors, *Generation Impact* speaks of their growing emphasis on seeing results, in measurable ways, with the broadest and most sustainable benefit. Carried along by compelling narratives more than dry research data, the reader comes away impressed with how much the current generation is striving to honor the past while energetically adapting philanthropy for the future. *Generation Impact* is a remarkable book that, like its subjects, renews optimism for the world ahead."

James Grubman, PhD
Family Wealth Consultant and Author, Strangers in Paradise: How
Families Adapt to Wealth Across Generations

"Sharna Goldseker has been the articulate voice of an inter-generational, reflective approach to philanthropy for decades. In this collaboration with Michael Moody, her experiential empathy is augmented with solid social science. Their inspired decision to let this cohort of emerging societal engineers speak "in their own words" has created a window into a history-changing phenomenon. The book reads like a great coming-of-age novel but carries the impact of a research classic – altogether a major step forward in our understanding of philanthropy, past, present, and future."

Kelin Gersick
Founding Partner, Lansberg, Gersick and Associates
Author, Generations of Giving: Leadership and Continuity in
Family Foundations
Clinical Instructor in Psychology, Yale School of Medicine

"By sharing firsthand stories of inspiring next gen donors and how they embarked on their philanthropic journeys, Goldseker and Moody provide a fascinating roadmap for how others might leverage their resources to change the world."

Coventry Edwards-Pitt
Chief Wealth Advisory Officer, Ballentine Partners, LLC
Author, Raised Healthy, Wealthy & Wise

"If you are looking for a primer on how the next generation of major donors will affect your organization, read Goldseker and Moody's *Generation Impact*. This is the source for understanding how wealthy millennials are reshaping philanthropy."

Derrick Feldmann
President, Achieve
Lead Researcher, The Millennial Impact Project

"*Generation Impact* is a masterful compendium of stories, interviews, and survey data that informs us all about the who, the how, and the why of next generation philanthropy. It is an important reference for multigenerational families and their advisors as they address the "now generation" of donors and their unique "tool boxes" of strategies. I particularly found the real life stories in their own words helpful to understand the alignment of the personal, professional, and philanthropic lives of Gen X-ers and Millennials. Sharna and Michael have written a well-documented and seminal book characterized by enthusiasm for the future of family philanthropy as seen through the lens of the next generations. At the same time, they honor the legacy of multigenerational family philanthropy."

Kathryn M. McCarthy
Independent Advisor to families and family offices
Director, Rockefeller Trust Company N.A.

"Even though the book looks at next-generation donors in the USA, most of the trends described in this overdue book can also be found in Europe and around the globe. There will always be cultural differences in giving but overall the book reflects the international perspective, the global connectedness that influences the actions of this next generation. The stories of this book will be a reference of identity for many."

Michael Alberg-Seberich
Managing Partner, Active Philanthropy
Managing Director, Beyond Philanthropy, Berlin

"*Generation Impact* shows how next gen donors tick, why and how they want to give, and keep giving. The next generation of major donors will change the world like no other philanthropists in history. That is a global movement. From New York to São Paolo, I can attest that Goldseker and Moody's snapshot of next gen donors is on point."

Daniela Nascimento Fainberg
Founder, Instituto Geração, Brazil
Global Philanthropist Circle Representative in Brazil, Synergos Institute
Family Philanthropy Advisor

GENERATION
IMPACT

GENERATION

IMPACT

HOW NEXT GEN
DONORS ARE
REVOLUTIONIZING
GIVING

SHARNA GOLDSEKER
MICHAEL MOODY

WILEY

Copyright © 2017 by Sharna Goldseker and Michael Moody. All rights reserved.

Published by John Wiley & Sons, Inc., Hoboken, New Jersey.

Published simultaneously in Canada.

No part of this publication may be reproduced, stored in a retrieval system, or transmitted in any form or by any means, electronic, mechanical, photocopying, recording, scanning, or otherwise, except as permitted under Section 107 or 108 of the 1976 United States Copyright Act, without either the prior written permission of the Publisher, or authorization through payment of the appropriate per-copy fee to the Copyright Clearance Center, 222 Rosewood Drive, Danvers, MA 01923, (978) 750-8400, fax (978) 646-8600, or on the Web at www.copyright.com. Requests to the Publisher for permission should be addressed to the Permissions Department, John Wiley & Sons, Inc., 111 River Street, Hoboken, NJ 07030, (201) 748-6011, fax (201) 748-6008, or online at www.wiley.com/go/permissions.

Limit of Liability/Disclaimer of Warranty: While the publisher and author have used their best efforts in preparing this book, they make no representations or warranties with the respect to the accuracy or completeness of the contents of this book and specifically disclaim any implied warranties of merchantability or fitness for a particular purpose. No warranty may be created or extended by sales representatives or written sales materials. The advice and strategies contained herein may not be suitable for your situation. You should consult with a professional where appropriate. Neither the publisher nor the author shall be liable for damages arising herefrom.

For general information about our other products and services, please contact our Customer Care Department within the United States at (800) 762-2974, outside the United States at (317) 572-3993 or fax (317) 572-4002.

Wiley publishes in a variety of print and electronic formats and by print-on-demand. Some material included with standard print versions of this book may not be included in e-books or in print-on-demand. If this book refers to media such as a CD or DVD that is not included in the version you purchased, you may download this material at http://booksupport.wiley.com. For more information about Wiley products, visit www.wiley.com.

Library of Congress Cataloging-in-Publication Data is Available:

9781119422815(Hardcover)
9781119422846(ePDF)
9781119422853(epub)

Cover Design: Kathy Davis/Wiley
Cover Image: ©Dimitri Otis/Getty Images

Printed in the United States of America

10 9 8 7 6 5 4

To Owen, Sasha, Logan, and Adrienne—the next "next gen"

CONTENTS

ACKNOWLEDGMENTS

First and foremost, thank you to the hundreds of next gen donors—the majority of whom are presented anonymously—who are at the heart of this book. A project like this goes nowhere without your willingness to open up to us, to reflect candidly on your hopes and fears, your dreams and difficulties. Thank you for trusting us. We hope we did you justice.

Special thanks to the 13 individuals who agreed to step out from behind the curtain and be featured in the book. Not only did you give so much of your time during the various stages of the writing and editing process, but you did so in a collaborative spirit. We hope this endeavor shines a spotlight on the issues you care about and encourages others to deploy the innovative strategies you have courageously offered. Thank you for being leaders of the next—and the now—generation.

Whether responding to the survey or sitting down for a long interview, the next gen donors profiled here took their integral role in this book seriously, like they are taking their outsized philanthropic responsibility and opportunity seriously. Candidly, many people asked us during our work on this project if these rising donors were really as earnest as we claimed. We think the evidence for this is clear as you read through the book. You will see their authentic generosity, sincerity, and even vulnerability in these pages, in what they say about themselves and their giving, and in their willingness to share with others. Both their hearts and minds are committed to helping solve problems that trouble us all.

An ambitious effort like this, taking significant time and energy over several years, requires resources, patience, and continual support from our core partners.

Sharna is grateful to Charles Bronfman, the late Andrea Bronfman, Jeffrey Solomon, and John Hoover from the Andrea and Charles Bronfman Philanthropies (which sunset in 2015) for their belief in her and their initial investment in 21/64, which inspired her work on this book. She also thanks the current board of 21/64, Inc., including John Hoover, Dorian Goldman, Marvin Israelow, Jennifer Grubman Rothenberg, and Gail Norry for their encouragement and support of her leadership, the team, and the organization's mission.

Michael thanks the supporters of his work as the Frey Foundation Chair for Family Philanthropy at the Dorothy A. Johnson Center for Philanthropy, especially the Frey Foundation and Grand Valley State University. The leadership of the center and the university took the long view and gave him both the space and the encouragement to see this project through. Special thanks to Dean George Grant, Kyle Caldwell, Paul Stansbie, and the late, great Jim Edwards.

We want to thank those early and committed funders whose support enabled the research, development, and production of this book, including Andrea and Charles Bronfman Philanthropies, Max M. and Marjorie S. Fisher Foundation, Shelley and Sheldon Goldseker, Tarsadia Foundation, Tecovas Foundation, and the

Youth Philanthropy Connect program of the Frieda C. Fox Family Foundation. Thank you to the Bill & Melinda Gates Foundation for allowing this new knowledge to be widely distributed to the philanthropic community and many other audiences, in the hopes that it can advance and expand effective multigenerational giving.

And thanks also to the funders of the original *Next Gen Donors* report and the *Next Gen Donors: The Future of Jewish Giving* report: Max M. and Marjorie S. Fisher Foundation, Joyce and Irving Goldman Family Foundation, Eugene and Agnes E. Meyer Foundation, Morningstar Foundation, and an anonymous donor.

The research phase and dissemination of the first report was enabled by a network of partner organizations across the country: Association of Small Foundations (now Exponent Philanthropy), Association of Baltimore Area Grantmakers, Bolder Giving (now part of the National Center for Responsive Philanthropy), Council on Foundations, Council of Michigan Foundations, Emerging Practitioners in Philanthropy, Forum of Regional Association of Grantmakers, Grand Street, GrantCraft, Indiana Grantmakers Alliance (now Indiana Philanthropy Alliance), Jewish Communal Fund, Jewish Funders Network, Jumpstart, Liberty Hill Foundation, The Minneapolis Foundation, National Center for Family Philanthropy, and Resource Generation.

Our deep gratitude to those close colleagues—past and present—in our organizations who supported this work over several years. To Danielle Oristian York, Barbara Taylor, Sara Finkelstein, Adina Schwartz, Erin Trottier, and Jos Thalheimer at 21/64; and to Tara Baker, Alicia Chiasson, Andrew Claucherty, Julie Couturier, Sherri Hall, Bev Harkema, Katie Kirouac, Allison Lugo Knapp, Pattijean McCahill, Heidi McPheeters, Mark Saint Amour, and Robert Shalett at the Johnson Center, we were privileged to have had you with us on this journey and thank you for your invaluable contributions along the way.

Thanks also to many other colleagues in this field whose experience, advice, and referrals played a role in the development of the book: Michael Balaoing, Rachel Bendit, Fredda Herz Brown, Chris Cardona, Leslie Crutchfield, Emily Davis, Adrienne DiCasparro, Coventry Edwards-Pitt, Derrick Feldmann, Jason Franklin, Ellie Frey, Mary Galeti, Joline Godfrey, Annie Hernandez, Andy Ho, Jay Hughes, Shawn Landres, Laura Lauder, Terri Mosqueda, Satya Patel, Ellen Perry, Ai-Jen Poo, Amy Rabbino, Nitika Raj, Ana Gloria Rivas-Vazquez, Roselma Samala, Katherine Scott, Paul Shoemaker, Doug Bitonti Stewart, David Stillman, Jennifer Stout, Urvashi Vaid, Jan Williams, Richard Woo, and Kim Wright.

This book was also made possible by a crack team of editors, designers, and other consultants. Our deepest gratitude to Heidi Toboni, who was a passionate and indispensable partner throughout the entire process—our best reader and savviest advisor. Huge thank you also to Lisa Zuniga, Laurie Fink, Karen Berry, Collette Shin, Peter Ruchti, Mark Fortier, and Mary Franklyn. Thanks also to Brian Neill, our editor at Wiley, for such enthusiasm about the project—and for putting up with all our quirky details.

Last but most significantly, special thanks from each of us individually.

From Sharna:

Since our initial discussion in Philadelphia's Reading Terminal in 2011, Michael, it's been a pleasure to collaborate. I look forward to our next project. Thanks Mom and Dad for instilling in me the spirit of giving and inviting me to the multigenerational philanthropy table. Simon, thank you for being the best husband and partner a next gen could want. And Owen and Sasha, you are my inspiration. I love you all.

From Michael:

Thanks to Sharna, for embracing this partnership in the best spirit I could have hoped for—with genuine goodwill, trust, and (alas) patience. Unending thanks to my family, who taught me from the time I could open my eyes that giving with an open heart *and* eyes is what good humans do, regardless of how much you have to give. And much love and thanks to my wife, Karen Zivi, for the encouragement, solace, and distraction whenever each was needed.

CHAPTER 1

Introduction: The Most Significant Philanthropists Ever

Justin Rockefeller grew up in West Virginia outside the purview of the family legacy of capitalism and philanthropy. Invited to a meeting at a café near Rockefeller Center in New York City as a college freshman, he actually had to ask where Rockefeller Center was. But during college, Justin began to appreciate the doors his last name could open and the opportunities he had to effect change for good. He has since worked to help one of his family's foundations divest its charitable endowment holdings of fossil fuels—a remarkable move for America's most famous oil family. Now in his 30s, Justin devotes a significant percentage of his time beyond his tech career to helping other families align their investments with their values.

Katherine Lorenz's grandfather, the late George Mitchell, became a noted Texas billionaire by pioneering the use of hydraulic fracturing to release natural gas from shale. But Katherine started her own career far away from the family business, creating and running an agricultural and nutrition nonprofit in rural Mexico. She eventually returned to take the reins of her family's foundation, guiding the family through a planning process to ramp up their support for environmental sustainability causes in Texas.

John R. Seydel grew up in Atlanta learning about giving from his parents and grandparents, in particular from his "Grandpa Ted" Turner, the media titan and founder of CNN who donated a billion dollars to create the U.N. Foundation. Together, they travel to tour the family's vast tracts of preserved open space in the American West and go on "learning journeys" to witness the impact of their international giving. Now a college graduate, John R. is determined to carve out his own identity as a donor and social entrepreneur. He knows he has big shoes to fill, and he wants to walk his own path in them.

—⟋⌃⟍

Most readers have likely never heard of Justin, Katherine, or John R. So why should it matter to us what they do or what they want for the future?

We should care because men and women like these three will shape our world in profound ways.

America's next generation of major donors, whether young Gen Xers or rising Millennials, will have an outsized impact on society and the planet we share, as people like Andrew Carnegie and John D. Rockefeller did in years past and as people like Bill and Melinda Gates and Warren Buffett are doing now—likely even more impact. Men and women we call "next gen donors"—inheritors like Justin, Katherine, and John R. as well as those from their generation who are earning their own wealth—will decide which diseases get the most research funding, which environmental organizations launch the biggest awareness campaigns, which new ideas for education reform are incubated around the country. And those decisions will impact, directly and daily, our health, our communities, our economies, our culture, and even our climate.

In fact, if current trends in wealth and giving continue, these rising major donors will be the most significant philanthropists ever. They not only have unprecedented financial resources but also big plans for how to wield their financial power. Simply put, they want to change giving in ways that will fundamentally transform philanthropy. And they want to do so *now* rather than wait until they accumulate all the wealth they can and then retire to a life of philanthropic leisure.

We need to get to know these next gen donors—find out what they're about and figure out how to engage them—so we can know what to expect from their emerging philanthropic revolution. More important, we need to make sure their historic potential is channeled in ways that make our world better, not worse. In this book, you'll meet these young men and women and learn about their ambitious plans to irrevocably alter the nonprofit organizations and social causes we care about. You'll hear them struggle to "find themselves" as philanthropists; you'll hear them make their case for a bigger role as rising leaders who simultaneously want to revolutionize the future while respecting the past.

Big Donors, Big Impact

Like most readers of this book, you probably have an idea of what a "philanthropist" looks like. You might assume philanthropists are wealthy older people who attend fancy galas. They give money and serve on boards, rarely rolling up their sleeves and pitching in to help when and where it's needed most. And while it's nice that they give away money, it mostly goes to causes that matter to wealthy older people like them. Their giving doesn't really make a difference to the problems *you* see every day in your community or the issues *you* are passionate about. Unless you visit a museum on your fifth-grader's field trip or find yourself in a fancy wing of a big hospital, how philanthropists give doesn't really affect your daily life that much.

But this portrait of a philanthropist is way off, especially in terms of describing the next gen donors we will introduce you to in this book.

Major donors affect your life more than you might know—maybe even more than you might find comfortable.

Ever been cared for by a nurse? Received a scholarship? Used a library? Consumed pasteurized milk? Then you've benefited directly from the decisions by major funders to support causes such as modern medical training, the arts, and public health. If you get your news from National Public Radio or allow *Sesame Street* to entertain and educate your preschooler, or if you're a woman who's had a Pap smear test, then your life is affected in a direct way by the actions of major donors. All of those innovations were driven primarily by philanthropic—rather than market or government—investments.

Many good things we take for granted are due in large part to wealthy donors giving big donations—things like community centers and local parks; beautiful churches, synagogues, and mosques; a world-class higher education system; and even the ideas for a 911 emergency system and white lines on the sides of highways. The same can be said for the eradication of many bad things we no longer have to worry about (at least in the United States), like sewage in the streets, children working in factories, and diseases like polio and yellow fever.

Philanthropists were primary funders behind the development of modern mental health treatment, hospice care, and autism treatments. They helped create many of our institutions serving widows, orphans, and people with disabilities. Medical breakthroughs such as the use of insulin to treat diabetes and antiretroviral drugs to treat HIV were made possible by donors with singular dedications to those issues. And of course, outside the United States, philanthropic giving by large donors, from the Rockefellers to the Gateses, has literally saved millions of lives, whether through the eradication of hookworm, the fight against tuberculosis, or the availability of antimalarial bed nets.

But as the history of international giving shows, how—and how much—major donors affect our lives can sometimes be controversial. While most of us are happy that big donors in the past were behind nascent social movements such as the abolition of slavery, suffrage, and civil rights, other movements funded by philanthropists divide us just as they divide the donors themselves. For instance, major donors are backing both sides of the marriage equality and the charter school debates, both the prochoice and prolife movements, and both the founding of the state of Israel and the Palestinian desire for a homeland.[1]

Still think your life isn't fundamentally different because of the choices that major donors make?

—☙

While they have a complicated and sometimes disputed legacy, the impact of philanthropic giants like Andrew Carnegie and Henry Ford on American life is undeniable. They created enduring institutions like hospitals, universities, museums, libraries, and the modern philanthropic foundation. Philanthropy today is based largely on the ideas and innovations of these corporate lions. They set the norms and shaped our collective image for how major donors give. Yet there are many others who fit into this category of "big donors" and who often had tremendous philanthropic influence but whose names and stories are not as well known. They, too, have affected our lives, but in often underappreciated ways.[2]

This pattern continues with major philanthropists today. Many people know of the work of big donors with famous last names like Buffett, Hewlett, Packard, Bloomberg, and Walton. And you most likely have heard of a few members of the emerging class of Gen X and Millennial megadonors, people like tech billionaire Sean Parker, who practices what he calls "hacker philanthropy."[3] But what do we know of the less famous next gen donors who have significant resources to give, who will be tremendously important to all of our lives? What about the donors in your hometown—some of whom might just be in their 20s or 30s—who write big checks to your community theater or that women's shelter you pass on your way to work?

As the influence and power of major donors—well-known or anonymous—expands, this lack of awareness becomes even more problematic. Those at the top of the donor pyramid have more and more wealth to give, and donors of the next generation—both young inheritors and earners of major wealth—are increasingly taking their place at that apex of giving, so our need to know about them is urgent and growing. Our current global and domestic political tumult only increases this need to decipher and then help inform the plans of the most powerful and generously resourced elites. In times of uncertainty, major donors can step into the fray and shape our lives and futures in even more profound ways.

Profiles of a few celebrated individuals won't suffice. We need to understand the collective mindset and plans of the donors of this generation, even if we don't yet know which of these donors will be the Carnegies and Gateses of the future.

The impact of the next group of big donors will eclipse even the giants who've come before them, in part because they are not content to just step passively into their predecessors' shoes; they want to forge bold new paths in those shoes—muck them up and wear them thin. If the philanthropists of the fabled Gilded Age of the early 1900s set the norms for our current giving, the donors of a Golden Age of Giving that is now dawning want to change those norms. They want even greater impact.

The New Golden Age of Giving

We are entering what prominent philanthropic observers are starting to call a Golden Age of Giving, a new era that will exceed in size and influence the Gilded Age of a century ago, when modern philanthropy was invented.[4] Like that previous period, this one is driven both by the bold, entrepreneurial ideas of big donors and by the sheer volume of resources they have to give.

We live in a time of incredible and rapidly soaring wealth concentration. We've all seen the numbers. The wealthiest 10 percent of Americans own 75 percent of all the wealth, while the wealthiest 1 percent own an astonishing 43 percent.[5] This discrepancy gets even more dramatic as you go up the scale. Advocacy groups like Oxfam and Institute for Policy Studies depict this wealth inequality in stark terms: The 20 richest billionaires own more wealth than the bottom half of Americans combined (about 152 million people), and the richest eight individuals in the world own more than the poorest half of the world's population (about 3.7 billion people).[6] The comparison is hard to wrap your head around: 8 versus 3,700,000,000—each with the same total wealth.

And this concentration is growing at a remarkable rate. From 1978 to 2012, the share of wealth owned by the richest 0.1 percent of families in the United States jumped from 7 percent to 22 percent.[7] Between 1978 and 2014, according to the Economic Policy Institute, CEO pay in the United States increased by almost 1,000 percent, while pay for the average worker went up only 11 percent.[8] Data from the annual *Forbes* lists shows that in 1987 there were 41 billionaires in the United States; 30 years later, in 2016, there were 540.[9]

So will this current era of extraordinary wealth creation and concentration also be an era of extraordinary amounts of giving? Research has shown that nearly every high-net-worth household (91 percent) reported some giving to charity, and that American families with $1 million or more in net worth account for 50 percent of the total amount of charitable contributions, even though they are only 7 percent of the total population.[10] Even if the giving rate stays the same for the wealthiest individuals, the sheer amount they will give will climb. How these big donors give will make a big difference.

Furthermore, as more wealth is held by fewer families, this wealth is being transferred across generations *within* those families. In fact, we are living in the midst of the greatest transfer of concentrated wealth in human history. A 2014 study by the Boston College Center on Wealth and Philanthropy estimated that just over $59 trillion will be transferred across generations between 2007 and 2061.[11] Not $59 billion—*$59 trillion*. Most of this wealth transfer is happening within a relatively small group of high-net-worth families. The study estimates that 20 percent of affluent families will account for approximately 88 percent of the wealth transfer.

This remarkable amount of wealth passing between generations also means a remarkable amount of money available for charitable giving. The Boston College study, considering both normal giving rates and the amount of transferred money earmarked for charitable purposes, estimates that during these same 55 years, almost $27 trillion will be designated for charity, either at some point during the wealth-holders' lifetimes or as bequests from their estates. Of course, if heirs decide to give more of their inherited family assets to charity, this philanthropic largesse will expand even further. Many of the next generation inheritors discussed in this book will be the active stewards of enormous assets for decades to come. Some have already taken on this role with verve.

At the same time, others in the next gen are busy making their own wealth, often in staggering amounts. Techies, hedge-funders, and other young entrepreneurs are becoming part of the 1 percent—or even the 0.1 percent—that owns a bigger and bigger slice of the pie.

In short, with these two socioeconomic dynamics converging, Gen X and Millennial philanthropists have access to dramatically greater resources than any previous generation. And more money means more potential for giving.

But we are entering a new Golden Age of Giving not just because donors will have more money to give. Even more significant is the fact that next gen donors want to revolutionize philanthropy to make it more effective. These leaders of the new Golden Age want nothing less than an Impact Revolution.

The Coming Impact Revolution

Next generation members of wealthy families, as well as our modern *nouveau riche*, are sometimes criticized for playing in the charity space merely because it is an expected accoutrement of privilege and status. Having a family foundation becomes de rigueur. Of course, this will be true for some of the next generation of prominent donors. But as the research in this book shows, we find that the next gen donors in the vanguard of philanthropic change don't conform to this image. In fact, they hate it. They certainly encounter peers who are just in it for the photo on the society page, but they emphatically scorn those kinds of donors.

And it is these active, earnest major donors who are emerging as the trailblazers of the next gen, setting the path for their generation's style of giving. What's different about them? They dislike the showy donor appreciation walls and fancy galas. They would much rather be out in the field contributing to programs that really work or trying out some experimental idea that has the potential to go to scale. They want to give for tangible results or not at all. What they have in mind for their era of giving is nothing short of revolutionary change.

Next gen donors are *so* focused on changing philanthropy to increase impact that we believe they are on the leading edge of what will become an Impact Revolution in philanthropy. They are eager to change whatever needs to change—even if that makes other donors, nonprofits, or anyone else uncomfortable—if doing so will help move the needle in a significant way on the problems philanthropy is trying to address. And they want to revolutionize philanthropy *now*, while in their 20s and 30s, rather than wait until their mature years. They want impact to be their generation's defining feature.

―⁓―

So how will big giving change during Generation Impact's evolution? These rising donors want to disrupt giving strategies, much like young tech entrepreneurs have disrupted business. They prefer to focus on fewer solutions and organizations rather than follow the "peanut butter" method of spreading their money around. They want to change systems not treat symptoms, funding change over charity. These rising donors also want to be bolder and more experimental; some might even say brazen. They want their tool belts to contain more than just grants and gifts. They are pushing for more impact investing and trying out microloans, giving circles, crowdfunding, and other nontraditional funding methods that blur the classic lines between for-profit and nonprofit ventures—all in the name of greater impact. Next gen donors want to go all in with the organizations they support, giving talent rather than just treasure, building more intimate relationships, and working closely as partners who share in the subsequent challenges *and* successes. They are, frankly, more high maintenance than their predecessors. But they say this makes them better donors who get better results.

A revolution designed to increase impact, to produce more good in the world, sounds wonderful. But even if this goal is eventually reached, revolutions are never easy. And the Impact Revolution that these next gen donors are pushing will do more than ruffle a few feathers. They plan to transform philanthropy in disruptive ways, not unlike what we've witnessed already in other sectors. Consider, for example, how streaming has transformed the music and home entertainment industries, or the changes we see in the shift to a "gig economy." Philanthropy, like those industries, will look remarkably different in 20 years.

It would be more dramatic—and more conveniently sound bite ready—for us to lament that these revolutionary next gen donors want to throw the baby out with the bathwater, that their passion for change will disrupt philanthropy in dangerous ways, leaving our core nonprofit infrastructure—libraries, hospitals, and so on—in the lurch and neglecting tried-and-true programs. Fortunately, our research shows this description of their plans isn't accurate. Most next gen donors we studied are exceedingly respectful of the philanthropic shoes they're stepping into; they're not bomb-throwers. Contrary to the "spoiled rich kids" image, this generation's more active big donors are driven by values and are keenly aware that "with great privilege comes great responsibility." They are asking questions and listening as they engage deeply with nonprofit partners or as they eagerly take their seats on the family foundation board. Those who hail from a legacy of giving are proud to carry that legacy forward, though they want to do so by innovating to improve that legacy. And while next gen donors see themselves as disturbance generators, they temper their drive for change with humility and a focus on change for impact rather than on change for attention or, perhaps worse, simply for the sake of change.

These next gen revolutionaries want to live out their values seamlessly in their families, their giving, and their investments—aligning their professional, personal, and philanthropic lives more than any previous generation. And while some newer causes—such as climate change and LGBT rights—will rise in importance, our research reveals that, contrary to popular predictions, traditional causes favored by their parents' and grandparents' generations will *not* be abandoned. In fact, as we will see, many next gen donors have a genuine respect for the legacy of past donors. Perhaps the most encouraging news is how focused Generation Impact is on finally making substantial progress on long-entrenched social problems. We welcome that as good news. It portends a more effective role for philanthropy in our world in the future.

Still, even a respectful revolution can break things it didn't mean to break. We need to be informed and vigilant to make the most of the coming Impact Revolution.

Who Are These Gen Xers and Millennials?

No doubt most of what you've heard about these generations wouldn't inspire much confidence in how the major donors among them will respond to their tremendous privilege and opportunity to make an impact. But a closer look reveals a nuanced picture of their generational personalities.

The Gen X Generation (born between 1965 and 1980) is the smallest of the generational cohorts alive today, stuck between the much larger and more widely scrutinized Baby Boomers and Millennials. Influenced in their formative years by Watergate, the Iran-Contra affair, the rise of AIDS, the War on Drugs, and the tripling of the divorce rate, Gen Xers in the United States are often seen as distrustful of traditional institutions—from government to marriage—and more cynical than Boomers about the possibility of mass social change. They are supposedly "slackers," individualists who want to be left alone to "do their own thing." The label "Gen X" itself was originally meant to signal their apparent apathy about big movements and causes and their lack of a defining, collective passion or identity.[12]

But this image of Gen Xers has softened over the years. What was mistaken initially for apathy is now seen more as a resourcefulness and desire to effect quieter but more lasting social changes. Gen Xers don't wait for movements or big institutions to solve the challenges of the day, nor do they wait for Boomers to retire to step into leadership roles. As the first "latchkey kids," they are independent and adept at coming up with their own solutions. For example, while Boomers were still chairing the boards of major nonprofit institutions in the United States, Gen Xers were creating new organizations (Teach For America and the Knowledge Is Power Program, also known as KIPP Schools, for example) to solve pressing problems in our country.

The Millennial Generation (a.k.a. Gen Y, born between 1980 and 1995) garners much more attention and speculation than Gen X, in part because it is the largest generation over age 21 today, and one with massive purchasing power. Growing up as impressionable witnesses to the Columbine and Oklahoma City tragedies, Hurricane Katrina, and of course the 9/11 attacks, American Millennials experienced trauma on their own soil unlike any generation since the Civil War. But they also grew up with the Internet, cell phones, and social networking and saw both the financial boom of the 1990s and the recession that followed. Raised by helicopter parents trying to protect them from these traumas and handing out trophies for participating rather than winning, Millennials have come to be seen as the Selfie Generation—narcissistic and entitled.

But this unflattering view has changed as more Millennials have come into adulthood. Research has shown them to be much more socially conscious and interested in collective social engagement than originally thought. They expect corporations to be socially responsible, and they see technology as a tool for human progress. They use their horizontal, social-network mentality to harness their peers for anything and everything, including social change. Raised to believe they can do whatever they want, Millennials now take that to mean they can change the world; better yet, they want to do so together. Maybe those participation trophies weren't such a bad idea after all.

If these are the generational personalities that inform how Gen Xers and Millennials in general engage in the world, will the major donors from these generations act and think along these lines? There is a growing body of research (cited throughout this book) on high-net-worth donors and lots of biographical accounts of big donors, but that research is focused almost exclusively on older generations. The social commentary on big Gen X and Millennial donors, by contrast, has mostly been about broad generational trends and/or based on second- and third-hand sources. We haven't heard much from major next gen donors themselves, much less in their own words.

This book fills that gap, pulling back the curtain to reveal the next gen, posing questions directly to the donors of Generation

Impact—people like Hadi Partovi, Hannah Quimby, and Alexander Soros—and recording their musings verbatim.

_____ ᴄ⸲

Hadi Partovi was born in Tehran, studied computer science at Harvard, and enjoyed tremendous success as a tech entrepreneur and early investor in companies like Facebook, Dropbox, and Airbnb. But instead of devoting himself to building an even bigger fortune, Hadi now funnels that business savvy into his work as CEO, cofounder, and principal donor to the nonprofit Code.org, pouring every asset he has—monetary or otherwise—into Code.org's mission of expanding access to computer science, especially for women and students of color.

Hannah Quimby spent her early years with her twin brother in rural Maine, in a cabin without electricity or running water. Her mother, Roxanne, met a beekeeper named Burt while hitch-hiking, and over time built their small lip balm business into the Burt's Bees phenomenon. The Quimby family is now one of the largest philanthropic funders in Maine, and Hannah has taken the lead, determined to invest the family's resources in grassroots, hands-on ways.

Alexander Soros is a PhD student in history at Cal-Berkeley. But he is unlike his fellow students in notable ways. For one, he is studying Jewish intellectuals, a research subject he feels connected to because of his own heritage. And two, he is shaping history around the world through his own activist style of giving and through his roles in the global foundations created by his father, billionaire investor George Soros.

These three next gen donors, featured in later chapters, help illustrate how they and their peers will be the most significant

15

philanthropists ever, not just because of how *much* they will give but because of *how* they intend to give.

—☙

To be clear, when we say the rising generation of big donors will be the most significant philanthropists ever, we are not saying that younger Gen Xers and maturing Millennials are more philanthropically minded or generous of spirit than previous generations.[13] Plenty of people in their 20s and 30s—and plenty of wealthy young people—are not all that interested in philanthropy. In fact, the historic wealth concentration might mean we'll see even more stories of inordinately wealthy young people making non-philanthropic choices (even downright misanthropic choices), relishing their position on top of the steep economic ladder without doing anything to help those below them.

But the fact remains that those members of the Gen X and Millennial generations who do want to give will have the unparalleled assets and entrepreneurial mindset to become the biggest, most influential donors in history.[14] And many of them want to give now, so how they approach their giving is already starting to change things. They see waiting until they retire to start writing donation checks as uninspiring and uninspired. They want to give throughout their lives. And they want to give in new ways from the very start.

These next gen donors want to "do good" in their personal and professional lives, as well as philanthropically. Whether as investors, consumers, employers, business professionals, or volunteers, they want all their assets directed toward effecting social change, and they're willing to invest their expertise, time, and networks in addition to their financial largesse. They care less about having their names on a building and more about being inside the building or "on the ground," sleeves rolled up, helping to solve problems. They want to use every tool available to meet their goals, including working closely with peers to achieve their visions. We'll explore this strategic, hands-on, innovative, peer-based approach throughout the book.

In Their Own Words

This book draws an in-depth picture of what this different philanthropic footprint of next gen donors in the Unites States will look like, capturing who they are, how they want to give, and what it all means. For the past several years, through both formal research and by engaging directly with these game-changing leaders, we've learned about their experiences, their strategies, and their dreams.

As we talked around the country about the results of our first phase of next gen donor research, we heard strong interest from diverse audiences in knowing more about this pivotal group of donors.[15] People are intrigued by the individuals who are starting to change the world of giving and nonprofits, and who promise to have such a major impact on our world in the coming years. Next gen donors themselves are eager to hear how others in similar roles are becoming the donors they want to be. And those who engage directly with next gen donors, such as fundraising teams and advisors, want insight into how they can best help these donors achieve the wide and deep impact they hope to have on our social issues, our communities, and our planet. This book is a direct response to that widespread interest.

As authors, we come to this work with different professional orientations and personal experiences with giving. Sharna brings the access and insights of a trusted insider—a next gen donor herself—and the field expertise of a consultant and specialist in next generation engagement and multigenerational philanthropy.

Michael brings his many years of scholarship and formal research training and his expertise as holder of the world's first-ever endowed chair of family philanthropy. We offer quantitative *and* qualitative research, as well as 40 years of combined experience with next gen donors and their families and advisors.

What we share is genuine curiosity about these rising donors and a firm belief that we must learn more about them at this historic juncture—both to understand the revolution they're bringing and to help all of us make the most of it. In this book, we show you what this new revolution will look like by going straight to the sources and hearing it in their own words. We bring you the voices of next gen donors who we believe speak to the shifting paradigm better than we ever could, and allow next gen donors to speak *for* themselves *about* themselves. The six donors you've been introduced to so far will be joined by a varied cast of seven others who share firsthand about their giving, many doing so publicly for the first time.

We also present insights we gathered from interviews and surveys of hundreds of other major next gen donors, including inheritors of family philanthropy and dot-com millionaires; those who have become financial advisors and stay-at-home moms; activists who consider themselves "radical donors" and religious conservatives who give primarily to faith-based causes; and some who are deeply engaged as professionals in this field as well as some who are just starting their philanthropic journeys. We intentionally sought to talk to donors interested in a range of causes, from health and education access to climate change and women's rights, and who give using a variety of vehicles and methods.

Throughout the book we also share what we've found to be most striking, surprising, concerning, or encouraging about the dreams and plans expressed by these earnest revolutionaries. We raise caution flags at times; we highlight reasons for hope at times. And then we offer what we think this means.

Taken together, the next gen voices and our commentary form a composite and compelling picture of a generation ascending to its historic role and an assessment of the Impact Revolution they want to lead.

Using This Book

We hope thoughtful readers interested in keeping up with today's trends and understanding the changing world will gain a better picture of the future we can all expect as these rising donors take the reins. You will get a sense of the likely impact of these next gen donors on your life, on the causes you also support, and on the organizations at the heart of your community.

Anyone working directly with this critical cohort of major donors—as well as the donors and their families—will find useful advice and insight here for making the most of this group's unprecedented potential to do good. Fundraisers and social entrepreneurs will learn how to attract next gen dollars for charitable, political, and religious causes and make next gen donors real partners in the work. Parents, peers, employers, wealth advisors, investment managers, and others will learn emerging best practices for guiding and helping these next gen donors as they make their mark on history. And we all will be better equipped to put this massive wealth to work in a way that makes a difference in a world with great need.

American society has experienced a long period of generational stability in the philanthropic world. The Traditionalists (born between 1925 and 1945) and the Baby Boomers (born between 1945 and 1965) have created and guided our key institutions for decades. But while we weren't looking, their children and grandchildren grew up. The future of philanthropy and the power to set the course of social change now rests in their hands. Let's see what they have in store.

PART ONE

The Impact Revolution

CHAPTER 2

Show Me the Impact

Picture a big thermometer, that well-known symbol of many a fundraising campaign. Each donation is documented in red, pushing the "temperature" higher and higher toward the campaign's total dollar goal. That image might be a fitting symbol for a previous generation of givers, but it is the antithesis of what next gen donors want to be a part of today and going forward.

For one, the thermometer metaphor focuses solely on dollars given, not on the results and impact fostered by those donations. The thermometer also makes it seem like the only role donors can play is to give cash—or encourage others to do so. Next gen donors insist that they have valuable assets to give beyond money, and those assets are valuable because they leverage more impact. Rather than measuring their impact as a line in a fundraising budget, next gen donors want to measure the real difference all their contributions make on the causes they care about. Seeing real-world impact is what gets them excited about giving.

Impact Obsession

We'd be hard-pressed to find any donors of any age who say they don't care whether their giving makes much of a difference. But for next gen donors, impact is everything. As the leaders of the new Golden Age of Giving, as donors with unprecedented resources and the power to revolutionize philanthropy, making a tangible difference is their top philanthropic focus. They want an Impact Revolution. They want to reshape philanthropy in ways they believe can finally lead to meaningful progress on our toughest challenges.

We can see this impact fixation in some of the philanthropic ventures already created by next gen donors. Facebook cofounder Mark Zuckerberg and his wife, Dr. Priscilla Chan embody Generation Impact. They created the Chan Zuckerberg Initiative (CZI) in December 2015, in celebration of the birth of their first child, and committed to using CZI to give the vast majority of their multibillion-dollar fortune to philanthropic purposes over their lifetimes.[1] CZI is a charitable LLC that reveals both the founders' hugely ambitious goals and their willingness to use a nontraditional approach to giving—one meant to allow them maximum flexibility to pursue promising solutions. In 2016, for example, CZI announced a $3 billion, ten-year investment in health care, with the audacious goal of "helping cure, prevent, and manage all diseases in our children's lifetime."[2] Whereas previous donors might have defined such an initiative around a particular treatment (e.g., "investing in new diabetes medications") or a particular institution (e.g., "expanding the endowment of the world-famous Mayo Clinic"). These next gen philanthropists defined their plans around a breathtakingly bold end result, a big impact.

Zuckerberg's Facebook cofounder, Dustin Moskovitz, along with his wife, Cari Tuna, have placed "measurable impact" at the center of their considerable philanthropic initiatives. Through Good Ventures and the Open Philanthropy Project, they make their giving decisions solely based on which investments or interventions will "do the most good."[3] The causes they focus on are not determined by their personal passions or experiences—as they are for so many donors—but by what data and research suggest are the issues or solutions that can save or help the most lives. If that means giving for criminal justice reform or malaria prevention rather than for rural libraries or urban green space, then so be it. The potential for maximum measurable impact on humanity is their deciding factor.

Another version of this impact-focused approach is the "hacker philanthropy" of tech billionaire Sean Parker. As a group, Sean says, hackers are already "intensely idealistic, so as they begin to confront the world's most pressing humanitarian problems, they are still young, naïve, and perhaps arrogant enough to believe that they can solve them."[4] So when he set up his own foundation, he declared, "We will only target very big specific problems that are 'tip-able,' where we see a path to victory and where we can make a catalytic impact."[5]

Impact is not just an obsession of next gen donors from the tech community, however. Our interviews with Gen X and Millennial donors of many backgrounds, from inheritors to earners, showed the same desire. Impact is what they want—and worry about—most. One talked about having "a nagging itch in the back of my mind: Am I really doing the most good I could be doing?" Another explained her primary challenge in giving as such: "When I look at my own giving, I get so overwhelmed because I go, 'Where can I have the most impact?'" Similarly, when we surveyed over 300 major donors in their 20s and 30s, we asked them to indicate the importance of various reasons for engaging in philanthropy. Out of 23 possible choices, they ranked "seeing that my contribution makes a real difference and the organization has real impact" as one of the top three reasons for giving.

Moving the Needle

Of course, younger donors are not the only ones who say they want to "make a difference" with their giving. This sentiment is a

25

common one found in surveys and interviews on the motives and goals of many types of donors, including older high-net-worth philanthropists and Millennial donors across the economic spectrum.[6] And research on how donors act suggests that impact matters. Experiments by psychologist Paul Slovic and others have shown that what really matters for people deciding whether to give to provide life-saving interventions (e.g., sending aid to a refugee camp) is *not* the sheer number of people who would be helped, but the *percent* of the total in need who could be helped.[7] Donors are more likely to contribute to help, say, 90 percent of 100 people in a single village destroyed by an earthquake than they are to help 10 percent of 10,000 people in a bigger region—even though the total number helped is much smaller in the first case (90 versus 1,000).[8] Most donors, it seems, don't necessarily want their contribution to be "just a drop in the bucket." They like to see that their giving matters.

So what makes the impact focus of next gen donors different from past generations?

What's different—and what leads us to call them "Generation Impact"—is how highly they *prioritize* impact, how much they emphasize *seeing* impact over all other criteria for judging their giving, how specific and passionate they are about what they want to *change* to achieve more impact, and how far they want to *innovate* to achieve this greater impact. They draw a line in the sand between the philanthropic approach of previous generations and the impact-first approach they want to take.

When we asked next gen donors how they were different from their parents and grandparents, in fact, the most common theme in their answers was impact. Many rejected quite strongly what they saw previous generations doing—giving to "gain social status or participate in the right social circles," giving merely out of "obligation," or giving for the quid pro quo exchange of "you give to my charity and I'll give to yours." Instead, they insisted they give in order to make a real difference, to "move the needle fundamentally and substantially on an issue." One donor claimed he was "impact-based rather than who's-who-based," unlike his parents, and another said she wanted to "be very focused on a problem," not just on "having a reputation." This donor made a similar stark comparison: "I want proof of impact. I believe my parents give much more for the 'feel good' feeling that comes along with giving, whereas I am dead-set on maximizing the impact of my philanthropic dollars."

Next gen donor and social entrepreneur Daniel Lurie has built a new model to address the age-old problem of poverty in the San Francisco Bay Area, and he has leveraged over $120 million from donors, including those who are considered next gen and believe he's onto something. He offers a terrific example of the next gen donors' distinctive—some might say single-minded—focus on impact, their willingness to try out new models to change the philanthropic landscape and to finally move the needle on long-standing issues.

Daniel Lurie

Being Part of the Solution

I was born and raised in San Francisco. My parents divorced when I was 2. My dad, who is a rabbi, remarried and has lived with my stepmother in Marin County ever since. My mom remarried also, to Peter Haas, who was a member of the large family of descendants of Levi Strauss, who have done so much philanthropically in the Bay Area.

Both my dad and stepmother, and my mom and stepfather, were really involved in the community and giving back, and they

(continued)

(continued)

each had their own traditions of family philanthropy. From an early age, the ethos that you had to be part of the community, that you had to serve, was imparted to my siblings. We had to be part of giving back, part of improving the community. We had to be part of the solution.

Not surprisingly, engagement in giving and serving in community started early for me. My brother and I sat on the board of my stepfather's and my mom's family foundation, the Mimi and Peter Haas Fund, from the time we were in high school. I went across the country to study political science at Duke University, where I became president of my class.

When I graduated from Duke—literally the day after I graduated—I was up in West Orange, New Jersey, trying to get a job on the Bill Bradley for President campaign. I ended up in Iowa for about ten months working on the caucuses in 1999 and 2000.

What I loved about Bill Bradley was that he always talked about issues of poverty. He talked about 12 million kids going to school hungry. He talked about the 35 to 45 million people who at the time were uninsured in this country. And it spoke to me that a guy with all the talents he had, all the smarts he had, wanted to serve. He wanted to talk about the less fortunate in our country. That spoke to me.

I moved to New York City right after the campaign and went to work for the Robin Hood Foundation there, New York's largest poverty-fighting organization. As it happened, I started work at Robin Hood one week before the attacks of September 11, 2001. The combination of Bill Bradley's ideals, the events of 9/11, and working at the Robin Hood Foundation crystallized for me what I wanted to do and how I wanted to do it. I have always had this desire to make my community better and to serve. But when I saw the Robin Hood Foundation at the epicenter of responding to the 9/11 attacks—responding with compassion and empathy and care for those hardest hit, low-income New Yorkers—that catalyzed me.

After a couple of years in New York, when I returned to the Bay Area for grad school, I started to work on a plan to bring a new model of philanthropy to my hometown. In 2005 I launched Tipping Point Community with a few board members and a group of about a hundred founding donors. Since then, we've raised over $120 million to support people in poverty in the Bay Area, and I still proudly serve as the CEO.

A Different Model of Giving

I think many family foundations do great work, and I consider it a great honor and responsibility to be involved with a foundation making smart grants in its chosen area. But I think of our family foundation more as my stepfather's and my mom's passion and legacy, and I am there to support those efforts. I don't necessarily think of it as mine. Tipping Point is my passion, my way of serving, my way of impacting the entire community. And I'm convinced it is the best model for achieving that impact.

Tipping Point exists to make our community stronger and to improve the lives of the 1.3 million people who are currently too poor to meet their basic needs in the Bay Area. Tipping Point's model is to search for and find the most promising organizations and then help them become more effective and efficient at serving children and families who are living in poverty. We are focused on breaking the cycle of poverty by funding critical areas such as housing, education, employment, and wellness.

While we have come to know something about these issues in San Francisco over the last 12 years, we didn't start out as experts on these issues. We felt we were really good at helping groups get better at what they do, building capacity, and supporting their back office, which is why we provide general operating support. This gives flexibility to the organizations that know their opportunities and challenges better than we do. As a result of this early decision, one of the biggest things that I have learned is the value

(continued)

29

(continued)

of general operating support, and the problems that arise for non-profits because most foundations don't provide this support.

Tipping Point wants to make our community better for every single person who lives here in the Bay Area, and that also includes our community of donors. Our model gives them a way to be involved, to be engaged in creating a stronger community. We engage young professionals in the community by helping them get onto the boards of our 44 grantee organizations through a board matching program. We also have a volunteer match portal on our website to get people engaged in volunteering with our grantees. By doing this we expand Tipping Point's impact even further, leveraging both our community's financial and human capital.

For many of us who work here at Tipping Point, we sometimes feel that we get more out of the work than anyone else. We like to think of ourselves as altruistic, but there is a selfish part because this work is so fulfilling and rewarding.

Finding What Moves the Needle

We have too many nonprofits—not only in this region, but in this country—that are well meaning and well intentioned but don't look closely at results. Good intentions are not enough. We need programs that are producing real results, because results are desperately needed. Poverty has not decreased in this country in the last 50 years; it's gone up. We are seeing more inequality of opportunity in this country despite all these nonprofits that exist to close that gap. In order for us to move the needle, we need programs to be really effective. And in order to know which ones are effective, you have to have some measurement.

Our primary focus at Tipping Point is always supporting our grantee organizations, helping them improve on what they do, get better at serving their clients, and help those clients move out of poverty for good. We want to help our grantees focus on the parts of their work that are the strongest and that have the intended impact they imagine. And in many cases, we try to help grantee groups shed those programs that are not having an impact, that are draining time and resources and aren't changing the lives of the people they are serving. We want grantees to get more bang for their buck.

To do this, we help grantees identify—using good data and impact measurements—which parts of their programmatic work are the real difference-makers. We love when groups go through their theory of change work and really figure out what is important and what is having an impact. We have had groups come to us and go through this process of real, deep self-reflection and end up eliminating entire programs. They look at the data and come to understand that a $10 million budget would be more impactful than the $15 million budget they could have, that they're wasting resources on something that is not having its intended impact.

We measure impact in this way—and have from day one—because we think it's the right thing to do. We don't want this measurement to be onerous on our groups, but we strongly believe we need better clarity on which programs are really making a difference.

R&D to Accelerate Results

We cannot continue to do the same thing over and over again and expect different results. It won't happen. Out here in the Bay Area, Facebook and Google and others literally spend billions of dollars on research and development because they know how that can lead to incredible results. But in the nonprofit sector, R&D dollars are essentially at zero. We at Tipping Point think that should change. We ask the nonprofit sector to do a huge lift in our society. We expect nonprofits to perform feats of strength and yet we don't give them what they need to perform those feats. We don't give them the general operating support dollars they need to run healthy organizations, and we don't give them any room to explore new approaches that might help them get better at what they do

(continued)

31

(continued)

and have a greater impact. If we think so highly of these nonprofits and their leaders, why are we not giving them what they need?

We see ourselves at Tipping Point as an engaged grantmaker, an accelerator. We help our groups get better, faster. Some might say this means we practice "venture philanthropy," a term made popular here in the Bay Area in the early part of the 2000s. But we steer clear of that label. The idea of venture philanthropy was that you should apply venture capital thinking to the nonprofit sector, but for some that term came to have a negative connotation. It suggested that venture capitalists lacking experience in the nonprofit sector should tell nonprofits how to run their business. That's not what we do at Tipping Point. We listen closely to our grantees to hear what they know is working and how we can help them get better, faster.

However, we do believe in some of the other principles of this "venture" approach—especially funding along a spectrum, taking risks, and supporting R&D. We fund some groups that have been around a hundred years and we fund start-ups. The R&D work at Tipping Point provides risk capital and partnership to our grantees so they can tackle big questions and ideas that could lead to the next big solution for issues our community faces.

The New Gold Rush

Whether you are at an "old school" foundation or a new school one, you want to have an impact. Donors have always wanted to have an impact. It was just easier in the early part of the twentieth century to build a library or a university. You could see a building, see students going in and out of it, see how many people took out books or graduated college. I think what's new over the last 10 to 20 years is this idea that you should measure that impact, hold groups accountable for achieving it, and try out new ideas to have greater impact. You can try something like Mark Zuckerberg and Priscilla Chan's new charitable LLC, the Chan Zuckerberg Initiative. Or you can try using the 1-1-1 model that

Marc Benioff started at Salesforce, integrating technology, people, and resources, which is great.

While we are good at measuring short-term impact, it is tougher to measure it in the longer term, I think. But that said, we can think long-term more readily now, as we have never seen people this wealthy at this young of an age before. The Carnegies were wealthy much later in life. Back then, no one was a billionaire in their 20s; it took time for people to build their fortunes, whereas now, especially here in Silicon Valley, we have seen billion-dollar fortunes built in a five-to-ten-year span. We're living in the new gold rush. It's incredibly exciting. But this also gives us the incredible opportunity to do better by those who have not taken part in this boom. We have the resources to do better, and I think we will do better.

I am incredibly optimistic because I do see these people starting to build the habit of giving at a younger age. There is a terrific crop of young philanthropic leaders who are engaged in and committed to improving our community, whether that's locally, nationally, or globally.

For nonprofits to take advantage of this gold rush and this new crop of young philanthropists, it's essential that they are able to communicate their impact. Many philanthropists are business leaders and want to see a well-run organization. They want to see strong leadership and strong financials. They also want to see the desire by the nonprofit to improve. This desire to become better is the standard, whether the investor is investing in a start-up or a high-performing nonprofit organization. Investors in Google and Apple want to see leaders adapt and change and try to improve for their shareholders. I think the same can be said for nonprofits. Tipping Point has 44 organizations we fund. We think we have great leaders at those organizations, but we also want to see them striving to improve, not being afraid to make mistakes, and admitting when those mistakes occur. Being able to admit mistakes should

(continued)

(continued)

be valued as a way to say, "we are striving to get better and here's how." That is something that we value at Tipping Point.

This isn't to say, though, that you have to be a tech billionaire to be a philanthropist and help make the community better. At Tipping Point, we believe that everyone can play a role, regardless of socioeconomic status. It doesn't matter what family you are from or how much money you are giving, you can be part of this community effort to solve big problems. You can be engaged and you can volunteer your time, you can serve on a board, you can give money at the level you can, you can be part of the community. Everyone has a role to play. But just don't wait. Get started now.

Daniel is clearly passionate about trying to alleviate poverty, but he doesn't think trying is enough. He wants results. And he's frustrated that despite the previous generations' efforts to fund poverty eradication programs, poverty continues to rise. Something needs to change to make more of an impact.

What Daniel has done to try to "move the needle" on poverty illustrates well what other next gen donors want to do to make philanthropy more impact-focused. They want to try different models, take new risks, and look for evidence of effectiveness. They want results.

The Power of Seeing

Next gen donors say they want impact, but what do they mean by that? Do they agree on the definition of *impact*? When we pressed our interviewees to describe what they meant by impact, we heard a number of explanations. For some it was about demonstrated outcomes—some sort of evidence that they had made a measurable difference, like the higher graduation rate among charter school students. This donor even said that seeing the impact in emotional ways was not as important as seeing these actual measurements: "Most nonprofits simply talk about the problem they're solving and what they're doing about it and show you pictures of happy kids to show that impact and to pull on your heartstrings. But they don't necessarily measure how much impact you get, how many happy kids you get per dollar that you give in. It is not exactly clear."

For others, impact meant clearer evidence that results were tied to *their* particular contribution, or that their contribution was being used effectively to help solve problems or create change. As one person explained, impact meant making sure that the money "actually is going to provide an added benefit to a user, a community, a school, or something, and to be able to see that happen."

Ultimately, the most common answer when we asked what impact meant was an indirect one. Next gen donors define impact as "being able to *see* something happen as a result of giving." These next gen donors might not have a single, shared definition of impact, but they know they want to *see* it. While this approach might not be the best definition of impact—as we will discuss later—it was by far the most common.

Not surprisingly, next gen donors are particularly enthusiastic about site visits. They love being able to "see the impact in front of your face." One donor called it her most "fundamental experience" to "both see need and see the nonprofit community step in and make an extremely concrete, real difference in people's lives." Another donor talks excitedly about a site visit he made to Central Africa: "I traveled with a small team, to kind of see the situation in person and to come face-to-face with what we have been discussing in what I thought was a more abstract way, sitting around the board table in a Manhattan office. That appealed to me. It was an incredible experience. Coming face-to-face with what I hoped we would support more in the future."

Next gen donors like site visits because they can see the outcome of giving *and* understand how this giving is working to make an impact. Sure they can read the mission statement for, say, the Boys and Girls Club they fund. But going to the club and hearing the children tell their personal stories about how specific programs helped them stay safe, build life skills, or prepare for college is much more powerful.

These rising generations—especially the Millennials—have grown up in a world full of screens, which may explain why they yearn to see the impact their giving has had "face-to-face" rather than virtually. One donor who works in computer science made this argument directly:

> I'm a tech guy. I love the virtual. But actually, a picture, a 3D video, whatever, will not convey the same feeling as if you just get out and travel there. When you go to a site visit or a town or a community [as a donor], you're not going to go there and walk around by yourself. You're going to get a tour, and a tour is going to involve other people. So you see that human emotion. You can see either the passion in their eyes or the gratefulness in their eyes or a bit of both. That's the driving force.

Many Gen Xers and Millennials have also been encouraged since they were very young to get out from behind their screens and get involved in community service and volunteering. So for some, their passion for seeing impact is tied to their passion for being hands-on in their giving. As with site visits, they feel that volunteering allows them to be physically present and to confirm, as one puts it, whether their money "is going to the right place, to the right people, where it can make a big difference." Another donor says that volunteering helps "me know who I'm helping, and how I'm helping them." Several also told us that this need to see, touch, and contribute in hands-on ways really distinguishes them from prior generations.

Of course, we must ask, will next gen donors, with all their earnest bravado, stick around to see those impacts that take longer to achieve and measure? Will they bring humility and openness to the process of changing practices that affect lives and livelihoods? These will be important questions as the Impact Revolution in philanthropy unfolds.

What Does This Mean?

The potential upside of the Impact Revolution is immense. If donors with unprecedented resources give in new ways that do in fact leverage significant impact, we can make progress on problems we've struggled with for a long time, and advance causes beyond what we've ever seen. We could, as Priscilla Chan and Mark Zuckerberg want, cure or manage all disease. We could, as Daniel Lurie wants, help millions more people find a path out of poverty. Big impact is possible if big giving envisions it.

But revolutions are messy—even revolutions driven by the haves versus the have-nots; even revolutions fighting for change in board rooms and institutions versus in the streets. Revolutions are messy even if the intentions of the revolutionaries are noble and positive. How can we prepare ourselves for the messiness? What changes should we brace ourselves for? And what unintended consequences or unforeseen pitfalls should we look out for?

The impact-first orientation of next gen donors can be a boon for nonprofits working to attract and retain these donors, but nonprofits need to think carefully and creatively about how they show impact. Fundraisers will certainly want to emphasize impact as the top-line message in their pitches to next gen donors. And nonprofits will want to find ways to put next gen donors in direct, personal contact with their organizations as well as with the people their organizations support, whether through site visits, volunteer opportunities, or simply the chance to hear the real stories of clients they serve.

Face-to-face encounters with impact are possible even if in-person meetings are not. Take an organization started by next gen social entrepreneur Charles Best. In 2000, when he was a 24-year-old high school history teacher in the Bronx, Charles founded DonorsChoose.org, a website where public school teachers post information about classroom projects and needs and donors choose which projects to support. DonorsChoose.org allows donors to see the teacher, project, and even the kids they are funding, providing both photos and details like budget and goals. They also get updates on the project's progress, and the DonorsChoose.org website has an ongoing "impact" page complete with an "explore our data" button. This approach appeals to the next gen because it gives these donors both a personalized sense of who they are helping and a clear sum of the impact they are making.

While seeing impact is exciting and motivating, providing personal meaning and fulfillment for the donors, we all need to be aware of some potential downsides of how zealous these next gen donors are for seeing impact. The primary focus must always remain on the real, complex needs and goals these donors are funding. Both nonprofits and donors need to be careful that the Impact Revolution doesn't devolve into misguided efforts to keep big donors happy with staged site visits showing only the positive sides of the hard work for social change. This is a worry that many nonprofit leaders surely have, and the savviest of next gen donors we spoke with share the concern. They still passionately want their giving to show impact, but they want that impact to fit what organizations truly need and to do what will lead to substantial change regardless of the optics.

Another challenge is that not all causes or organizations do work that produces impact that can be monitored in clear, "face-to-face" ways. The outcomes that some groups fight for can be too big, too remote, too complex, or too subtle and intangible to see easily (think of changing attitudes about racial violence). And some of the solutions that will ultimately produce the greatest cumulative impact won't be able to show tangible, donor-pleasing results in the short-term (think of basic scientific research to understand what causes cancer).

While it is vital that nonprofits try to show their impact—and the process of getting to that impact—in all its complexity, they also have to think carefully about how they can show donors their outcomes in appealing ways. It can be a tall order to highlight your positive outcomes for donors while still defining those outcomes in ways commensurate with the nature of their cause *and* in ways that demonstrate evidence of long-term change.[9] We believe nonprofits and next gen donors can become better partners in effecting change if the donors learn about and witness the challenges nonprofits grapple with. The good news is next gen donors say they are eager to have this sort of close, honest relationship with the nonprofits.

Ideally, nonprofits and next gen donors can develop enough of a relationship that they define impact *together*. Donors can express the change they want to see in the world, and nonprofits can explain the complex nature of the problem they address and the struggles they face in fighting it. The two parties can mutually agree on what impact means in each complicated case and come up with the most appropriate performance and impact measures.

Both parties then buy in to that meaning of impact and hold each other accountable for achieving it.

—☙

But again we have to ask this: Will next gen donors, with decades of giving ahead of them, have the patience to stick around to see the real change their giving can have on long-term, complex issues? Time will tell. But some of the next gen donors we talked to were keenly aware of this challenge and tried to take the long view. One thoughtful donor explained, "You're investing in an organization; you want an ongoing relationship with them. It's probably long-term. Real problems take several years to solve, laying the groundwork and identifying areas of need, and going through many, many different stages. You might not see the outcome for a while. But I think we're able to operate at a scale where our giving would be most effective over a period of time rather than just a one-time, one-year thing."

Next gen donors will certainly push philanthropy to be even more focused on vehicles that allow "giving while living," preferring this to setting up perpetual foundations or waiting to make "planned gifts" from their estates after they pass away.[10] As we will see throughout this book, they dislike waiting until they retire to give, so waiting until they die is even less appealing. This means that raising money from next gen donors for endowments or bequests will probably be more difficult. But again, they want to develop close relationships with organizations, and if doing so shows them that the organization needs such deferred-impact gifts, they could be persuaded to give them.

A related challenge is whether donors want to fund specific programs or core operations.[11] We know that donors of all sorts often

prefer to fund programs, especially programs with visible beneficiaries or easy-to-see outcomes and new programs that are full
of promise and innovation. Surveys and experiments consistently
show that a primary concern people have about giving to charity is
the worry that too much of their contribution will go to overhead
or fundraising costs.[12] But as nonprofit leaders—and many of the
emerging donors we spoke with—know all too well, the greatest
resource they need in order to increase their impact is either unre-
stricted funds or support for talented staff, adequate space, and
even core "R&D."

Because of their special, outsized role, next gen major donors
have an opportunity to help shift the field beyond this simplis-
tic approach of making funding decisions by looking at overhead
costs. Yes, these rising donors want to see impact, and yes they are
excited about funding new ideas and new tools, tendencies that
might lead them to prefer program funding. But as Daniel Lurie
knows, funding organizational capacity and operations is often the
best way to accelerate impact, especially over the long term.

—☙

Revolutions are never easy, but revolutions designed to create
more good in the world can be worth the trouble. The coming
Impact Revolution in philanthropy could be so, if we all go into it
with eyes wide open.

CHAPTER 3

Changing Strategies for a New Golden Age

As we've talked to people around the country about our research on next gen donors, we've encountered enthusiasm and concern in about equal measure. The enthusiasm leads them to ask a number of unanswered questions: What are next gen donors interested in? What kinds of changes do they want to see in our world? What's the secret to getting them more engaged? The questions of concern are: Will the next generation give at the same level as previous big donors? If I want next gen donors' support, will I have to change how I appeal to them? Just what kind of donors will I have to work with?

But hands down the most common question we hear is this: Are they going to give to the same causes and organizations as big donors of the past?

We get this question from nonprofit leaders concerned that their organization will no longer be a priority. We get it from current donors and socially conscious citizens worried that the causes they care about will be of little interest to the very Gen X or Millennial donors who could potentially make the biggest difference. And we get it from older members of philanthropic families who fret that the younger family members will abandon what they have long supported.

Our answer to this question is mixed. These rising next gen donors are, on the whole, interested in the same big causes and social problems as their parents and other older donors. They don't plan to cut off major funding for health care or education or basic needs or other causes. Nor do they plan to give up on local communities.

In our survey, we asked next gen donors a straight question: Overall, do they support similar or different causes than their extended families and previous generations? Roughly two-thirds (67.1 percent) answered "similar." When asked to explain, many donors said being active with their families expanded their issue knowledge and built close relationships with specific organizations, so they want to stay focused on those same causes.[1]

But (and this is a critical clarification) next gen donors want to support those causes and organizations in fundamentally new ways—ways that they feel will make a much more significant and tangible impact. They want to revolutionize *how* we give, not necessarily what we give to or for whom. They believe strongly that we need to retool philanthropic strategy if we want to make better headway on substandard education, health disparities, poverty, and other long-entrenched social problems. And this means they won't necessarily want to support the same organizations in the same ways. As we warned, the Impact Revolution will surely ruffle more than a few feathers.

Passionate about Strategy

When next gen donors talk about changing how they want to give, they often characterize these strategic changes as part of a momentous generational shift, not a minor tactical tweak. One donor in her early 20s eagerly proclaimed that "we are really blazing a trail that is very different from the generation that came before." Next gen donors are excited about making the shift they already see as their generation's historical contribution to improving philanthropy.

In this way, next gen donors are certainly in tune with a significant trend in philanthropic circles toward emphasizing strategy. Calls for "more strategic philanthropy" have dominated the publications and conferences in our field for the past couple of decades, even as that term has been defined in many different ways.[2] The main thrust of this "new" strategic approach—which, to be honest, connects back to threads interwoven throughout the history of giving—is to give "more from the head and less from the heart." Strategic philanthropy is driven by sober-minded judgments of how to give most effectively and by close attention to choosing the right methods and means for giving, not just by giving to the right cause. It criticizes donors who are driven solely by their passions or their emotions.

We can see why this approach might appeal to these emerging big donors. They are becoming aware of the philanthropy field right at the time when this is the dominant discourse, and this focus on "better strategy for better results" is extremely attractive because it prioritizes impact. In fact, we think next gen donors want to take this emphasis on strategy to revolutionary levels, not just make incremental or tactical shifts.

But it would be wrong to say that they don't have passion and that they want to give solely from the head and not the heart. Rather, *their passion is strategy*. For Generation Impact, good philanthropy is always strategic philanthropy. Giving from the head warms the heart.

Same Issues, Bigger Impact

We, too, were curious to know whether there was a coming shift in the cause areas that major donors fund, so we asked next gen donors

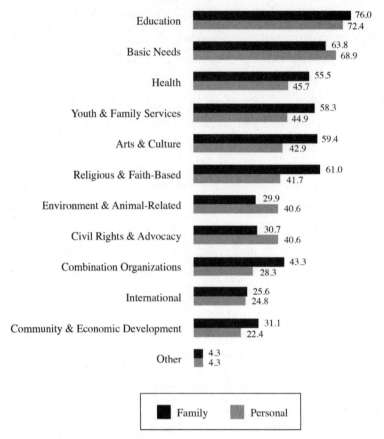

Figure 3.1 Family and Personal Giving to Issue Areas

which issue areas they support personally and which issues their families support.[3] Figure 3.1 shows the top two causes for both as the same: education and basic needs. Many of the other issue areas fell into similar tiers of preference for the next gen donors and their families, though with some obvious variations that we'll discuss later.

Here again we see that the similarities in causes across generations are more striking than the differences. The next gen *is* focused on meeting basic needs like shelter and food, just as its parents have been. These donors still want to give to health care at some level. In fact, if we look over the long history of major giving, we note more continuity than change in issues across generations of donors.[4]

But what about the differences that clearly show up in Figure 3.1? Next gen donors show somewhat less interest in giving to some traditional causes, like health, youth and family, arts and culture, and religion—though those four causes are still in the top half of the rankings for the next gen. And next gen donors were more likely than their families to give to civil rights and advocacy as well as environmental and animal-related causes.[5] In fact, unlike their parents, they rank those two causes above the so-called combination organizations—traditionally popular organizations such as the United Way or Jewish Federation that act as a "middle man," raising money and then distributing that to charities working in a variety of issue areas.

We know that most Gen Xers and Millennials are less engaged in formal religious practices than their parents and grandparents, that as a generation they are more supportive of civil rights for the LGBTQ community and people of color, and that they have grown up surrounded by more widespread environmental awareness.[6] But what can explain the relatively lower interest in areas like health, arts, or those middle-man organizations?

We think the answer relates to impact. It isn't that these causes are of less interest; it's that it's harder for the next gen to see how it can make a direct, meaningful impact by giving to the types of organizations working on those causes. It is harder for the next gen to develop a close, personalized, strategic relationship with such groups. The health care field has some of the largest nonprofits in any area, and the arts and culture arena is chock-full of traditional institutions known more for their gala events than their dashboards showing improved effectiveness.

This preference for seeing impact (and avoiding large-scale, traditional institutions) might also partly explain the next gen's relatively lower interest in giving to religious organizations. In fact, when we looked at the young donors who said they attend religious services frequently, we actually found they give to religious causes just as much as previous generations. We believe it is partly because they know those organizations firsthand, have a relationship with their leaders and participants, and can see from the inside the impact of giving to them.

These next gen donors we surveyed were echoed by those we personally interviewed. One interviewee explained that he wanted to get away from funding "traditional, big institutions" and instead "get more toward a portfolio of grants that really move the dial on an issue." Another said that on her family foundation's board, the next generation pushed the family to stop "funding one another's private schools" and instead look for how it could have "an outsized impact for our actual dollars."

The same can be said for any large nonprofit. Many of the next gen donors told us they much prefer to give to smaller organizations because they can have—and see—a greater impact; they can make a personal connection and catalyze change using innovative strategies. One donor put it simply: "I would rather be involved with a small organization where I can make a big impact than a big organization where I make a little impact. If I work with a small organization, I can make a significant impact, and I can help them drive the change that they need."

When they were involved in giving to larger institutions, their engagement with specific programs or campaigns is what kept them active. They gave to the piece of the bigger organization that they felt connected to, that they could observe closely.

The lesser interest among the next gen in funding the middle-man fundraising operations like the United Way or Jewish

Federation probably has something to do with this size issue as well. Being just a line on a fundraising thermometer is of little interest. Next gen donors struggle to see the impact they are having when giving to umbrella groups because there is too much distance between their giving and any clear outcomes generated.

Strategies for Success

Saying that next gen donors want to change *how* they give to causes (their strategies for giving) more than the causes themselves begs this question: What strategies do they want to change specifically? As they take the reins of big giving, these donors can't change everything all at once. They need to prioritize which strategies they consider the most essential for expanding philanthropic impact.

When asked to assess the current or traditional ways of giving, some next gen donors got specific about criticizing how previous generations' style of giving was too "informal," "ad hoc," "personality-driven," and "based on connections with people, not necessarily the actual program." They wanted to move from "passive checkbook philanthropy to more active, catalytic strategies." They felt like "the traditional philanthropy of writing checks to the Breast Cancer Research Foundation Dinner . . . lot of that will die off as grandparents die off and there will be a shift." Katherine Lorenz, a donor we introduced at the start of the book who is deeply involved in her family's multigenerational giving (and who is profiled in Chapter 10), still notes a distinct shift: "We view philanthropic strategy differently from our grandparents. We worry more about the programs *inside* the buildings rather than the bricks on the *outside*." .

Other donors saw the shift less as a wholesale replacement of new strategy for old and more as a necessary improvement of past strategy alongside an introduction of the new. This wasn't always easy for them to explain, though. One helpful attempt: "I think it is a blend of accepting, learning, and carrying out some established best practices and in other places pushing back or challenging other best practices or habits that have existed."

We asked next gen donors what they consider the most important components of philanthropic strategy, choosing from a long list of statements. Figure 3.2 shows the top five vote-getters:

1 I conduct due diligence and do research before deciding who to support.

2 I first decide my philanthropic goals or ideal solutions, and then search for potential recipients who fit those.

3 I fund efforts that address root causes and attempt systemic solutions.

4 I prefer to have information about an organization's proven effectiveness or measurable impact before deciding whether to support it.

5 I often recommend a cause or organization to others.

Figure 3.2 Top Five Most Important Components of Philanthropic Strategy

Our data confirmed the appeal of these five elements of strategy over and over. One donor we interviewed succinctly captures the sort of research-based, focused, impact-driven philanthropic strategy the next gen wants to embrace: "Personally, if I had my own foundation and was controlling it with nobody else, I would be very strategic about what I was interested in and narrow it down, educate myself in that area, and make some plan that I felt was going to accomplish some sort of result."

Below we summarize each of the first four elements of strategy and show how next gen donors see each as essential for greater impact. We also give illustrative quotes from our in-depth interviews with next gen donors to provide supporting examples in their own words. Chapter 7 deals extensively with the fifth component of strategy, "recommending causes or organizations to others."

1. Conducting due diligence.

Next gen donors want to make more careful, research-based giving decisions, using their information-gathering skills to investigate problems and solutions. They believe organizations should be transparent in providing the information they seek. They want to conduct due diligence (a term they used a lot) about their potential philanthropic investments like they would other financial investments.

"Let's say that I'm giving away $1 million. I am not going to go spend $1 million on a house without really doing my research on what the neighborhood is like, when the house was built, when was the plumbing done, et cetera. I want to know everything about that house, because $1 million is a big investment. Same with giving to an organization. I don't want to give $1 million to an organization that I don't feel intimately familiar with. I want to see exactly what I am getting there and to be research- and information-driven."

"[My father] has a list of a dozen nonprofits that are well-meaning and do great things, but I might come at a problem

(continued)

51

(continued)

differently. Where he's got a list of actual nonprofits, I may have a list of problems I'm interested in and then try to research what is the best way to attack that problem."

2. Being proactive and focused.

Next gen donors want to make a deeper commitment to a few proven solutions or organizations rather than try the traditional "spread the love" or "peanut butter" method that they feel would spread their money around too thinly. They want to be proactive rather than reactive, unlike big donors in the past. They want to first determine their goals and theory of change, find recipients who fit these, and then stick with those recipients over the long haul.

"You can be so impressed with all these great people who are doing great things but, unfortunately, you don't have an infinite amount of money. There's a finite amount of money. You can't just divvy it up among everyone. If you start divvying it up too much then it makes no impact for anybody. So it's better sometimes to just pick an organization and give them the full boat because they can do more with that than either one of those organizations can do with half."

"I think too many family foundations don't focus. They don't stick with a program area over time and so they end up funding in areas where they aren't experts. I always advise people to pick two or three things to focus on. Being able to say no is just as important as being able to say yes in this work."

3. Addressing root causes.

Next gen donors want to give in ways that address the root causes of problems, in the hopes that perhaps someday we will solve some of our most persistent social ills. They want to change systems, not just treat symptoms. They want to fund change, not charity.

"I would target more money toward organizations, individuals, and groups that are doing 'root-cause' work to eradicate larger social and justice problems."

"My grandparents often focused on individuals, looking at ways to help them navigate a broken system. Our generation looks to fix the broken system so that all individuals have an equal opportunity at success."

"I personally think, in an ideal world, every nonprofit should aim to go out of business. If you want to try to solve problems, you should solve the problem so that it completely goes away."

4. Measuring effectiveness and impact.

Next gen donors want to see evidence of the proven effectiveness and demonstrated results of the organizations they support. They make giving decisions in part based on the potential return on investment (ROI) of their contributions, what one donor called their "ROI for the world." They are frustrated by the lack of impact and effectiveness measures in the nonprofit sector and want better metrics to inform their giving.

"We believe that the nonprofit sector is going to evolve and transform as the [older] generation retires and moves off of the boards. As they do so and our generation takes over that role, we see a major transformation in the way that our generation will expect nonprofits to act and the results that I think we expect them to gain."

"Measurement is critical to me because otherwise how do I know if I'm being successful? How do I know if it's a good use of time? How do I know that we made the world a better place? We have a choice between being fuzzy and feel-good versus being more metric-driven and measurable. Given that I'm intentional about all this stuff, I need to know that I can measure my own success."

The donor profiled next, Mary Galeti, distinctively illustrates both the desire to change strategy and many of the specific strategies we just reviewed. Mary inherited her role as a donor. Actually, she was thrust into it. Due to the sudden and unfortunate passing of her mother and aunt, Mary found herself with significant responsibility in the family foundation—a foundation that would soon grow considerably in assets due to those deaths.

53

Faced with such loss, one might assume a woman of 22 might be too overwhelmed by grief or too absorbed in coming of age to serve as a thoughtful and engaged donor and leader. However, Mary's maturity is evidenced in the questions she posed for herself at the time, which exemplify the mix of earnestness and assertiveness we found to be hallmarks of next gen donors. She asked herself, "What kind of donor do I want to be? How can I honor my family's legacy and make an impact with these funds?" As we'll see, her responses to these questions are fascinating.

Mary is keenly aware that this tragic turn in her life also dropped a tremendous opportunity in her lap. She decided to embrace the opportunity by crafting a highly strategic approach for her family's giving, one that makes responsible use of all their assets while still being entrepreneurial and forward-thinking.

Mary Galeti

The story of wealth in my family is somewhat unique. For starters, it is closely connected to the invention of barbed wire, of all things.

In America in 1870, during the great migration west, post–Civil War, people were buying up huge tracts of land and needed a way to fence off their property so that thieves or animal predators would not come in the middle of the night and steal or kill their cattle or their sheep. From this need came the invention of barbed wire.

My great-grandfather, William H. Bush, happened to have been apprenticed to a guy named Joseph Glidden, who eventually won the patent war for barbed wire. Joseph Glidden sent my great-grandfather down to Texas to buy up as much land as he possibly could with all of his money. He ended up with 500 or 600 square miles in the Panhandle, through what is now Amarillo.

After my great-grandfather Bush had started setting up the ranch, he came back and married Joseph Glidden's daughter,

---

which was the way those things tended to go at the time. Unfortunately, both Joseph Glidden and his daughter died within about six months of each other, within a year of her wedding. So my great-grandfather found himself very wealthy in a short amount of time.

Soon after becoming a widower, my great-grandfather got remarried to the woman who would become my great-grandmother. She came from a very prominent, established family that was spread between England and the Midwest. My great-grandparents' legacy to me, then, is half "deeply established" and half "the great American success story." We are now in the fourth generation of wealth on my great-grandfather's side and the eighth generation of wealth on my great-grandmother's. So my relationship to money is, at this point, a deep feeling of responsibility and of stewardship—not just to the money but to all the assets, including the ranch.

My great-grandparents had two daughters, my grandmother and my great-aunt, who enjoyed the ranch thoroughly. Over time our family developed assets around the ranch, so while the patent on barbed wire has by now expired, the family business includes land management, cattle, grass, and wind.

I was born in Cleveland, Ohio, but I consider my family to be both from Cleveland and Amarillo because the working cattle ranch requires so much of our attention and energy. We also have a family foundation called the Tecovas Foundation, named for a natural spring on the ranch.

Both as part of my family and independent from them, I do a lot of work in philanthropy and in the social entrepreneurship space. This includes managing the operations of the Tecovas Foundation, based out of our current hometown in Washington, D.C., or wherever I and my laptop happen to be. I live in D.C. because my husband, Russell, works here as well. We recently had our first child, Bizzy.

(continued)

(continued)

Renewing a Legacy of Innovation

The modern story of philanthropy in my family began in 1998 when, at the tender age of 89, my grandmother wanted to do one last big project in Amarillo. Her "theory of change"—though she never would have used those words—was that for young people to be able to innovate, they need an arts and humanities education to balance out their science and technology education. Amarillo already had a thriving arts community, so my grandmother said, "We will build this performing arts center to support the arts community in Amarillo, and we will wire it for distance learning." In 1998, she created the Tecovas Foundation with the idea that the majority of the assets would go to build this performing arts center, and then there would be $500,000 or $600,000 in a small grantmaking pool for her children and grandchildren to utilize for philanthropy.

Then, in 2004, after my grandmother had passed away and as the arts center was nearing completion, everything suddenly changed. Both my mom and one of my two aunts passed away within four months of each other. They both left much of their inheritance to the foundation, which meant it was more significantly endowed much earlier than anyone thought it would be. We went from having about $500,000 in assets to about $14 million. But the majority of the people taking over the board, including my two cousins and me, were very young—younger than 25 and, in one case, under 18 and not out of high school yet. We wondered, "What are we supposed to do now?"

I became vice-chair of the foundation board, and my aunt was chair. We had no paid staff. I was 22 and getting married, graduating from college, and grieving pretty significantly, so this was a tough time to be thrust into a major role in my family's philanthropy. I ran off and worked on the 2008 campaign trail and then for a tiny nonprofit called Grassroots.org. I learned from that nonprofit experience that I was terrible at fundraising but really wanted to make a social impact. It dawned on me that I already had a vehicle by which to change the world—the family foundation.

I started taking over the foundation in early 2009 and tried to improve how we do our grantmaking—how proposals are brought to us, what due diligence looks like, how we work with potential grantees, all of that. But I soon realized we could best fulfill our potential if we started thinking even more proactively about our giving. In a sense, we had a legacy of being forward-thinking and innovative from my grandmother, who was thinking about distance-learning opportunities for a performing arts center in the late 1990s, way before that sort of thing was happening in arts education. But I felt we hadn't embraced the full potential of that legacy. Our family needed to start looking for a niche we could fill. We needed to be even more innovative to truly carry on that legacy.

To help me lead this innovation, I did a fellowship called the StartingBloc Social Innovation Fellowship. That program distinguished between social entrepreneurs (those who want to create their own thing), social "intrapreneurs" (those who want to work within a large organization to create a new program or project), and social "infrapreneurs" (those who are the systems thinkers focusing on social infrastructure change). I found that I self-identify mostly as a social infrapreneur and decided I wanted to bring that approach to our family's philanthropy.

Strategy for Further Out

To focus our strategy, our foundation started working with small organizations that were reaching a point where they needed one or two infusions of cash and a stamp of credibility to get to the next level. Often in this field, nonprofits are in a "catch-22" where they can't get funding from foundations unless they have already received some other foundation funding. So we decided we could make a real impact by being the first institutional grant for those nonprofits in which we believed. We conducted due diligence, did

(continued)

(continued)

not require the nonprofit to fill out a mountain of paperwork, and held a lot of dialogues to figure out how to do this strategy right.

This funding approach meant we ended up spending time with a lot of social entrepreneurs and others who were focused on deep systems changes. Over time, we also ended up looking at tax structure issues because social entrepreneurs more often than not are now filing as for-profits even when conducting mission-based work. We funded Program-Related Investments (PRIs) through no- or low-interest loans and entered the impact investing space. All of these sector-crossing innovations are fundamentally changing philanthropy, and my family and I want to incorporate them into our evolving strategy when we can to increase our impact. Indeed, I think one of the dominant questions about philanthropy going forward is how much the vehicle type matters. There are some for-profit organizations and investments doing more to change the world than many nonprofits. Being clear about your goals for impact may change where and how you choose to deploy your capital.

The other new reality in philanthropy that I'm watching closely is where the philanthropists from newly earned wealth will invest. For many of us who have inherited money, "from shirtsleeves to shirtsleeves in three generations" is a distinct possibility. But what about the number of people creating new wealth from New York to Silicon Valley, Austin to India, Poland to China? There is so much wealth being created, but how those new wealth-holders interpret "being philanthropic" is very different from what's been the traditional American style. Many of these people have created wealth by inventing something new, so they are predisposed to apply this entrepreneurial approach to their philanthropy.

I think we can't even envision yet some of the innovations in the way our world and our nonprofit sector will evolve, especially as technology evolves so quickly. Like Peter Diamandis, chairman and CEO of the X Prize Foundation and author of *Abundance*, says, if you are a Maasai warrior in Africa and you have a cellular phone, you have more connectivity than the president of the United States did 25 years ago. And if you are a Maasai warrior and you have a smartphone with Google, you have more access to information than the president of the United States did 15 years ago. So we can't even imagine what the next 20 years are going to look like.[7]

Let's be clear, though, I don't think the philanthropic community should stop funding endowments and the arts or education. But there have to be some funders thinking further out, being proactive, and looking at different kinds of investments and solutions so we can best respond to the uncertain changes ahead.

Still, philanthropy can't always be as agile and fast to respond as I think my generation would like it to be. That isn't always a bad thing. Sometimes it is good to slow ideas down. But I find, walking between those two worlds, that they do not yet feel aligned in the way I'd like them to be.

It's funny, but now, many years later, I'm considered a senior citizen in the social entrepreneurship movement! But in that time, I think I've learned quite a bit about how the next generation of donors, volunteers, and social entrepreneurs think. And I've come to see how the field can do a lot more to respond effectively to what the next generation wants, without throwing away everything that has gone before.

Balancing the Old and the New

Ever since I was very young, maybe 3 or 4 years old, I have felt an intense responsibility to "the family," which means all of the assets of the family—the people, the land, the resources. I was taught that the assets of the family are going to allow me to have opportunities in life, and my responsibility is to take good care of the family while the family enables me to pursue whatever else it is that I want. This sense of responsibility also affects the attitude and approach I take as a funder. I am privileged to get invited into a lot of rooms that I otherwise would not be invited into, and I take that very seriously. I try hard to steward these resources in a way that hopefully does a

(continued)

(continued)

lot of really impactful things, even if that means changing how we as a family give. Stewardship and strategy juxtapose and complement each other, in my view, and I've learned how to take advantage of this balance of the old and the new.

Looking to the future, in 20 years I want the foundation to have a clearer philosophy, a better articulated theory of change, and a more defined ethos about how we engage grantees. I hope at that point I am tapping into even wider resources and communities in my giving and seeing the best that is out there to fund.

In 20 years we'll also have the fifth generation of our family engaged. I hope as we bring that generation in we'll be modeling good behavior, both in the foundation and in the family business. We want the rising generations to share our view that we all need to work together and we all value stewardship and good care of family resources.

I imagine it will be hard to hold space for our kids to start designing strategy, especially as I imagine it will look very different from what my cousins and I have built. With any luck, they will show up with this chapter in hand, to remind us that this strategy work is ultimately about being forward-looking, about serving the future, and about experimentation and unexpected opportunities. I look forward to that day.

Mary's experience diving deeply into the world of philanthropy and social entrepreneurship is a dramatic illustration of points we heard from many other next gen donors. She sincerely wants to be a good steward of a family legacy and to pass that on now to her own children. But she is also excited over how much more impact her family can have if they adopt an innovative philanthropic strategy—if they are more *focused, proactive, entrepreneurial,* and *systems-oriented,* yet still careful and smart. In fact, for Mary, being innovative is her family's legacy. And she hopes her kids will adopt and carry on that legacy as well.

In another sense, however, Mary is unlike many other next gen donors. She inherited a family legacy of innovation, yes, but the foundation itself did not have much of a preestablished strategy, nor a strong-willed old guard. She was able to introduce her revolutionary strategy without having to overthrow the old one. Many other next gen donors face a bumpier path to changing strategy.

Give Local—But Differently

We know Gen Xers and Millennials are extremely globally aware generations, growing up in a time of easy access to information. They might, in fact, know more about hunger in Sudan than they do about hunger in their hometowns.

But we also know that they have an ardent desire for personal engagement and for seeing their impact. This desire helps explain a somewhat surprising finding from our research: Next gen donors still want to give to local organizations. "Addressing problems in my local community or hometown" was still rated as one of the top five reasons for engaging in philanthropy. One donor offered an interesting metaphor to explain why she wanted to focus on local giving: "It's almost like when you're sitting in a café and you hear the cacophony all around you, and you literally just want to put your headphones in and stare at your computer. The more globally aware you are—you know of all of these things happening all over the world—the more you really want to hunker down and focus right where you are and see how much of an impact you can make." This finding will likely come as good news to those who worry that local causes will lose support as the next gen members become big givers.

But remember, *how* next gen donors want to support local communities, and the types of organizations they want to support, are changing. They want to give locally, but with a new strategy and using new tools. This means that although local causes in general will still get support, some local charities serving those causes will struggle to retain next gen donors unless they offer them new ways to engage.

Similarly, a concern we often hear in the family foundation field—a field dominated by foundations that have deep connections to place—is that next gen donors may never live in those communities. Here, too, we have somewhat good news. Next gen donors connected to place-based family foundations repeatedly told us they are committed to maintaining a focus on their legacy communities, even if they don't live in those communities now. This was Mary Galeti's story, of course, and we heard similar stories from others. To compensate for not living in the town where their families give, these donors often seek out site visits when they are in that area. They also try to develop close working relationships with the organizations their foundation supports. Without those local touch points, the giving from a faraway foundation would be less inspiring and interesting to them because they could not see, hear, or touch the impact.

Local giving can also offer an olive branch to siblings and cousins who serve as trustees of family funds and foundations but who may have disparate interests and community commitments. Here we see the key strategic priority for the next gen that we highlighted earlier: its desire to focus their giving on just a few causes and organizations. Consider how one donor, who is now on the board of his family's foundation, explained a decision he and his cousins made: "We are pretty spread out geographically, so we have decided to focus on the city where my mother and her generation grew up and where the money was actually made and created. It has been nice to keep us focused on something that we all love and care about and also not splinter the focus of the foundation."

This finding reinforces that there is not going to be a revolution in the causes preferred by the next generation of major donors. The revolution will be in their strategies for giving to those causes.

What Does This Mean?

The next generations of big donors follow their passion in their giving, like other donors. But their passion is to improve philanthropic strategy itself, to maximize impact. This desire to change giving worries many people. Will the next gen give to the same causes and communities? Will it revolutionize philanthropic giving so much that it becomes unrecognizable or, worse, will philanthropy's positive impact on our lives and communities be lost in the shuffle?

The findings we've reviewed in this chapter likely give some comfort, but there is reason for caution as well. Big changes are certainly coming. And like other parts of the Impact Revolution, these changes in how the next gen gives will be messy and frustrating for a while. They will certainly force many other people around the philanthropic and nonprofit table to change in turn. But we believe that if we can adjust to this new reality, and if the next gen donors themselves approach the process with humility, sincerity, and patience, then Generation Impact might just make headway on some of our most persistent and troubling social problems.

This coming transformation in philanthropic approach by the biggest donors of the future means they will favor certain organizations, which in turn means other organizations will likely suffer. This is the harsh reality of the Impact Revolution.

While all nonprofits will have to adjust to the strategic approach of these new major donors, some will have to adapt more than others. Large, traditional institutions will not be able to magically transform into smaller ones, but they can be creative about making themselves seem small to next gen donors. Instead of asking these new donors to contribute to your big fundraising campaign, get them connected to a special program or new initiative, one where they can see their contribution bringing about tangible and meaningful impact. Combination organizations like United Ways or Jewish Federations will have a special challenge. They need to discover ways that next gen donors can feel more connected to the ultimate beneficiaries of their contributions or can feel like they are supporting a strategic, evidence-based solution that gets at root causes.

Next gen donors also want more information and impact measures from nonprofits, and this desire requires nonprofit professionals to be open to gathering and giving that information. The next gen donors' desire to educate themselves about issues and to focus on proven solutions can make them better thought partners for nonprofit work if nonprofit professionals find greater ways to engage them at that substantive level.

As we've seen, next gen donors want to change how we do philanthropy not because they are bored with traditional giving but because they are convinced these changes will lead to better results. They are so convinced of this, in fact, that they feel they have no choice but to make these changes. And they plan to do so whether the older generations come along with them or not—though they'd welcome the company.

This means conflicts over strategy might be a chief source of friction within multigenerational giving families and vehicles like foundations. As Mary Galeti's story illustrates, next gen donors want to lead their families into more proactive, focused, effective, and entrepreneurial approaches. But in families where older generations have long-standing, ingrained commitments to certain conventional methods or favored organizational partners, this eagerness to shift to a new approach will meet resistance. And this resistance—or perceived inflexibility—might lead to the next generation opting out of the family giving process altogether.

Philanthropic families looking to engage the next gen better would do well to find ways to accommodate the passion these rising family members have for new strategies. They can also help these up-and-coming donors feel more connected to the local impact the family has, giving them the chance to see the results of their new plans.

We also advise next gen donors to be careful as they implement their changes so that good intentions do not lead to unintended consequences. The keen focus on attacking root causes and funding "change not charity," for instance, can sometimes mean neglecting essential, even emergency, services and aid. Focusing so much on upstream causes for future systems change could mean we overlook those drowning downstream today, so balancing the portfolio of giving to address both should be an intentional strategy.

Finally, the call for greater transparency and reporting from organizations could be helpful despite the extra work involved. But it could also tip the balance of power in philanthropy even more toward the donor side, giving donors more control over organizational choices like how to define success or determine which programs take priority. Donors should be sure that their desire for information and research actually becomes their practice, not just something they demand of organizations but then don't use. As one donor we interviewed lamented, "Would I like to be researching organizations and the different types of things that they do, and developing an opinion on what the best way to go about it is? Yes. Am I doing that now? No. Is that a conflict internally? Yes."[8]

—◌—

Next gen donors want to transform giving, even if it means some rough sailing along the way, because they are convinced their changes will improve giving. As this next gen donor reflects, "The vision I have for how [my giving] might work takes a lot of time; it takes a lot of energy. It is more labor-intensive than the traditional models of philanthropy. But I am really committed to putting in that time. It feels like my calling in life right now."

CHAPTER 4

Why Not Innovate?

Next gen donors find many faults in old-school philanthropy, the greatest of which being that many of our most troubling social problems persist despite decades of philanthropic giving. If all that giving to education has led to the largely dysfunctional system we have now, something isn't working. If we still have dramatic, rising economic inequality despite hundreds of millions of dollars in philanthropic giving to address this specific problem, then maybe, next gen donors reason, it's time we try a new approach.

Their desire to make seemingly intractable problems tractable motivates next gen donors to try innovative methods. In fact, their willingness to veer away from the usual suspects in the philanthropic lineup and experiment with new approaches is perhaps their most revolutionary characteristic. To achieve the big impact they long for—revitalizing education, eliminating health disparities, and so on—they feel they need a bigger and better tool belt. And sometimes they feel the need to take more dramatic steps, even if that means blurring the lines between the nonprofit sector and other sectors.

Next gen donors aren't just less afraid than previous generations to experiment with unlikely mechanisms for change; they're downright eager to try nontraditional funding vehicles. In a way, they want to disrupt philanthropy, just like Amazon disrupted the publishing industry, and Airbnb the hotel industry.

Experimentation, like revolutions, can be chaotic and risky. Failure is a very real possibility. But if the payoff is progress on our toughest social problems, then next gen donors think temporary chaos is a small price to pay.

Excited About Innovation, Okay with Blurriness

Next gen donors have the advantage of being new to the philanthropic game. Or at least they see this as an advantage. As one donor put it, the next gen donors in his family "aren't shackled by inherited wisdom about how things are done and should be done," and this "naiveté" is a "great asset," because they can "come into the room and ask very basic questions" about why things are done a certain way and why other options aren't being explored.

Our interviews revealed that next gen donors love to shake things up with these sorts of questions, in part because they have a profound belief that "there has to be a better way." They believe in the power of innovation, and they want to design that better way. "We want to invest in innovators because these problems have been happening for a while, and they're not going to be solved by the same type of approaches," explains one next gen donor.

Another donor underscored how this was part of a generational shift, a willingness to let go of assumptions about what has been and an open-mindedness to what could be: "I think there is an element in this next gen of being totally open and okay with things that were taboo not too long ago. There's an element of accepting things that the older generations just didn't. Boundaries are just being completely obliterated, for better or worse."

If not all boundaries are being "obliterated," lots of them—especially the boundaries between the traditional for-profit and nonprofit sectors—are being blurred by the innovations that so excite this next generation. They see this as a positive shift and even a harbinger of changes across the philanthropic landscape.

Maybe the most visible example of this blurring is the Chan Zuckerberg Initiative (CZI), which we introduced earlier in the book. CZI was established not as a traditional family foundation or charitable trust but as a "charitable limited liability company (LLC)." This variation on the for-profit legal form allows Mark Zuckerberg and Priscilla Chan the freedom to deploy their assets for good across multiple sectors. They can make philanthropic gifts but also invest in socially responsible companies or support public policy advocacy and campaigns without the restrictions that traditional nonprofit entities would have. And while critics argue that by funneling their philanthropy through an LLC, Chan and Zuckerberg skirt certain transparency and disclosure requirements, the founders insist that their justification for this unusual path is to be able to use as many mechanisms for change as possible and to avoid the limitations of purely charitable vehicles.[1]

Though older generations are often uncomfortable with blurring boundaries—they worry about a slippery slope toward commercializing charity, for instance—Gen Xers and Millennials have a much higher tolerance for this approach. In fact, they are excited about it: "I think it's a very exciting time to be involved in this [field.] People are just thinking differently about philanthropy. They are not just writing checks to established nonprofits, to the United Way or the Red Cross. They're saying, 'Well, there are these Kiva loans and there are these social businesses and there are these double-bottom-line, triple-bottom-line investments.' There are a million different ways to be philanthropic in 2012 that there weren't in 1985."[2]

It isn't hard to understand why these generations are more comfortable with this blurriness when we consider that they were steeped in sector-blurring innovations throughout their formative years. They grew up buying pink M&Ms that both tasted good and funded breast cancer research, choosing among various fair-trade coffee options that offered a great beverage and supported indigenous farmers, or buying fashionable Feed brand handbags stamped with numbers to signify the number of meals or micronutrient packets provided to hungry people as a result of its purchase.[3] Younger generations grew up in a time when companies marketed themselves as "socially responsible," especially Millennials, whose cohort recently surpassed the Baby Boomers in size and who represent a massive consumer block.

But we should be careful not to assume that this embrace of blurriness—and of tools that borrow business methods, logics, and language—arises out of a heightened commitment to or infatuation with capitalism among rising generations. Rather, it stems from their desire to have more "tools in their tool belt"—a metaphor we heard a lot. They want to design the best solutions to problems. If that means trying out ideas from the business world, then why not? Sector boundaries are not sacrosanct to the next gen. If crossing or blurring boundaries in smart ways can help those in need, advance environmental sustainability, or improve health outcomes, then why not embrace this?

The New Tool Belt

We heard this revolutionary call for trying new, innovative methods loud and clear throughout our years of research. Next gen donors talked about a litany of particular methods they want to add—or maybe already have added—to their philanthropic portfolios. Below are the most common new tools they want to explore as they become the dominant donors in our society.

Impact Investing

Traditional 501(c)(3) private foundations in the United States are legally required to pay out a minimum of 5 percent of their endowed assets each year on grants, operations, and other program costs. In recent years, critics have argued that traditional donors see this 5 percent as the only portion of their considerable assets that can or should be used for good; they ignore the other 95 percent of the endowment left in investments.[4] Many next gen donors we spoke with agreed strongly with this criticism. They think investing the 95 percent in the right ways might even do more good in the world than making grants from the 5 percent.

In fact, what has come to be known generally as "impact investing" was the most commonly discussed new tool among the next gen donors we talked with. They want to invest many if not all of their assets in ways that advance their social, not just financial, goals. Impact investing can be both about *divesting*, or avoiding companies doing bad in the world, and *investing* in companies doing good. It can mean—as Justin Rockefeller, featured in this chapter, describes—divesting a foundation's endowment from the fossil fuel industry, or it can be about investing in clean energy start-ups, unionized hotels, or organic farms. And as impact investing rapidly gains popularity among foundations and individual donors alike, many of the primary cheerleaders for it are next gen donors.[5]

In a way, though, this keen interest in impact investing among next gen donors is not surprising. As we've seen, they have considerable, even unprecedented, financial assets (inherited or earned) that they must now decide how to invest. And they know their financial assets give them the sort of power that can get things done in our society. Why not use this power for good?

This approach reveals a cautiously pragmatic attitude of next gen donors toward capitalism. They realize it is a system that can cause global problems and foster deep inequalities—inequalities that they have personally benefited from, in some cases to an astounding degree. But rather than overturn capitalism, they want to use it to redress inequality, maybe even to stave off global problems at their source.[6]

Funding beyond Grants

Next gen donors are also intrigued by a number of creative new funding mechanisms, now emerging in the philanthropic space, that move beyond the traditional grant. Most popular are no- or low-interest loans. These include microloans to support small business entrepreneurs—for example, tailors looking to open a small shop in Nairobi. On sites like Kiva.org, donors can "choose a borrower" by seeing the faces and reading the stories and business ideas of real people looking for microloans and then get periodic updates about the progress of the funded venture. The microinvestments get repaid, and donors can then reinvest the money in another worthy project. Another sort of alternative financing method, called program-related investments (PRIs), is being used increasingly by foundations—as Mary Galeti described in Chapter 3. PRIs can be loans, loan guarantees, or other methods more commonly used by banks.

Next gen donors are deeply attracted to these alternatives to grants as ways to better leverage their assets for bigger impact. Some like the idea of loans because it helps get past the traditional power dynamics of grantor and grantee that make them uncomfortable as major donors.

Crowdfunding and Giving Collaboratives

Giving alongside other donors isn't a new tool for philanthropy, of course, but the development of some new methods—especially giving circles, funder collaboratives, and online crowdfunding platforms—has certainly changed how collaborative giving can happen. Younger donors are particularly attracted to these new ways to "give together." Next gen donors are the driving force behind many growing donor collaboratives, especially those in the progressive giving space such as Solidaire and Funders for Justice. As we will see in Chapter 7, they are also particularly excited about giving circles. In fact, in our survey "giving circle or pooled fund" was one of the few charitable vehicles that next gen donors said they already use personally (14.8 percent) more than their families do (4.8).

While many of the new online crowdfunding sites are not explicitly philanthropic, many can be used for philanthropic purposes, and some are intended to raise funds for charitable projects only. We heard a lot from next gen donors about crowdfunding ventures like DonorsChoose.org for education giving, GlobalGiving for international projects, and Kickstarter for the arts. Like with Kiva for microloans, these charitable crowdfunding sites allow next gen donors to see who they are funding—a key element of their desire for impact, as we saw in Chapter 2. The sites humanize the recipients in a respectful and engaging way. Next gen donors also appreciate the leverage and the collaborative, peer-based spirit of crowdfunding. They can make larger grants by pooling their assets, and they get the many benefits of collaborating with other donors. We will hear more about the appeal of Kickstarter from Victoria Rogers, a donor featured in Chapter 5, and more about this peer orientation, which drives many next gen donors, in Chapter 7.

Social Business and Social Enterprise

For some next gen donors, promoting and funding "socially-responsible businesses"—those with a double- or triple-bottom-line—can actually be a better alternative to funding nonprofits. If an entrepreneur wants to help, say, girls in impoverished regions get better access to health care, many next gen donors feel like that entrepreneur would do better to start an innovative "social enterprise" business to serve this need rather than found a nonprofit.

The Acumen Fund and d.light are great examples of the appeal of social businesses to next gen donors. Acumen Fund is a nonprofit through which donors can invest in social businesses and entrepreneurs in the developing world. Among other initiatives, Acumen invests in new factories and provides jobs for women in Africa to make and sell mosquito nets to ward off malaria instead of just giving charitable money to women to buy the nets. Founded in 2006 by two Stanford MBA students in their mid-20s, d.light is a social enterprise offering affordable solar lighting and power solutions to people around the world who lack reliable access to electricity.

Domestically, new for-profit/nonprofit hybrids like B Corps or charitable LLCs also intrigue these donors.[7] They see great potential for B Corps that know how to make a profit but formally commit a portion of that profit to social benefit, like Patagonia did in 2016 by donating 100 percent of its global Black Friday sales to "grassroots organizations working in local communities to protect our air, water, and soil for future generations."[8]

Advocacy, Policy, and Movement Giving

The desire to find strategies that address root causes and result in system changes leads some next gen donors to fund advocacy, policy reform efforts, and movement organizing, especially at the grassroots level. They see previous generations of donors as wary of such giving, in part because they wanted to avoid sticking their necks out and taking a public stand with their giving. But next gen donors believe activism is sometimes necessary and that going public can have benefits that outweigh the downside of public scrutiny. One donor explained, "In my parents' generation, every instinct is to say, 'I don't know, do we really want to put ourselves out there? We could end up in the media.' Whereas for my generation it's like, 'Well, the whole point would be about telling other people about it and getting other people to do it and being a voice for it.'"

Many in the next gen want to be "louder" about their giving, whether in social media or otherwise. Some believe they had a special calling to fund grassroots organizing and movements like the marriage equality movement or Black Lives Matter, even if doing so brings more attention to them and/or their families as major donors. They see that such movements garner less attention from traditional donors than museums, hospitals, or universities do, and they feel the need to shift major giving in their direction. Advocacy and policy giving are championed as "important strategic levers" and a means of having a "much bigger impact" than giving for direct services. Some donors emphasize the importance of political giving alongside philanthropic giving. Others, like Alex Soros featured in Chapter 9, talk about actively donating to 501(c)(4) organizations, not just (c)(3)s, or about why giving for public policy research or advocacy can lead to greater social change—you just have to wait longer to achieve it.[9]

Using Every Tool for Impact

Say "philanthropist" to someone today, and one of the names likely to come up is Rockefeller—a name synonymous with extraordinary giving in this country. Most people know the Rockefellers for having made one of the largest fortunes in American history from oil and for being affiliated with Rockefeller Center in midtown Manhattan. In addition, the family has founded many universities, cofounded institutions like the Museum of Modern Art, generated 24 Nobel prizes out of Rockefeller University, and guided several philanthropic foundations, starting with the Rockefeller Foundation in 1913. Rockefeller philanthropy was behind Grand Teton National Park, the yellow fever vaccine, and so much more.

From the beginning, the Rockefellers have been concerned with giving efficiently and effectively.[10] John D. Rockefeller Sr.'s great-great-grandson, Justin Rockefeller, is deeply proud of his family's philanthropic achievements. But like other next gen donors, he thinks his family can and should evolve its approach to increase their impact.

Justin Rockefeller

What's in a Name?

My father grew up in New York City with the already famous moniker John D. Rockefeller IV, going by "Jay" to lessen the burden of that name. After college and studying abroad in Japan, he moved to D.C. and in the early '60s worked in the Peace Corps and at the State Department, becoming friendly with Washington movers and shakers such as Robert F. Kennedy, Dean Rusk, Sargent Shriver, and Roger Hilsman. He became a VISTA (Volunteer in Service to America) to serve Americans who were gritty and valued hard work but were in a really tough situation. He moved to West Virginia in the mid-1960s and fell in love with the state and the people, eventually working his way up the legislature to become governor in 1976. That's why he

---

and my mom, Sharon Rockefeller, who has been WETA Public Television's CEO for nearly 30 years, raised me along with my three siblings in West Virginia.

The reason I mention this is because my father made both a geographic and a psychological shift away from New York City and many things Rockefeller. I didn't grow up hearing about wealth or philanthropy at all, but I did hear a lot about public service and public broadcasting, witnessed my parents work extremely hard, and heard each of them express the value of hard work. I knew that we had resources because we lived in a big house, but my father didn't speak much about our family members' institutions or history. Household discussions usually revolved around politics. At Princeton, I studied politics because that is what I knew—though I was also introduced there to philosophers such as Peter Singer, who was the first to introduce me to the notion that "what you do with money has moral consequences," which profoundly influenced who I am and what I do.

In my freshman year, my older brother was already living in New York City, and he said, "You really should come here and start learning about this city. Come spend the weekend, and let's meet for lunch near Rock Center." I said, "Okay cool. Where is that?" That was my cue that I needed to start learning about the family. I read the book *Titan* about John D. Rockefeller, and decided I would move to New York to learn more about family institutions and get to know more cousins.

So after college, I went to New York City and worked at the Museum of Modern Art (MoMA) in government relations, partly because of the intersection of my interests in art and politics, and partly because my great-grandmother cofounded it and it was high on my list of family-related institutions to get to know. While at MoMA, I joined the board of the Rockefeller Family Fund (RFF), a grantmaking foundation established by my family's third and fourth generations that is relatively smaller than the two older family foundations—about an $80 million endowment when I was

(continued)

(continued)

on the board—which provided me with early exposure to philanthropy in general.

The Power of Social Entrepreneurs and the Private Sector

That experience led me in my mid-20s to develop ideas of my own and cofound a social enterprise called GenerationEngage focused on connecting community college students to the political process and politicians to community college students. I helped build GenerationEngage for five years and learned a lot along the way.

During this time, I also met many social entrepreneurs who became heroes to me, such as Bill Drayton of Ashoka, Charles Best of DonorsChoose.org, and Linda Rottenberg and Peter Kellner of Endeavor. I asked them what was and wasn't working and learned one of their common frustrations was around scale: A disproportionate percentage of their time and effort went to fundraising. So I thought, "I know that the nonprofit sector has quite limited scale; government has considerable scale but is bureaucratic; the private sector has by far the most scale." And I realized I knew too little about the private sector or the capital markets, so I decided to learn more about those.

I made a deliberate and unsubtle shift to a fund of hedge funds called Uhuru Capital Management, which donated 25 percent of its general partnership performance fees to a foundation that would invest in social businesses and write checks to Ashoka and Endeavor—social enterprises supporting high-impact entrepreneurs in emerging markets. In 2009, when the very concept of capitalism came under scrutiny, Uhuru's Jed Emerson and Managing Director Peter Kellner convinced me that capitalism was ripe for a new chapter and a better way. I loved the Uhuru model, but the timing was unfortunate and the fund did not survive the Great Recession.

I then moved into venture capital to work directly with entrepreneurs. I did that first in New York City and then in Palo Alto after my wife matriculated at Stanford Business

School. In Silicon Valley in early 2012, I joined the financial technology company where I now work, Addepar, which makes complex portfolios easy to understand, allowing investors and advisors to make more informed decisions. Addepar helps its clients understand what they own, which is the critical but harder-than-one-would-think first step when aligning values and investments.

Naïve Questions about Maximizing Impact

Meanwhile, my involvement in the family foundations continued, and I joined the board of the Rockefeller Brothers Fund (RBF). It was founded in 1940 by the five brothers who were sons of JDR Jr., including my grandfather, JDR III, and, different than RFF, is comprised of half family members and half nonfamily members to bring additional expertise to bear on the subject matters we're funding. From 1940 to 1953, there was no endowment, but in 1953, because JDR Jr. felt very proud of his five sons and their work—much of it focused on postwar rebuilding—he decided to endow RBF.

RBF's mission is broad: to advance social change that contributes to a more just, sustainable, and peaceful world. The program areas support peace building, sustainable development, democratic practice, and the arts. We also support what we call "pivotal places," or specific geographies where we do most of the spending on those four themes. We calibrate funding levels among those programs, and also among the strategies that constitute the programs, as the times dictate.

Within RBF, I saw my best opportunity to add value not on the program side—where the brainpower and expertise around the table is extraordinary—but on the investment committee working on how we invest the endowment. I used my naïveté about investment management for what I hoped would be the good of the foundation as a whole. For example, I asked questions such as, "If we are spending almost $10 million a year fighting climate change,

(continued)

(continued)

why do we have a $2.5 million position in Coal India, the nationalized coal company there? I don't understand all the nuances of finance yet, but that seems strange to me." Fortunately, the president and other staff of the foundation were already interested in this idea and for years had worked on shareholder activism. But the foundation hadn't yet changed the investment policy statement or taken meaningful board action.

In 2010, we as a board decided to issue a mandate to our outsourced chief investment officer to invest up to 10 percent of the endowment in a way that aligned with our mission. At the time, RBF's endowment was approximately $750 million, so 10 percent would have been $75 million aligned with the mission. In February 2014, we started to divest of fossil fuels as part of this alignment strategy. We started to divest at around $106 a barrel of oil—and now oil is less than $40 a barrel; while the decision ended up being a good one financially, we did it for moral reasons. We're now down to less than half of our initial exposure to fossil fuels, and eventually we are going to come to as close to zero exposure as is realistic. Overall, the RBF endowment is now up to about $850 million, and 40+ percent—a percentage that will continue to grow—of that aligns with our mission through ESG and impact managers. I'm very proud of the work we're doing there.[11]

Ultimately, the key questions that RBF was asking were, "What does our tool belt look like? What else besides grants does it include? What are our resources for effecting change? How do we maximize the positive impact of the foundation as a whole?" I hope maximizing positive impact is every foundation's goal.

In asking those questions at RBF, we realized the endowment itself is one of our key tools for effecting change. Frankly, we also appreciated that the Rockefeller name is a powerful tool in the climate conversation given its historical ties to the fossil fuel industry. So we intentionally announced our plans to join what is called the "divest-invest movement" during Climate Week in 2014 to further stimulate public discourse and move the needle on climate change. We hoped people would ask, "If a Rockefeller family entity can divest fossil fuels—the family fortune having come from oil—could our pool of capital do that as well without compromising financial returns?"

More Impact for Everyone

All of this work with RBF inspired me to ask myself similarly thoughtful questions such as, "What does my tool belt look like, and how do I maximize it for social change?" If my tools include credibility with an influential network, a surname that opens doors, time, energy, motivation, relevant experience, limited personal capital, and working at a company that has best-in-class technology, then how could I use these tools for change in deeper ways?

This has led me to use my unique tool set to engage ever deeper in impact investing and to look for ways to help others in this work. When I ask other families why they do not align their values with their investments, I hear the same responses over and over: "I don't know what works and what doesn't work. Do I have to compromise returns? Who are the great managers out there? What are the trends? I'm excited about the idea but nervous about dipping my toes in these waters."

I decided there needed to be something like The Giving Pledge (in which billionaires pledge to devote more than half their wealth to philanthropy), but for impact investing. Over lunch with my friend Josh Cohen, the managing partner at City Light Capital, an impact investment venture firm, we decided to cofound The ImPact, a nonprofit network of family enterprises (family offices, foundations, and businesses) committed to impact investing.[12] Its purpose is to improve the probability and pace of solving social problems by increasing the flow of capital to investments that generate measurable social impact.

To achieve its mission, The ImPact provides families and their organizations with the knowledge and network they need to make

(continued)

81

(continued)

more impact investments more effectively and uses sophisticated technology—Addepar donates its software to The ImPact—for data aggregation, analysis, and reporting. The ImPact is a tool for its members to learn both from each other and from impact and financial data that have been largely missing from the conversation. The Impact provides a safe space, so members can share with one another what they are invested in, their interests, and the problems they are hoping to address.

We want to shift the narrative of philanthropy and impact investing from one of inputs (dollars committed) to outcomes (impact created). The Giving Pledge inspired The ImPact and is a wonderful thing for the world, but, on a surface level, is primarily about the input of billionaires giving away half their money and less about the outcomes of what actually results from that. With The ImPact, we want the focus to be on the outcomes and impacts.

The next generation wants to use all the tools on our tool belts and even invent new tools that can create lasting change and maximize positive impact. That impact, ultimately, is the goal.

Justin could easily assume the prestigious mantle of his family's philanthropic empire and do a lot of good in the world by carrying forward what they've done for decades. He sees the power in the assets he inherited—the famous name, the endowments and institutions already built and designated for charitable use. But he wants to be an innovator—not because he just wants to "make his mark" somehow instead of only being known as the next one up in the Rockefeller line; he wants to prove a new approach because he's convinced that is what's needed to maximize impact.

To make real change now, though, he wants to add new tools like impact investing or other innovations from social entrepreneurs—even if doing so means his family foundation divests from the very sources of capital that made the fortune in the first place. And he is working to help others in his generation do this as well, to build a movement of entrepreneurial next gen donors and impact investors who have the chance to transform the landscape of major giving in the future.

Aspirational Innovators

Unlike Justin, not all next gen donors are avidly using the range of new tools available, at least not in their current giving. In fact, our survey showed that next gen donors still primarily give through traditional vehicles—as part of a family foundation; through a donor-advised fund; online to organizations or through giving portals; or by check, cash, or workplace giving.[13] But when we asked them about their future giving, we found clear evidence that many are eager to expand their repertoire of vehicles. "There is a difference between what I think is important and what is actually reflected in my current giving," one explained. "There are many ideals I strive for that I have not yet hit." And those who *were* currently experimenting with new tools were, like Justin, exceedingly passionate about them. They often proselytized among other rising donors, cajoling them to try new approaches.

For those next gen donors who still give primarily through a family foundation started by previous generations, their excitement about new tools means they find themselves lobbying for change within their families. Many talked about pushing their families to do more impact investing of their charitable endowments, for instance, or to think about investing in PRIs or funding more advocacy. Some were just eager to see their family foundations embrace new ways of working; as this young trustee exclaimed, "I wish they would just knock down all the walls at the foundation and put drafting tables in the middle of the space and everyone could just work together!"

Keen next gen changemakers know this sort of transformation in family institutions can be slow, but they see pushing for it as their objective. One donor who was active in her family's large foundation explained the challenge well: "I think there is a certain appetite [among older family members and staff] for exploring different models, but at the same time, I think as an organization it's just inevitable that change is going to be very, very slow. I think it's that metaphor of the cruise ship versus the speedboat. A cruise ship is not going to turn on a dime when you start swinging the wheel; it might be five minutes before the thing starts to turn because it's just so massive."

To be clear, pursuing a range of new methods doesn't mean abandoning the traditional tools. Rather, next gen donors want to *add* these innovations to the portfolio of options they have for doing good.

Being Unreasonable to Do Something Extraordinary

Making the sort of changes to philanthropy that next gen donors want to make—and using the innovations that so intrigue them—is, as we've said, disruptive. Interestingly, we met many younger donors who define their emerging philanthropic identities around this disruption. They want to challenge the status quo, to fund neglected ideas, and to be "unreasonable" in a field that values everyone getting along. For them, the payoff from this disruption is more impact, perhaps even extraordinary impact.

Scott Belsky is one such disruptor. A successful tech businessman and investor, Scott is also an inheritor of a family tradition of philanthropy as the grandson of the education entrepreneur Stanley Kaplan. Scott cut his philanthropic teeth at the family foundation table before growing and selling his own company to Adobe and then creating his own foundation with his wife, Erica. His current approach to giving—which he calls "responsible" yet "contrarian"—also owes a great deal to what he has learned as an entrepreneur and early-stage investor. He is adamant that the same strategy of searching for innovative models that he uses as an investor can serve him well as a donor.

Scott Belsky

My grandfather was an entrepreneur, and I have always been interested, like him, in starting and building teams. That interest has evolved into wanting to help other people who are starting and building teams, which is what I do currently.

In college I studied design and business and then, after Harvard Business School, I started a company, Behance, focused on connecting the creative world. The business was bootstrapped for five years. We went through the trenches of being a few months away from breaking even, sometimes close to not making payroll. I learned so much during that five-year experience.

Fortunately, we had one product, a network, that grew very quickly, so we raised venture capital funding and continued to grow the business until we were acquired by Adobe in 2012. This was an incredible opportunity for the team members. We had not sold a lot of the company to other investors yet, so a number of us were able to benefit significantly. I joined the parent company after being acquired and worked there for over three years before leaving to start a new company as well as become a venture partner at a venture capital firm based in the Bay Area.

(continued)

(continued)

Experiential Education in Philanthropy

I had been exposed very early to philanthropy through a family foundation that my grandfather, Stanley H. Kaplan, founded when he sold his business, the Stanley H. Kaplan Educational Center, to the Washington Post Company. Similarly, when I sold my company, Erica and I created a foundation for our own philanthropy. I feel like the background and experience I had with my family helped prepare me to be a donor, even though my wife and I certainly do our giving now in a different way than my grandparents did.

The Rita J. and Stanley H. Kaplan Family Foundation, established in 1984, was meant to exist in perpetuity by bringing new family members to the board. My sister, my parents, and my aunt are also involved in the foundation. My grandparents were very much engaged in Jewish philanthropy, health, and education, and they set some parameters that we are expected to follow as we fulfill their mission.

While serving on the board, each family member can allocate an amount of grant funds to support causes he or she is interested in. I recall joining the board while in college and having a budget of approximately $20,000 then, which was an incredible opportunity at that age. So while I didn't receive a financial inheritance from my grandparents, I did get to participate in a large foundation and to allocate my own budget. Experiencing that level of responsibility at such a young age was both a burden and a source of excitement. I took the role very seriously and found that it provided me with an experiential education in grantmaking.

I love the way that I was brought into the world of philanthropy. It was such an amazing honor. In fact, I would encourage other families to start their next gen donors off by giving them autonomy over their own grants budget—even a small one. By doing so, the next gen can feel that sense of responsibility, and also that sense of pride in becoming involved with organizations they decide to support. I think it's powerful to let the next gen make decisions as individuals and to learn from those. In fact, as the cofounder of my own foundation now, I'm cognizant of the lessons I learned, and plan to use those to help my own children, who will participate in our philanthropy someday.

Responsible yet Contrarian

I try to remind myself not to just fall into the rut of getting involved with things because I was asked to support them or because it strokes my ego to do so. Instead, Erica and I try to identify a few issues in which we are most interested and then take advantage of the opportunity we have to learn more about those issues, and support them with our time and our passion, to make the most impact.

I am always most impressed with philanthropists who have this sort of deep commitment to education and a passion for what they support. Bill and Melinda Gates are icons of being the most knowledgeable about the things they are investing in. I think this is actually a component of fiduciary responsibility. If you're going to give away money that the public has some right to—based on the fact that it is tax-advantaged to give it away—you have a responsibility to understand what you are supporting and to be connected to it in a meaningful way.

While responsibility is important, I also want to be strategic and even take some risks. I have developed a somewhat contrarian approach to philanthropy, focusing on orphan causes that, if supported, can have a disproportionate effect on society.

An example of this is an organization that Erica and I support called Defy Ventures. They equip formerly incarcerated people who want to be entrepreneurs with feedback, coaching, mentorship, and funding to help them get their businesses off the ground. We find society tends to write off people who've made a mistake and become incarcerated. When they are released, they can't get jobs and are ostracized from society, even though they might have more hunger to prove themselves than anyone else, to turn their lives around and reestablish their names and credibility. To me, those are people we

(continued)

(continued)

should be betting on, and so we make strategic gifts to help people like this who are underserved yet have high potential.

As I've developed this approach, I've evolved how I want to engage in philanthropy. In my early 20s, I had the opportunity to attend a lot of conferences with my family foundation, to benefit from educational opportunities, and to participate in networks like Grand Street—a network for 18- to 28-year-olds who are going to be involved in philanthropy and want to clarify their values, vision, and philanthropic direction among a group of peers. These opportunities played a huge role for me at that age, helping me develop my voice and feel confident about my role in a family foundation. It had a very profound impact on me.

Now, in my 30s, while I still want to increase my surface area and knowledge about philanthropy, I don't value spending time at conferences. Instead, I want to be doubling down on understanding the issues that are interesting to me and where I could have more impact. I want to focus on results. I want to focus on what I can do to make the most impact in the world. So I don't find sitting on nonprofit boards to be the best use of my time right now. Those boards seem to be too much about coddling and appeasing donors so they will keep giving money. I will keep supporting an organization as long as I believe in it and have an interest and passion for it. And I try to support our grantees beyond just the dollars I give, but in a way that I feel can make an impact. For example, I like to do specific things that help organizations, such as making certain calls or giving feedback in an area in which I have an expertise.

Innovation at the Edge of Reason

My approach to giving has also been influenced by my experiences as an investor. For example, in the investment world, if you ask too many people what they think and you take their feedback to heart, you will never make a good investment because you will always end up regressing to what is familiar. And everyone will find fault with anything that is not familiar. Similarly, if I'm thinking

88

about making a grant to an organization that is doing something differently, the more people I ask for feedback, the more people will tell me what's wrong with it because it deviates from the mean of what is already known. If you keep hearing that cautious kind of feedback over and over, you start to doubt the thing that lured you to this organization or cause in the first place.

For this reason, I don't like angel investment groups where investors join together. I think those defy the whole point of investing, which is to see things that other people don't and to make decisions independently without being skewed by what is trending or popular. I don't want to be influenced by too many other sources of noise, not as an investor nor as a donor.

The other principle from great investing that I apply in philanthropy is that innovation happens at the edge of reason, so sometimes you have to be a little unreasonable. If you are too reasonable, if you are always anchored to the business models that are known to work or the marketing strategy that is known to work, then you are always going to pick the company that may be a safer investment, but it is never going to be the one that has the 100x-multiple return. The greatest investments in the world are brand-new business models, brand-new market strategies, brand-new concepts that change an industry rather than just make it more efficient.

Similarly, with philanthropy, if you want to do something really extraordinary—or if you want to address causes that have never been addressed properly—you have to be able to think at the edge of reason; you have to be a little unreasonable. Unfortunately, in a field that prioritizes collaboration, that strategy can make you a bad group member. No one wants to be in a group with someone who is being super unreasonable. But I think that's the way to have the most impact.

This mindset is definitely informed by my work in investing. In fact, I think there is a West Coast tech-investing way of thinking in which people don't conform that is changing philanthropy out here. While there are some things that we shouldn't reinvent all

(continued)

89

(continued)

the time, I believe there are some things that should be questioned, which is what West Coast philanthropy is trying to do. It's adopting an entrepreneurial approach, applying a nonconformist mindset where people are willing to fund something bold.

Said another way, there is less desire among the next gen to contribute to large organizations and keep funding the status quo. I understand someone has to fund those organizations. It's not always the right answer to be contrarian. It's important that we keep museums running. But I don't think this is the role next gen donors should play. I am especially good at funding the stuff on the edge of reason, and this is where I get most excited. So I'd rather do that than just write a large check to a massive status-quo organization, knowing that older donors will support those. I want to make more strategic gifts, and I believe next gen donors like me want to support organizations that can affect change.

I also don't identify with giving for status. I saw this on Wall Street early in my career, where older colleagues stood publicly and announced how much they gave to a particular cause, which seemed to me like they were proclaiming their wealth and self-importance. It rubbed me the wrong way. If you want to give for the right reasons, to support an organization's mission because it echoes with how you want to change the world, I think that the ego can get in the way of that. Of course the ego is always there, but I try to ground my decisions in knowledge and passion for an idea. I think next gen donors are ultimately not as motivated by seeing our name on a list, having it on a building, or standing in front of your peers and are more focused on doing something significant.

Again, I have learned from business that if you're going to invest in something that everyone else thinks is right, you are too late. The space will be too crowded, and it will be too competitive. That ethos carries over on the philanthropy side for better or for worse. A great investor invests in something that everyone else thinks is wrong, because that is how you do something extraordinary. Same with philanthropy.

Scott certainly highlights many of the strategic preferences that we identified in the previous chapter—being responsible about due diligence, focusing on results, and so on. But we can sense from him that these strategic imperatives to be serious and responsible do not mean being cautious. We sense from him the excitement that next gen donors have for exploring new terrain and embracing innovation even if that means being nonconformist. He wants to take risks on orphan causes and neglected people and organizations—on ideas "at the edge of reason"—because those are the ones that could create epic change.

Taking Risks and Failing Forward

Next gen donors like Scott insist that to have the impact they want, they will need at times to experiment, to be bold, and to take risks that seem unusual or even unreasonable to many others. They want to take risks on new ways of attacking the causes they care about, not just trying to make the old ways more efficient. And they accept that the price for taking these risks is the possibility of failure.

These donors reject the risk-averse approach of much of traditional philanthropy. That approach, they insist, is a recipe for continued mediocre impact. Here again, many of the next gen donors advocating for more risk-taking see that mindset as something philanthropy would do well to adopt from the business world. Next gen donor Hadi Partovi, a successful tech entrepreneur and an investor like Scott who will be featured in Chapter 6, echoes this critique of traditional philanthropy and the call for emulating the risky "big-bet" approach of the tech world:

> Traditional foundations are extremely risk-averse. If you wanted to get $1 million from them for some really bold idea

that has no evidence that it could work, but it could be really big, it's just impossible. But that's where the most impact is doable. If you look at the for-profit landscape, the highest-impact companies started out that way, with this crazy idea that nobody thought would make it. But somebody took the bet on it and suddenly it's the next Uber or the next Facebook. There's no reason that shouldn't be happening in the nonprofit space.

Accepting the reality of failure is something that other prominent next gen donors, like Cari Tuna and Dustin Moskovitz, who we introduced in Chapter 2, consider essential to their improved philanthropic approach. As Cari has said, "I actually expect that most of our work will fail to have an impact, and that is part of doing high-risk philanthropy well."[14] Donors we spoke with agreed that their new approach requires what one labeled an "appetite for risk."

But what does this "high risk, high reward" giving look like? For many it means making a bet on untested, often smaller organizations with big ideas. Giving to these organizations "could make a huge difference, but with no guarantees." For others, risk involved trying out new funding models like low- or no-interest loans, funding nascent movements, or being the first funder to commit to a potential collaboration without any promise that others will join.

The possibility of failure always lurks behind this sort of risky giving. But these younger donors have a strong belief that failure can be helpful at times. It can lead to learning and improvement. "Failing forward" is considered a virtue. As one said bluntly, "Some organizations are going to fail. They're going to die and pass away. But to me that's okay, because they inform a new model for how things are done going forward."

What Does This Mean?

We argue in this book that the next generation of major donors will be the most significant philanthropists in history. This is not just because they have unprecedented resources to give. It's because they want to fundamentally change *how* giving happens. This often means trying new methods and new tools, even if these entail greater risk.

We should all brace ourselves for this potentially tumultuous time of trial and error, and for a "new normal" in which the pace of change and innovation in philanthropy moves at a much faster clip. Donors have always tried to improve philanthropy, inventing new vehicles like foundations or community chests or matching grants. But the next gen wants to accelerate that innovation dramatically. Generation Impact is willing to make bigger changes faster than previous generations.[15]

We should also prepare for failures. And next gen donors themselves need to be aware that, while failure when pursuing some idea or approach can lead to positive learning, it can also affect people's lives and livelihoods in real ways.[16]

The next gen's clear "bias toward the new" is itself reason for caution. As research has shown, innovation is not a silver bullet for solving social problems.[17] Successful implementation of innovations requires much more organizational work and faces many more obstacles than most innovation champions acknowledge. And sometimes the tried-and-true solutions of old are still the best; they've been used for a while because they work. The next gen needs to recognize these difficulties and acknowledge that its powerful position means it could force innovation into spaces that are not ready or not right for it.

93

Further, the specific innovations that are capturing much of the attention from next gen donors—those that blur the traditional boundaries between for-profit and nonprofit sectors and encourage social change efforts to use market mechanisms—make a lot of people nervous, sometimes for good reason. Some worry about the slippery slope these create toward the "commercialization of everything" and the "marketization of philanthropy."[18] Borrowing too directly from business models and translating them too quickly to the philanthropic context can ignore the subtle but vital differences in how the nonprofit sector works (e.g., how success is measured and in what time frame). One of our next gen interviewees even pointed out that there are a lot of problems in the world that markets, even socially responsible ones, simply cannot solve.

> There are many problems in the world that are almost entirely created by financial markets and by the way that we do business. And because impact investing is sexier than philanthropy, there is a danger that we will all just say, "oh, this is the answer." That is very, very dangerous because there is a high risk that it perpetuates the systems, the structures of power that exist in the world that do need to be profoundly disrupted in order to effect the social and environmental change that needs to happen.

Despite these cautions, these powerful next gen donors will continue to pursue their passion for impact investing, social businesses, loan funding, and other new approaches. And if managed carefully, these methods for social change could reap huge social benefits and even make it possible for many others in our society to use these new tools.

For instance, other, smaller investors now have the luxury of making informed impact investments precisely because many next gen individuals with considerable resources to invest are asking for ways to fit their investments to their values and for more transparency from the financial industry. The next gen didn't invent impact investing, but one could argue that next gen donors' demand for it has caused financial advisors to bring more impact-investing options to market.[19] The same can be said for the clear shift toward socially responsible businesses. Millennials calling for green products, social enterprise options for buying jewelry or eyeglasses or other items, or even jobs with multiple-bottom-line companies are certainly pushing the economy decidedly further in those positive directions.

The next gen's interest in new tools like impact investing, microloans, or advocacy and movement funding will certainly be a boon for groups providing those opportunities for rising donors and social investors. But existing nonprofits, even large ones, can adapt in ways that keep them relevant for the next gen as well. They can try to adapt to the faster pace of change and innovation that these next gen donors want, avoiding the problem that one donor worried about, when "foundations innovate faster than their grantees." They can also actively collaborate with eager next gen donors in experiments with new tools—like new funding mechanisms beyond grants—and create designated paths for their next gen donors to explore new ideas inside the organizational context (instead of looking for those exciting opportunities elsewhere).

Philanthropic families can similarly adapt, widening their tolerance for risk and using this excitement for innovation as a way to engage the next gen even deeper in family giving. Families might even creatively use family history. Many family fortunes were built as a result of entrepreneurial risk-taking and innovation, a fact noted by several next gen donors. They see their passion for finding

95

new avenues for change as "continuing the legacy of innovation" that their parents or grandparents started; they are merely translating that legacy into the family's philanthropy. Older members of current families could frame this as permission to innovate, helping next gen donors see how they can pursue their passions within the family foundation context.

For now, next gen donors are clearly excited about trying new approaches to doing good and having greater impact in the world. They might not be using all the innovative tools they want to yet, but they aspire to once they have the chance in their families or in their own giving. It's just a matter of time before these new approaches become the norm. And after this Impact Revolution, philanthropy will never be quite the same.

PART TWO

Going All In

CHAPTER 5

The "Do Something" Generation

In Part 1, we introduced the giving revolution that Generation Impact wants to lead, and demonstrated how that revolution was about changing the *ways* big donors give. In Part 2, we explore three of these ways in more depth—three ways next gen donors want to go "all in" in their giving: giving their time, giving their talents, and giving with peers.

⁓◌

Ask next gen donors—like we have—to describe bad philanthropy and their answer will likely include something along the lines of "just writing checks." The next gen wants impact, first and foremost, and merely giving money is not the best way to achieve real impact.

For these rising donors, good philanthropy is hands-on, engaged philanthropy. It involves donors giving their time as well as their treasure. Good philanthropy also means donors cultivating close relationships with the organizations they fund, seeing firsthand the impact of their gifts of time and money, and being able to ascertain what organizations really need. Put simply, next gen donors believe that getting close to organizations helps them be both better and bigger donors. Engagement is their path to bigger impact.

Get Out There and Do It

People in their 20s and 30s in the United States today grew up at a time when they were constantly encouraged, if not mandated, to volunteer and engage in community service.[1] As adults now, they associate giving with giving of time. As one younger major donor who has been involved in family grantmaking for a long time put it, "That's just how I function. From a young age, I really wanted to do hands-on things and go on site visits and see the program in action and be at that level. I didn't want to just write a check. I wanted to take full advantage of the opportunity to do something good. In this generation, [with] community service that's done in schools, I feel like there's been a culture that we've grown up with of doing things in a very hands-on kind of way."

John R. Seydel, the grandson of media mogul Ted Turner and an emerging Millennial donor who is featured in Chapter 8, ties this to the idea that in his "Trophy Generation," everyone got a trophy just for being active in something, awarded for not being "complacent." He says, "We want to be fulfilled and inspired in every little thing we do because that is what we were taught. We have grown up with a mentality that 'I have to find the organization that fulfills me and that is where I am going to give my time.'"

It is not surprising, then, that a refrain we heard over and over from next gen donors was that they want to "do something."[2] They want to get their hands dirty, to "experience something real" or "get out our tool belt and just go out there and do it." They don't want to just go to fancy events for donors, write big checks, and watch what happens. As one explained, "I was going to all these cocktail parties with my family and just lamenting. I kept saying, 'I want to get more involved with something that actually *does* something.'" Fittingly, one of the largest and most active organizations promoting volunteer engagement among young people these days is called DoSomething.org.

Our survey results reinforce this do-something orientation, as well as its origins in early volunteer experiences. While giving online was the most common type of philanthropic act—with 77.7 percent saying they have given this way in the past 12 months—this doesn't mean they don't want more direct involvement. Volunteering was the third most common activity (70.2 percent), not far behind giving through a website or donating in-kind materials like a car or computer. Other informal, person-to-person helping activities ranked high as well. And nearly 8 out of 10 next gen donors (78 percent) reported having volunteer experiences before the age of 15, and 35.5 percent before the age of 10. As one donor said bluntly, "I don't want to go push a button and give $100,000 to an organization without ever having to interact further. That is not appealing to me." Others even said they consider giving money alone to be insufficient at best, and at times even ineffective or outright harmful.

These donors weren't always specific about *what* they wanted to do as a volunteer. They just wanted to be connected, in person, to the nitty-gritty work of the organizations they support—to get in the game, not cheer from the sidelines.

—◦—

Of course, the idea of hands-on donor engagement with organizations is not new, and previous generations of donors have done things like serve as fundraising campaign volunteers or board members. But for younger major donors, this hands-on approach is a primary way they define themselves, and they often point to it as a clear distinguishing feature of their generation. "It seems to me that in older generations, [they have] a very hands-off approach to funding. 'We write checks, or we give money, but we are separate from the work that is happening.' But I want to be very much in relationship to the work that is happening. I don't want to be standing on the sidelines. I want to be part of that work for social change."

Another donor set up the contrast that while her parents gave out of "obligation to give back," her generation's approach is "very much about engagement." And donors like her are proud of this do-something orientation. They see it as an indispensable part of their generational personality.

Even these members of the generation who have the chance to give substantial treasure still consider giving their time to be more valuable. That's pretty startling when you think about it. If this is their mindset, it points to significant shifts in the nonprofit/major donor relationship in the years to come.

Part of this yearning for on-the-ground action stems from a desire for learning. In our survey, we asked donors about various influences on their development as a donor. Seventy-two percent said "personal experiences as a donor, volunteer, board member, etc." were "very important" to their learning—clearly the most important influence among a list of options.

Next gen donors say experiences and close relationships make them better donors by giving them more insight into the areas they want to fund and by letting them cultivate the skills and expertise they will use for years to come as major donors. "It's very easy to do this work with your head in the sand. It's a very insular role, the family foundation trustee. You don't have to 'do' anything. There's no accountability. You can go to a board meeting once or twice a year and never get outside that bubble. [But getting better] means going out and learning directly. We call our grantees 'grantee part-ners' for a reason. They are how we learn about what is going on in the fields that we're trying to support."

Victoria Rogers is a next gen donor who believes deeply in volunteering as a path to being a better donor. She is grateful to her parents for providing her opportunities very early in life to contribute her time as well as her wealth and giving her the chance to learn through those experiences. As a child, she attended the well-known Lab School in Chicago with a diverse group, including then-Senator Barack Obama's daughters who were a few years younger than Victoria. She learned about philanthropy and investing from her father, who had founded a mutual fund company and became one of the most successful and philanthropic African Americans in the United States. Now working at Kickstarter, Victoria exemplifies how the Millennial Generation thinks about the groups they work with. They want to "see behind the curtain" and "feel close to the work."

Victoria Rogers

I grew up in downtown Chicago but went to school on the South Side, which is a big part of who I am. Hyde Park and, in particular, The Lab School were a defining part of my life. It was an open-minded place that fostered independence, a place that gave kids the freedom to be exploratory rather than didactic. We had the freedom to have an education that encouraged us to find our own way. I did that with the same people from age 3 until 18, and it was helpful to explore with a steady group of friends, many of whom I'm still in close touch with today.

There is something special about Hyde Park as a context for my upbringing, as it is a community that is very diverse and brings a lot of different voices together. My fellow students had parents who were nurses at the University of Chicago as well as Nobel Laureates and businesspeople from downtown. You add in the professors, and it was diverse and dynamic with a sense of openness and cross-cultural exchange that felt unique. There was also a lot

(continued)

(continued)

of mixing of students from different backgrounds, but I never felt like I was at "the black table" or "the white table." Of course, President Obama was a U.S. senator from Illinois at the time, and his political career was developing then. Though younger than me, Malia and Sasha went to Lab. It was a magical time to be in Hyde Park. My friends and I volunteered on both his senate and presidential campaigns—driving to Iowa on the weekends to canvas and giving of our time to be a part of that energy for change.

My dad had grown up in the neighborhood and also went to Lab and raised me very much immersed in different communities across Chicago. When I was growing up, for example, he would take me to Cabrini-Green, a housing project, to meet people and talk. And we participated in Reverend Jesse Jackson's initiative to visit prisons on Christmas morning. Part of life was understanding differences and also feeling like people weren't necessarily that different because we are all part of the same fabric.

Empowered to Learn by Doing

Personally, I volunteered at the Sue Duncan Children's Center, which was founded by former Secretary of Education Arne Duncan's mom. My dad went to Lab with Arne and introduced me to the place when I was in seventh grade, explaining that Duncan grew up volunteering at this place, too, as his mom had started the afterschool children's center. As I was growing up, I found it eye-opening to see the difference between the kids who attended the Duncan Center and often didn't have the same resources or access as those of us living in neighboring Hyde Park. For example, I had always loved making art, and it was clear that a lot of those kids didn't have an experience of art at their schools. The Sue Duncan program was primarily geared toward tutoring kids in math and helping with their homework, but I asked Sue if I could offer an afterschool art class as well. It started as a once-a-month offering and evolved into a weekly art class that I would plan and facilitate from seventh grade until I graduated high school.

That was my entry point into volunteerism and into the power of art to influence people, to bring people together, to foster a place for dialogue. It felt like this language that was unspoken became a means of connection and communication where words might not have come so easily. This thread has run through everything in my life, from the Sue Duncan Center to art history at Yale, to arts institutions where I worked during the summers, and now as a donor and board member of Creative Time—an arts nonprofit in New York focusing on how art can engage with public space and the publics who view them. And, of course, as a thread through my professional role at Kickstarter today.

My dad always wanted me to be conscious of a world that was beyond myself and empowered me to be able to not just volunteer but also to give financially to projects that I am interested in. Early on, he invested some financial resources for me that have grown over time, and I've been able to contribute to nonprofits from income off the investments. Of course, in addition to becoming involved as a donor, my dad also encouraged me to learn by doing. Sometimes an opportunity would come by that he thought I would be interested in, like a theater company, and he would say, "Do you want to invest in this together?" With his encouragement, I jumped in perhaps at an earlier time of my life than I would have otherwise, as I felt empowered by him to learn by experience.

Perhaps that comes from my dad's own history. He started a business when he was 24, a financial mutual fund company in Chicago, Ariel Investments, when there weren't other African Americans running their own investment houses. He sits on the corporate boards of Exelon and McDonald's and also serves as trustee to the University of Chicago, is a member of the American Academy of Arts and Sciences, [is] a director of the Robert F. Kennedy Center for Justice and Human Rights, and recently joined the Barack Obama Foundation's board of directors. My mom, too, has been an active participant in the world around us. It didn't matter to them

(continued)

(continued)

what I get involved with, just that I found a way to be involved. And my parents' involvements informed my early experiences.

Seeing Behind the Curtain

My role as a donor and volunteer at Creative Time, which commissions and presents public art projects around the world, emerged in that vein. I had been an intern at the organization and loved its mission. I was passionate about the work and close enough to know there was a financial gap to be filled. My dad and I discussed if there was some way after serving as an intern and volunteer that I could help them financially as well as become involved with the organization in my own right.

I had several conversations with the director to figure out what being an involved donor would look like for me. I ended up joining the board, making a contribution, committing my time, advocating for them in different spaces in the art field, offering advice on their work, and serving on the search committee to find a new executive director. My involvement has been very multidimensional, and the relationship has been reciprocal. It has been a great learning opportunity for me. I think it feels a lot like a family, too, which is particularly lovely at this stage in my life.

To be clear, to me giving is much more than sitting on a board. Sitting on a board can sometimes feel like you are making decisions from on high. My experience with Creative Time showed me that my board perspective would be different had I not worked there previously. For example, when our director left to join the Brooklyn Museum, my experience working directly with the staff was helpful in understanding the implications of this for the team. Knowing the place from the inside has been an illuminating board experience.

My generation wants to see behind the curtain in order to see how organizations work. As someone interested in art, I want to visit an artist's studio, have dinner with an artist, and spend time getting to know how she thinks. For me, and for many people in my generation, I think it's about following our hearts and getting involved. That leads me to ask, "How can a nonprofit allow me to feel close to the work so that I can be a part of it?" Or, "How can they help me try it out?" Taking risks is okay, especially at this stage of my life. I have room to try something out and see if it feels right and give it a chance rather than being paralyzed by the options.

Professionally, I work at Kickstarter, which helps artists, musicians, filmmakers, designers, and other creators find the resources and support they need to make their ideas a reality. To date, tens of thousands of creative projects—big and small—have come to life with the support of the Kickstarter community. I've actually backed 386 of them. In my role I focus on art and help projects find support both financially and in terms of people-building—like when you have the power of a thousand people behind you saying that they want your project to exist. Kickstarter was founded seven years ago by an artist who wanted to enable people to make something happen in the world without having to go through all the traditional channels. And for backers, one can feel they have a role in what gets made.

Kickstarter is democratizing the way in which things get funded, and thus changing the landscape of what gets made, because everybody now has a voice to empower someone to create something. We ask ourselves, "What does it mean to make an album without a record label or make a film without a producer or for a painter to make work without gallery representation?" I think that appeals to my generation because it enables everyone to be a donor in a sense. The lowest you can pledge is one dollar, and so it really opens the door. I am drawn to this place because I'm excited by this opportunity to get away from what I believe could feel like an ivory tower and to think about the way in which art and culture impact everyday people. Unlike previous generations, who came together to fund a museum or gallery, Kickstarter is an online space where you can post a project and someone in Japan can learn about it a second later. I think our

(continued)

(continued)

generation expects art and design to meet them where they are because technology makes that possible. So this is a powerful new concept.

Giving for Life

At 25, my peers and I are primarily asking ourselves, "Am I in a space where I'm learning and being exposed to new things?" It still feels like I'm a sponge more than I have a direction. I think there certainly are doors that have closed and things that will not be in my future, but I'm in a stage of exploration still. I'm pretty certain that I want to be always working with art, but I think that could mean a ton of things, including a pruning down of what that looks like.

Ultimately, my dad really cares about financial literacy, and while I think that's important, it's not my passion. To his credit, he hasn't pushed me to support financial literacy programs but to find and follow my own passion. And that's what I'm working on now—in life and in philanthropy. I have been surprised when I've been in next gen donor settings that the same flexibility hasn't seemed to always be there in other families. I think it has been meaningful to me to grow up with the encouragement to explore and experiment and experience things firsthand. It has made giving fun and interesting, like something that is more than a financial commitment but also a life commitment.

Victoria's story illustrates how this hands-on, do-something approach of next gen donors is often tied to their early and ongoing explorations of self. They aren't just excited about this approach because it feels more real and rewarding, though that matters. They are excited about it because it helps them figure out how they, as individuals, are best suited to doing the good they want to do in the world.

Looking for a Real Relationship

Victoria also illustrates how and why next gen donors crave authentic relationships with people doing real work for the greater good. We heard this wish for close connections from many next gen donors. One said he won't give money unless the organization can "connect me with someone I can talk to on the inside." Another talked about wanting to have "ongoing engagement and investment of who I am and my time and my resources" so that he can "become part of the community" of the groups he supports.

Next gen donors seek to connect not just with the leadership of organizations but also with the people on the front lines doing the work and even (when possible) the beneficiaries of the work. This makes giving so much more fulfilling for them and impactful for the organizations. "I am more of a mile-wide, hundred-miles-deep guy, where you just get to know everybody very well, you have a very close relationship, you really believe in the organization, and your money just makes a big impact on that organization," says one donor.

The relationship next gen donors seek is not only a "hundred miles deep" but also long-term. One described it as an enduring investment, explaining, "We're investing in a relationship. We're investing in a partnership with people who have shared goals." For many, having deep relationships means imposing limits. A donor who described turning down numerous requests to serve on boards said he did so because "I'm super committed to this one organization [and] I don't take board duty very lightly."

Like all relationships, for these partnerships to work they need to be open, honest, and transparent. Next gen donors highly value being shown the inner workings of the organization, the full picture of the groups they are funding, "warts and all," just as Victoria did after Creative Time's director left to take another position and the remaining staff rallied.

Authentic relationships build trust, next gen donors insist, and the most effective giving partnerships require that sort of trust. Conversely, these donors say they are very aware when they are not entrusted with the full story. "If you're in philanthropy in any way, whether you're on the fundraising side or the giving side, you can sniff out bullshit. People are imperfect; they make mistakes. They are not going to get it right every time. If it looks that way then it would be manufactured. You can see straight through that when someone is not being genuine."

While next gen donors' desire to have such close relationships can be of great benefit to the nonprofits on the other side of the partnership, this closeness also makes it harder to keep the relationship strong. This was abundantly clear in one donor's story about a partnership that went awry:

> It wasn't on purpose, like "We're cutting her out." They just had such poor management of their communications that once I wasn't regularly interacting with them, I just wasn't a priority anymore. It was like, "I'm a person, right? If I'm not a priority to you, after all of these years and time and money and sweat and tears that I have contributed, how am I supposed to invest in you? It is a relationship; you have to be willing to invest in me as I'm investing in you." We talk a lot about Millennial donors and impact, but I actually think it's not just impact, it's *relationships*. I know dating is, like, the worst metaphor, but you have to have a relationship with these [donors] for 20 or 30 years, so you have to think about that and actually care about them as people. Know when their birthday is.

With Great Power Comes Great Responsibility

A big barrier to achieving these sorts of close, honest, productive relationships is, of course, the fact that the donors inherently hold greater power because they ultimately make the decisions about who and what gets funded. Even when the donor is a hands-on partner working side by side with staff and other volunteers, it is hard to ignore this reality.

Many next gen donors yearning for close engagement in their giving recognize this and are looking for ways to work through the power dynamics. For some, like Mary Galeti, the key is acknowledging that power dynamic and understanding the role she plays in it. "I try to manage expectations and be modest about what role I actually play as a funder. This means being an equal with our grantees, acknowledging that our grantees are the ones who are actually producing the work and I am just funding it." For others, working closely and honestly with "people on the ground" and touching their experiences goes a long way:

> How do you break down the barriers that exist among people
> and create the possibility for real collaboration, real
> partnership, mutual exchange, and mutual creation of value?
> I hope [this happens when] others are forced out of their
> comfort zone, when their own sense of comfort and being is
> disrupted by the experience of a radical encounter with
> people who are different from them, people who suffer and
> people who are poor and disempowered and disenfranchised.
> I think empathy is the most powerful force in our world, and
> you don't develop empathy by writing checks. If anything, it
> has the opposite effect, because you write a check and you
> think, "Oh, I'm a powerful person."

For others, the key is listening—really hearing what the grantees have to say: "It is important to be in long-term, sustainable relationships with the people and organizations you give to. The communities that are experiencing injustice or systemic issues are the ones who best know how to solve those issues. And as people with resources, our call is to deeply listen to those people, not try to dictate their actions."

Perhaps the most common suggestion for dealing with the power dynamics, though, is the time-honored relationship advice to be honest and open, and to speak frankly.

> No matter what you say, [nonprofits] are always going to treat you like you hold the power because in the end, you kind of do. I try to be really honest and express that we're not looking for perfection. We understand that things aren't always going to go your way, and that doesn't mean we aren't going to fund you anymore. I always try to keep really open lines of communication, to show that we are genuinely invested and support what they're doing. It's building a relationship that's more friendly than, "I'm holding a check over your head."

Another donor echoed this worry about being seen as taking advantage of her power. Avoiding this image requires regularly "checking in, just to make sure that what you're doing and how you're engaged with that nonprofit is not suffocating. I think it's trying to have a more honest connection with the people you're supporting. I don't want to be a 'helicopter funder.'"

Hannah Quimby thinks a lot about these relationship challenges, in part because she's been on both sides of the relationship. A woman who grew up "living simply" with modest means, Hannah has now found herself in charge of a well-known foundation—and part of a well-known family—that is one of the biggest funders in her home state of Maine. But she also has experience as a volunteer and staffer for a nonprofit. She knows on-the-ground experience is the best way to learn how to be more effective. Now, as a funder, she takes the same approach. She wants to get out of the office to see the work firsthand. In this way, she embodies the hands-on approach that is a hallmark of this next generation of donors.

Hannah Quimby

I grew up in northern Maine. My parents were part of the Back-to-the-Land movement in the late '60s, early '70s. I have a twin brother, Lucas St. Clair, and we were raised without electricity or running water in a cabin in the woods. My mom, Roxanne Quimby, didn't change her last name when she and my dad married, so when they had twins, they decided to give my brother my dad's last name and give me my mom's last name. Needless to say, we grew up different than most kids.

In 1982, my mom met a man named Burt Shavitz. Burt had been a photographer in New York and moved to Maine to live a simpler life. He learned to keep bees and supported himself by selling jars of honey off the tailgate of his pickup truck on the side of the road. One day my mom was hitchhiking to her waitressing job and Burt picked her up. When she learned he was a beekeeper and had been storing up beeswax, she struck up a deal with him; she would help him with the bees in exchange for the beeswax. She had gone to art school in San Francisco and was always creating art and crafts, and with the beeswax she began making hand-dipped candles, labels for the honey jars, stove polish, and lip balm. She began taking these to local craft fairs.

Burt's Bees was officially incorporated in 1989, and they grew it slowly without taking out any loans. Looking back on it now, it's

(continued)

(continued)

nice to remember how exciting it was to be a part of this. When we got home from school, my mom would put my brother and me (and often our friends) to work packaging soaps or pouring lip balm. On weekends, Lucas and I would help pack up our beat-up old Ford Econoline van—which had blue shag carpet and a lightning bolt up the side!—to go to craft fairs around New England. It was great to get out of our small town and see new places.

Living Simply, Still

While I don't mention the connection I have to Burt's Bees very often to people, I am very proud of my mom and what she has accomplished. I admire that while she didn't have an Ivy League education, an MBA, or a business background, she grew a successful company. It is a great example of how hard work, creativity, uncompromising values, and a greater purpose can serve someone just as well as a more traditional route. I'm also thankful that Burt's Bees wasn't financially successful until I was in college, because it meant we were raised very simply, without many material possessions, and that completely shaped my own values. I doubt money would have changed my childhood that much because of what my parents cared about, but I imagine it is just trickier to raise children with certain values when there is a lot of wealth in the family. I guess that is why there are a lot of books on the topic!

My mom has never desired the lifestyle that you often see with someone who has great wealth. She took the proceeds from the sale of Burt's Bees and established three foundations and now finds maximum enjoyment on her farm with horses, chickens, turkeys, rabbits, a huge garden, and her farm stand. I find that really admirable.

The philanthropic story of our family grows from these core values, and is tied to the story of the company as well. When I was growing up we didn't have the financial resources to be philanthropic in the traditional sense, but from the beginning of Burt's

Bees the way that the company operated was philanthropic. When it started to make more of a profit, some of the profit went into land conservation in Maine. Then, as Burt's Bees became larger and more successful, we were able to give more, both through the company and through a family foundation my mom set up in 2004.

My brother and I ended up going to boarding school in western Maine, and I went to Prescott College in Arizona, which is a small liberal arts school that mostly has a focus on environmental studies. After graduation, I ended up working for Burt's Bees, doing corporate training and sales, for about six years until the company sold. I saw while working in the family business that everyone at the company knew the value of having an impact with conservation. This was a big part of why my mom was motivated to continue growing the company.

It's a big part of me, too. I just have this inherent desire to be involved with environmental nonprofits. I see the opportunities that I had as a kid to spend a ton of time exploring the outdoors. We had total freedom to spend all day outside, all summer long, and the way that impacted my life was enormous. Here I am in my 30s, hiking mountains on the weekends. So that environmental focus is very much connected to the value system that was demonstrated by my parents when growing up, living simply.

Our Learning Curve

After working for Burt's Bees for six years, I went to graduate school to study integrative health. While in San Francisco, I got very involved with a nonprofit organization based in Oakland, California, called Bay Area Wilderness Training. I was doing a lot of volunteer work with them, and even met my future husband there. We both eventually travelled the country to help take their model nationwide.

Around the same time, I also started working full-time for our family foundation, though I had been on the board for nine years.

(continued)

115

(continued)

When my mom decided to form the Quimby Family Foundation, she had asked my brother and me—we were 26 at the time—to be on the board, and we all sat down together to develop a mission and geographic focus. But eventually we saw that we really needed a full-time staff person for the foundation. I just didn't expect to be that person.

I have grown to love the work, but I have to say the decision to become a staff person of the foundation didn't come that easily for me. It was hard to feel confident that I would do the job as well as someone with years of experience. Did I deserve to have this role? Ultimately, I decided it was an incredible opportunity for continued learning, an opportunity to do meaningful work, and I didn't want to pass that up. There was so much support with conferences and organizations and even consultants that we worked with, from whom I have been able to continually learn. It has been really fantastic, and I believe I've brought more depth to this role than I think I had anticipated.

At the very beginning of our foundation, we had to learn the real nuts and bolts, such as how do we present our mission? And how do we communicate that with the community? After 10 years now, we are asking, "How do we take a step back and see if we have moved the needle at all? Have we really had an impact? Are there other things that are happening in Maine right now that are a good reason to cause us to shift our mission? How do we do that in the most respectful way? How do we communicate that to past grantees and communicate that change in a way that is going to be the most helpful to the largest number of organizations?"

As the primary staff, I did a bunch of informational interviews in order to answer these questions and to ascertain what the needs are. I wanted initially to look at agriculture. The local agriculture movement in Maine is really starting to grow and thrive, and that was one thing we wanted to support. So I met with some farmers. I got a lot of feedback from the community about where there is a need, and that is where we started our funding. It has been great to see how many people—both other funders and nonprofits—are willing to sit down and talk with you and share their ideas and opinions.

Building Close Relationships

I really enjoy meeting with the nonprofits. The site visits are my favorite part of the work. I like being really engaged with the non-profits, hearing the stories of the people who are affected by the programs, and witnessing some of them in action. It is different than with organizations where I'm just reading their applications but we are not actually meeting—like with organizations based in New York but doing some work in Maine. There is such a huge difference between that and going to this land trust that I went to last week where they had kids that were doing navigation lessons and a woman outside teaching a painting class. I loved being in the barn that they're trying to renovate, and then meeting with their board in person. It was such a rich experience, as I gained a greater understanding of the organization as a whole and saw the people who were directly benefitting from the programs. I know some funders don't want to take up too much of an organization's time, but I feel like at least having that initial conversation, and being introduced to the program and the people who are part of those programs, establishes a relationship that you can then build on later, whether through a phone call or through mail.

I also love meeting with volunteers of an organization, partly, I think, because of the work that I've done as a volunteer with wilderness training. I am so passionate about that work, and when I meet other passionate volunteers I see what perfect advocates they are for an organization because they wholeheartedly believe in the mission and give their time and talent in support of that work. So I really love listening to volunteers at other organizations about why they're giving so much of their time because I can relate to their passion.

(continued)

(continued)

Now, my mom likes to be more behind the scenes and doesn't necessarily like big events or meeting with nonprofits as frequently. But I love doing these meetings and site visits, and my brother is also more interested in getting together with funders and grantees. In fact, I would say that meeting with nonprofits and establishing close, candid relationships with them has now become a core part of my approach to being a funder. I've learned a lot of lessons about how to make these relationships work best for both sides.

I've found in these meetings that it is easier than I would've thought to have pretty honest conversations about what we are interested in or what we're able to provide for funding and what we are not able to do. We have this open process—and as a small foundation we are not able to fund a lot of the organizations that submit. But I have a lot of conversations around why we've made that decision and that we are very much open to having more conversations in the future about different projects that they might be working on with better alignment.

The Benefits of Staying Close and Being Honest

I heard a donor say once that they try to get as much information from an organization as possible—especially if it is struggling or if it was provided funding and then didn't meet its goals—and then the person will almost always reward the organization's honesty. If an organization tells you, "This project didn't actually end up going as we planned—and this is why," and if you still have a lot of faith in their work and the leadership there, it's good to still provide funding. I can really see how important that is. You develop a closer relationship with the organization.

We have seen it happen in one organization that we funded for six years, a school that does documentary photography, writing, and radio. Their enrollment was down and they lost the ability to provide credits to college students who were coming, and a whole series of things were happening. Ultimately, after 42 years, they decided that they had no option but to close their doors. There was a backlash from alumni, saying, "Why didn't we hear about this? Why couldn't we have been involved? Why are we just finding out about this now?"

Over time, I had gotten to know the executive director there pretty well. We had provided grants and a loan for student housing. So I sat down with this executive director and she told me the situation. We spoke candidly, and it felt like she was behaving more like a friend. She told me about the struggles and challenges at the school. Then she met with a couple other board members from our foundation and we talked with another art school. We brought them all together and had a two-hour strategy meeting. We decided that we were going to provide funding for the school to continue to operate with their own unique programs and branding, but with the support of this other art school. It has been very positive, and I think that came from me having put the time into developing that relationship, bringing all of them together. That wouldn't have happened if we had never met, just sent a check and that was it.

In other cases, seeing an organization firsthand and getting to know them over time has helped me recognize that what might seem like an organization that is just struggling to get by is in fact really entrepreneurial and could be doing even more. In Maine, it is hardscrabble; there isn't that much funding available. There are a lot of organizations that have really small staff and small operating budgets, that can't take the next step to grow their programming and are trying to get volunteers to help them write grant proposals. But these organizations have strong leadership and great ideas. We often decide to fund them because we see the potential and value of their entrepreneurial spirit, and we have faith that with more funding they would be able to really thrive.

Looking back on how much I've learned as a funder in these last few years, I recognize just how much I have learned *from* non-profit organizations. I see them as the experts for sure. It's great to see how much I have learned from the people who are *actually doing the work*. I'm eager to keep building these kinds of close relationships and to keep learning.

Hannah aims to get close to the organizations her family funds. She doesn't want to just read their applications, make a decision about funding, and then send checks and wait for reports at the end of the grant cycles. Instead, she wants to meet the volunteers, listen to the staff leaders, have candid conversations about strategy and problem-solving, and see the impact they're making as they make it. She's even willing to open herself to their critiques. Unlike the tendencies of her mother's generation, this, for Hannah, feels like a more authentic and effective philanthropic relationship. It feels like the best way to work through the power dynamics.

Engaged Donors Are Bigger, Better Donors

The upside of next gen donors wanting to be so directly engaged is that they are convinced that this actually, as Hannah noted, makes them both bigger *and* better donors.

Another interviewee who was part of a group of cousins beginning to get more involved in their family foundation's decision-making said they were pushing for all the family trustees to volunteer for the groups that received the biggest checks, to be sure "that it's going to the right place, to the right people, where it can make a big difference." Others said they used volunteering as a way to decide whether to give big: "My strategy has been to volunteer with them first a little bit, because I want to get to know the people behind the name of the organization. I may give a smaller gift and actually see how they treat that gift, and then slowly deepen the relationship."

This can end up being good news for those nonprofits that engage donors well. While it means nonprofits need to open up more and spend more of their limited time with donors, it can pay off. One donor insisted that to be a "responsible" donor he needed to be "very actively involved in those organizations I give to. I want to see financials, know the staff, and know the board. There is no substitute for direct involvement." So what's the pay off? As Jenna Segal, an active board member and donor, says in her profile in Chapter 6, this hands-on approach means that while "I'm probably going to be more of a pain in the ass, I'm also going to give them more money."

Many of the donors we spoke with pointed to this approach as a paradigm shift—from donors telling nonprofits what they have to do to get money, to nonprofits telling donors what they need money for. This next gen donor said responsible and responsive giving is "about listening to what people really need who are in communities that are more removed from power and disenfranchised, not just saying that we think we know what they need."

As we saw in Chapter 2, next gen donors want to see the impact of their giving. This desire motivates them to give more and shows them how to give for more impact. What better way to see impact than to be a hands-on volunteer, meet regularly with the staff, or connect with beneficiaries in some way? As one donor insists, "Experiencing it with your own hands and eyes is a must." Another explains, "What I always tell other young people who are getting involved in philanthropy [is], 'You have to go see the groups you are working with.' Because you can read the most compelling proposals in the world, and you can go to their websites and you can look at pictures, but if you don't actually meet the people and talk to them and hear their stories, there is a disconnect."

For some, the biggest benefit of volunteering for the groups you fund is to be sure you are getting an authentic, complete picture—again, seeing the work, as one put it, "warts and all." "I think there is a really powerful connection from actually rolling your sleeves up and getting in on the ground and using that to inform how you allocate your 'treasure.' Because if you are just sitting back and writing checks, I think it's very, very difficult and challenging to really understand how a nonprofit works. I think [in] the standard site visit there is some risk of them sort of prettying up the pony when the donor comes."

What Does This Mean?

So what does it mean when the major funders of the causes we care about expect to have close, sustained relationships with the organizations they support? For one, it means they will be much more high maintenance and high touch donors than previous generations, who were more comfortable giving money from a distance.

With the Do Something Generation, nonprofits will have to retool how they engage donors and rethink what counts as donor engagement. Engagement will be less about lavish galas once a year, direct mail drives, and token seats on symbolic boards. It will be more about hands-on volunteering and regular meetings focused on the most difficult organizational challenges. It will be about cultivating the candid, authentic relationships these next gen donors crave—what one donor called a "two-way dialogue and partnership."

Gen Xers and Millennials are calibrated to detect cynicism, though, so nonprofits that manufacture empty opportunities for engagement or try to pander to the egos of next gen donors won't be well received.[3] An active donor we feature in Chapter 7, Jenna Weinberg, laments this problem:

I feel like I've gone to too many places where I've wanted to volunteer and some organization has made up a volunteer opportunity for me as an "engagement tool" rather than something that's actually helpful to the organization. We can see right through that. And I feel like if more organizations are able to create real, meaningful volunteer opportunities—ones that are actually in line with the organization's mission—it will allow people to become more hands-on and feel like they're part of the organization's work beyond writing a check.

The good news for all of us, though, is that when next gen donors *do* feel connected and engaged in a genuine way, they can become the biggest and best supporters an organization has ever had—and could remain so for decades. The relationships they have are likely to be long-term and perhaps even exclusive, with donors committing most or all of their unprecedented resources, time and treasure both, to a small handful of groups they believe in. And having loyal, dedicated major donors like these means considerably more resources potentially will flow steadily to the good solutions, good causes, and good nonprofits.

There is positive news here as well for those who might still be worried that the next gen in philanthropic families, when they take the reins, will stop funding the local organizations and causes their families have long supported. As we described in Chapter 3, while the next gen is highly aware of international causes and global non-governmental organizations (NGOs), and less rooted in a single community than previous generations, they still want to give to local organizations and their hometown communities. We can understand this impulse more now that we know just how passionate they are about getting close to the work. Simply put, it is harder to be deeply engaged on the ground with organizations on the other side of the globe.

Another benefit might be a growing willingness among donors to support the core organizational budget and capacity of nonprofit organizations—funding operations, not just programs—a possibility we discussed in Chapter 2. Too often this debate pits nonprofit advocates (in favor of overhead funding) against donors (in favor of targeted funding). But donors who are closely involved in the inner workings of the organizations they support might bridge this divide. Like in Victoria's story about being a better board member when she knew intimately the inner workings of an organization, more engaged donors can understand better the need for core operational support and see the organization's point of view.

For these relationships to work, though, the donors will have to remember the warnings we heard here about hubris or suffocation. They will need to keep the inherent power divide in mind, to check in with their partners on the other side of the funding table, and, above all, to listen to what people and organizations really need. If they do, we can all enjoy the potentially enormous benefits of having highly engaged, well-informed, active big donors.

CHAPTER 6

More Than an ATM

Next gen donors clearly want to be engaged in their giving. They want to be hands-on, giving time and not just treasure. But the "Do Something Generation" is a far cry from the "Do Anything Generation." Not all engagement is the same.

Ask next gen donors to just give money, and they will feel like a bank account. Ask them to contribute their skills, knowledge, or hard-earned expertise, and they will go all in.

Valuing Me for Me

Even though they are only in their 20s and 30s, these next gen donors are, for the most part, highly educated, and many have substantial skills and experience. Some are successful entrepreneurs, some are lawyers, some run their family's large foundations, and so on. But just because next gen donors are eager to give their talent doesn't mean it's easy for them to do so. Some find that organizations only see them as a source of financial capital, not human capital. Others find that nonprofits that do try to engage them do so only in superficial ways that make little use of their specific skills and experience. Either way, the result is that donors feel underutilized, undervalued, and even disrespected. Obviously, donors who feel that way are not donors for long.

The worst case is when next gen donors feel they are treated "like an ATM and not like a person." They want to be taken seriously as capable contributors who have more than money to give. They want to be seen as having both "means *and* a brain," to be appreciated for "the skills and the smarts that I hopefully bring to the table, not what kind of car I drive."

Next gen donors coming from families with a philanthropic legacy experience their own take on this, as they want to be seen as more than just a formidable last name or inexhaustible revenue source. They want to be recognized for the professional competencies and expertise they can bring to the work. One such donor explains how he is just now starting to feel more appreciated and useful as he is getting more widely known for the talents he brings: "I know that people involved in the community see me for me. They don't see me as my mother's son or my grandfather's grandson; instead, I bring a lot to the table in my own regard. Even though I'm not yet 30 years old and don't have a lifetime of experience under my belt, I'm still valued in terms of who I am, what my experiences are, what I bring to the table on my own merits, rather than on the merits of my last name."

This person still acknowledges that a famous last name and family legacy helps and that "I can tweak that to my advantage at some points." But when he feels most valued—and most committed—is when it's about him, not his name.

Some especially thoughtful donors we talked with, though, raised a caution about this desire to give talent. At times, some next gen donors can begin to value their own skills and expertise more than others—occasionally more than the professional staff of the groups they support. One donor calls for more "humility" among her peers:

There's definitely a segment of us in my generation who are very much the "I've made lots of money and I'm going to be an angel investor and bring my business skills" [type]. I think there are pieces of that which are really good, but there are times when the nonprofit sector professionals are not really given the opportunity to show they know a lot about the field they're in, or the problems they're trying to solve in the world, because a donor has "a better idea." I think that we have to be very careful because we do have a lot of power in that situation and, whether or not our ideas are good, they might be adopted because our money is needed in order to do something for that nonprofit.

More Than a Party Planner

Next gen donors want to give their whole selves in part because doing so is important to their emerging identities as donors. They reject traditional check-writing because they want to make sure the organization appreciates their other assets as well and because—as we've seen—they want to get close to the real work organizations do. "It can feel like I'm giving my money and it's detached from me. So, what about my self-worth, my identity, and who I am? How can I contribute the other things that are integral to my self-worth and my value? If I'm just giving money, it can make me feel that my value is just associated with that, rather than my time and talent. My voice and my experience are of value, too."

On-the-ball nonprofits are definitely looking to give their future major donors ways to engage beyond just opening their wallets. But this works best when nonprofits offer outlets for engagement appropriate to the donor's skill set, making it personally meaningful. Says one, "I really don't want to go out and volunteer a day to go feed people at a homeless shelter. It is just not where my skills are best used; it is not what I do best. What I'm very good at is selling, marketing, and communication. Those are areas that organizations need a lot of help with."

The next generation is savvy enough to spot the types of token engagements often offered to younger donors—like asking their friends to give, or sitting on a powerless "youth advisory committee."[1] They'd rather have the chance to be an advisor to the staff on, say, legal or technological questions—whatever best matches their skill sets. They'd rather serve the organization than sit on a board.

Mary Galeti, who we met in Chapter 3, talks passionately about this point, echoing what she's heard from many of her peers:

> Young people are often relegated to a committee that plans a party for young people. Awesome. That is fun to do for a year or two, but many of my friends [say,] "I spent three years at McKinsey [consulting]. I have worked for three years at Goldman Sachs. Did you know that I am much smarter than throwing you a damn party? I have more to offer than that." We want to feel valued for our talent and our time. Next generation donors want to see a clear path to where we are going and to understand what our role will be in that. I tell nonprofits that want to build a community of engaged young people. "Give us a clear call to action. Let's problem-solve together. Tell us what you are working on, and let's work on this together. Tell me what you need me to do." We want to be valued as professionals with time and talent to give.

It often comes back to respect for these donors. They want nonprofits to respect that their time is valuable. They want to be a valued and valuable partner. One next gen donor expressed, "I don't make my contribution by choosing the colors for a party or by figuring out what the gift bag is going be. That is not exciting to me. I haven't gone to stuff envelopes in this stage of my life because they make it into a big ladies' luncheon tea thing, and I'm like, I don't need this tea party. I don't have time to be here right now and do this. [I'd rather be] more involved, maybe as a very modest, humble thought-partner."

─◌

Jenna Segal, a Broadway producer, women's advocate, and next gen donor in New York City, devotes a significant percentage of her time to philanthropy and insists on not being treated merely as an ATM or a party planner. She has thought a lot about how some organizations utilize her talents better than others, and she commits her whole self to those that take her seriously.

Jenna Segal

I grew up in North Brunswick, New Jersey, a middle-class town with a multicultural community of people. I'm married to some-one I went to high school with, although I didn't connect with him until we reunited in New York years later. Between New Jersey and New York, I went to Washington, D.C., for college, as I have always been interested in politics. I discovered I was also interested in entertainment, and so after graduation I worked at CNN in Wash-ington, D.C., MTV in Los Angeles, and then Nickelodeon in New York, where I felt like I had finally found the right city for me.

My parents don't have significant wealth but raised me to be philanthropic (even though that isn't the language they would

(continued)

(continued)

use). My mother was an ESL (English as a Second Language) teacher and administrator in a public school district for 40 years, and my father has always believed in giving. My in-laws came with my husband as Refuseniks from Russia and built an incredible business which my husband now runs, and we are fortunate to have an opportunity to have philanthropic resources.

Finding the Right Fit, Even in Established Institutions

My on-ramp to the philanthropic world came when I had children and was no longer working in an office full-time. I deliberately made the time to do all the things I had always wanted to do but didn't have time to do before. I took a class at the Junior League of New York about nonprofit management and board governance that taught attendees how to be board members. It was the best thing I could have done before joining a board. It gave me the tools I needed to sit at a board table and not feel intimidated. That said, after the course I was assigned a board placement and joined a board whose mission I wasn't passionate about.

That experience taught me a valuable lesson. I discovered that one could be on a board that didn't align with one's interests, and I knew that would never again be me. Finding the right fit with an organization is essential because even when one is passionate about an organization's cause, board service can be hard work. There is a learning curve to figure out what being a board member means. You need to find your role as a board member, which means, on the one hand, not just sitting on a board passively and, on the other hand, not becoming an unpaid staff member involved in the day-to-day until you find how you're going to be involved. Going through this learning curve takes time and patience, and I only wanted to do that with organizations where my interests were aligned with their missions.

I've come to believe that finding the right fit with an existing organization is better than forming your own philanthropic venture. It can even improve those organizations. I like using my skills to help established institutions be recycled for the next generation. I feel it's such a waste to have people spend so much time and money building up an institution and then for the next generation to let it go underutilized. Instead, why don't we ask, "How can we build on the assets already invested?" Philanthropic resources are hard enough to find that communities can't afford to squander established institutions. Instead we need to reinvent them, reimagine them, and even recycle the aspects of those institutions that can be sustained and utilized in new ways by the next generation.

I've followed this approach in starting new programs at a few established institutions, bringing my skills and experience to bear. Unequivocally, my greatest success in philanthropy has been a partnership with the Jewish Community Center of Manhattan, located on the Upper West Side of New York City, where I initiated a program called Passport to engage people returning from Israel after the immensely successful Birthright Israel program. Birthright sends 18- to 26-year-olds for a free 10-day trip to experience the land of Israel and to become connected to its heritage and people. Receiving a "passport" to take classes at the JCC upon their return from Israel, these younger members of the Jewish community become connected to an institution and come to see it as a place to connect with their peers and the community. Initially, the program began with 30 participants, but [it] has grown so much that now over 3,000 young people have come through the JCC's doors in the last five years.

Of course, I believe if you've started something—if you've planted the seed and helped it grow to be successful—you have a certain responsibility to continue watering it until you find a method for it to gain water without you. So I've stayed involved and invested in this program at the JCC for years in order to help it grow, and I've also asked the JCC for some agreements so that we both continue to invest in our side of the relationship.

(continued)

(continued)

Thinking even bigger, I'd eventually like to see this Passport program replicated in JCCs nationally.

Playing the Right Role

From this venture, and from other work I've done over the years, I've learned a few things about successful nonprofit engagement. First, if I am thinking about becoming involved with an organization, I try to gauge the flexibility of that organization. Knowing now that I am good at bringing new ideas to existing institutions, I look for organizations that are not resistant to change. I ask, "Would you be willing to try this new idea or that?" and if the first answer I hear back is, "That wouldn't work here because . . . ," I see they might not be as open to new ideas nor a fit for my approach to funding. Looking at my role in the organization, I ask, "Am I here to catalyze change and be an activist or to rubber stamp the status quo?" If the latter, it's probably not a fit for me given what I've learned about my hands-on approach as a funder.

If I *do* find an organization where I'm aligned with the mission and it is interested in trying out new ideas, then I turn to a second lesson I've learned. I try to come to an agreed-upon set of expectations about what we're going to do together. For example, in the inaugural year of the JCC Passport initiative, we didn't have our expectations aligned, and I became frustrated at times when I expected something the organization didn't. In the second year, I worked with a consultant to help me draft a donor agreement with the JCC, where we put in writing what we both expected. We now have a shared set of expectations for what the realistic results of our partnership are, from quantitative performance to how the program staff will keep me in the loop to how much funding I'll provide and/or help them to raise from others.

If I'm not just investing in a program but joining the board of an organization, then I may ask additional questions. I usually start quietly, listening for at least two full meetings before I take on any issues. That's not to say I don't talk to staff or the board president after the meeting if I have questions; however, I learned it is easy to become unhelpful in a boardroom when I don't know the history of the organization or have a gauge for the players at the table and the roles they play. So now I survey the landscape first and then decide the role I want to play.

At times, I am not yet giving as much as other funders around the table. I'm humble to learn first from the more experienced board members while I offer my time and talents, and then I contribute when I'm more familiar with the organization and its needs. I believe this is particularly important for us as next gen donors, so I give my resources where it's most useful to the organization.

Not a Party Planner

Now that I'm nearly 40, I've grown enough to know that I look at the different roles I can play in philanthropy distinctly. I can donate, volunteer, or serve on a board, and I don't find they're all interchangeable. I feel my real contribution is thinking through the vision for a specific program and raising money toward that vision like I did for the JCC program. In those cases, I give of my time, talent, and treasure, and I get something back in what I learn and whom I can learn from. I'm interested in the goal and making an impact more than I am in the title of board member.

I have to be especially careful about finding the right way to be involved as a woman in philanthropy. When I join a board, without a doubt, the first thing they want me to do is fundraise or to be the committee chair of the fundraiser. I have produced a Broadway show and worked for MTV, so yes, I can plan a gala or throw a hell of a party, but that's not why I join a board, as that's not going to fulfill me. So now when I join a new board, I try to step back and speak little, and then only contribute to things that have nothing to do with fundraising at first. It's a choice I've made to shift my role and the way the organization perceives me. Bringing strategic ideas to an organization has moved me from being seen as "party planner" into other, more meaningful roles.

(continued)

(continued)

Ironically, after a significant number of years on a board, I would likely plan and execute a fundraiser for that organization. But that is because by then I would understand that nonprofit and its mission inside and out, and I'd be glad to use my knowledge and skills to champion it with a fundraiser. Until then, I think fundraising is the worst place to put someone who first joins the board of an organization because it sends the message that the organization doesn't care about who that board member is, what their skills are, and what they want to give or get as a volunteer. Instead, it conveys that the organization only cares about that board member's money. I want to say to organizations, "Your board members could just write you a check, but if they're spending time to serve on your board, it's because they're passionate about the mission and they want to have more meaningful involvement on a higher level."

The Next Gen Way

In my experience, all next gen donors try to find the best way to be involved, a way that suits their skills. Actually, I've never met two young people who are philanthropic in precisely the same way. I'm not sure that was true with previous generations. There seems to have been more of a "way" to do philanthropy in the past. You were on a board and you called your friends for support. Now I think the major donors of my generation and the younger generation are all trying to figure out what works for them.

But despite the diversity of ways of being a donor, I think next gen donors share this desire to find the way that fits them best, including a desire to be actively involved. There are very few young people I know who write big checks who don't want some kind of substantial involvement with the organization to which they're writing that check. I wouldn't, for example, go into a clothing store and say, "I have $500 to give you; please just hand me $500 worth of clothes." I guess it's that simple to me. I don't feel comfortable going to an organization and saying, "Here's $500; do whatever you want with it," and then finding out later that that $500 might have been spent on things that I don't agree with, don't excite me, or don't make an impact.

It's funny that out in the community, I hear both that next generation donors *don't* want to be involved and I hear we want to be *too* involved. Personally, when I'm passionate about an organization's mission, I might be considered "too involved"; I might even be a pain in the ass! But ultimately, I'm going to be more involved *and* give more money. And I see this in other next gen donors as well. We're out there, and we are passionate if we're engaged in a meaningful way. If we are, we will be highly involved and generous donors for a long time.

Rules of Engagement

I would encourage nonprofit leaders to foster as much inclusion as possible for next generation donors. At least in the beginning, I wouldn't push next generation donors to fundraise or even give at a level that leads to discomfort financially. With next gen donors, it is a marathon, not a sprint. I think if you go for the sprint in terms of money, then you're going to wind up with a one-time donation. If you go for the marathon of building trust in a relationship, it will be more fruitful for years to come.

And, of course, to bring us full circle, if a new next generation board member or donor has an idea for your nonprofit where they want to give money and get involved, please don't say, "We'll take a look at that." It seems almost a catchphrase for nonprofits. I hear executive directors and development professionals say, "We'll take a look at that," and then I never, ever hear back from them. Even if the answer is a disappointing one, like "Here's why we don't think this will work for our organization," that at least communicates that you have respect for the person you are soliciting and that you care and have spent time thinking about what it was that they wanted to contribute.

I know some organizations don't want their board members or donors to be actively involved in the hands-on work of the

(continued)

135

(continued)

organization. They feel they have staff members to do that. Nonprofits may want my advice, but they didn't want me to be an employee. I understand that. But I also think it can keep organizations from making the most of their donors' passion, time, and talents—especially when working with next generation donors. Nonprofits need to listen to what our passions are and put our skills to good use. Doing so just might turn into something great for the organization. So many of my peers are extremely reliable and genuinely want to get involved in philanthropy in a hands-on way. I know a lot of younger donors like this. And I'm proud to be one.

Jenna's sentiments speak to something we heard from many of her peers about a dilemma they face. Thoughtful engagement demands a lot of time, but it does so at a stage in their lives when this resource of free time is particularly scarce—as they launch careers, start families, and so on. This makes donors like Jenna very discerning. Yet they are unwilling to say the solution to this dilemma is to take the easy way out and just give money. They still want to go "all in"—giving time, talent, and treasure to one or two organizations—or not go at all.

The Value of Talent

Nonprofits and others doing good work for good causes certainly need money, especially the sort of significant and sustained gifts that Jenna says properly engaged next gen donors can give for the long run. But they still insist giving talent *and* treasure is better than treasure alone. One next gen member of a long-standing wealthy family explained, "I don't want to underemphasize the importance of the financial support, because I think that's something that all of the organizations are in dire need of. But I think if you're only looking at it from the financial perspective, it leaves an incredible amount on the table, especially the degree to which time and talent can influence the treasure in terms of how that's allocated."

Other donors see the value of talent in a more personal way, pointing to the special skills they can use—and eagerly want to use—in their philanthropic work. One talked about the value he can bring as a lawyer helping nonprofits work on their legislative advocacy: "For me, it gets personal. Since I have a law degree and I have all of these skills, this was something I wanted to do to make the world a better place." Another emphasized being of specific use to the groups she funds: "I'm pretty useful at creating companies and building companies, and I imagine I can be pretty useful to nonprofits as well. So that's where I try to spend my time."

You can see a familiar thread running through these statements: the desire for a close, highly engaged relationship with the groups they support, where they are helping to advance each organization's mission by lending meaningful expertise. Donors insist this relationship works best because they bring needed skills as well as funds to the table. Again, going "all in" is better for all involved.

Hadi Partovi believes in going all in. As an extremely successful tech entrepreneur and investor who was wealthy at a young age, Hadi knew he wanted to use this wealth to improve the world, especially the American education system, as his father had done in their native Iran. But unlike other wealthy young entrepreneurs he knows, he doesn't think his best strategy is to keep making more and more money. So after earning more than he and his family will ever need, he now gives more than just money to charity. Instead, he went all in by founding, funding, *and* running full-time a nonprofit dedicated to making computer science education accessible to every child.

Hadi Partovi

I was born in Iran, in Tehran. My family—my mom, dad, my twin brother, and I—moved back and forth between the United States and Tehran when I was very young. We are one of the only Iranian families who left Iran and then returned in the late 1970s, at a time when most people were leaving the country. I was 6 years old when the Islamic Revolution changed the country, and war with Iraq broke out and changed our family life tremendously. When I was 11, we left Iran permanently and moved to the United States.

My father had been a founding professor at Iran's main technology university, and he is my role model. He completely lives his life for others, frankly in a mind-blowing kind of way. As soon as we arrived in the United States and my father felt his family was safe, he decided to go back to Iran. He felt he had helped to found this university there and wanted to make sure the education system that he helped to set up didn't fall apart. So once we were settled in the United States, my father went back and spent another two years living apart from us, all to help the education system there. That left a big impression on me, obviously. I think every way he's lived his life has been dedicated to education and to helping others. His journey has informed mine.

Early Success in Tech

When I was 10, my father had brought home a computer, a Commodore 64, possibly one of the only PCs in the entire country. He said, "This doesn't have any software or games or apps," but he gave my brother and me a book to learn BASIC programming. Then, when I was a young teenager in the United States, my friends would get summer jobs working at restaurants or gas stations, and I'd get high-paying coding jobs at tech companies. I later majored in computer science at Harvard University and got an early start in the tech industry working at Microsoft.

My career since has basically been as an entrepreneur and then eventually as an investor. I started two tech companies, Tellme

Networks and iLike. One was really successful; one was almost successful. I have been very lucky as an investor and advisor to tech start-ups and to be early on the ground floor at a number of the most successful start-ups, particularly Facebook, Dropbox, and Airbnb.

I have always had the philosophy that beyond a certain amount, making money is about helping the world. Once my own personal financial needs are met and my family is taken care of, I'd rather use the money I earn to help make the world a better place. So that is how I live my life. And again, those values come from my father.

I started making small gifts a few years ago and realized as a new philanthropist that giving was really hard. I was asking questions such as, "What were good nonprofits to support? How does one decide where you're going to make more of an impact?"

In the investment world, I know how to invest in start-ups and tech stock, but in the world of nonprofits, the science of it or the measurement of even just how you report on it is much less well developed because there isn't a standard for the bottom line of a nonprofit. For a for-profit, the bottom line ends up being earnings or stock price, but for nonprofits, there is no standard of how you measure success.

Going All In

I started out writing checks and, together with my twin brother, started a donor-advised fund. But over time, I've realized that what I can do by giving my time and talent is far, far greater than what I do by just writing checks. The primary way I've done this is by starting a nonprofit called Code.org with my brother. I now work on Code.org full-time—and it is both my full-time job and my life's mission.

Ironically, I didn't start out with a grandiose plan for Code.org; rather, it started out as a one-off project to create a video—the video that is still on the Code.org homepage—to promote computer science and convince people that our schools

(continued)

(continued)

should teach it. The launch was beyond my wildest dreams: That video had 10 million views in a week, and we had tens of thousands of schools and educators reach out asking for help. Now, at the time, Code.org was literally just me and some volunteers who helped with the video, so there was no staff to respond when those 10,000+ educators reached out to us. I quickly realized this needed a whole organization.

Three years later, Code.org is now a 50-person organization whose mission is to help bring computer science to every school in the country. We believe that every school should teach computer science and every child should have the opportunity to learn the basics about how technology works and how it is changing the world around us.

While I have other interests, I would say 95 percent of my time, talent, and financial resources now go to Code.org. My brother and I together have given about $2 million to Code.org and then, most important, it has been my full-time job for almost three years. Choosing to go all in with my time was a big deal. Considering how well I was doing as an investor in technology, taking time out from that very lucrative career to run this nonprofit full-time is a pretty big financial sacrifice for me—or a financial contribution, whichever way you look at it.

I remember very well, before I started doing this, somebody said to me, "The most impactful thing you can do is to make a lot of money—because you're clearly good at that—and then give that money away." But I believe the exact opposite. If everybody followed that advice, you'd have only "B-team" players left in the nonprofit world, while all the best entrepreneurs stayed focused on making money.

So I both fund this nonprofit and I run it. Most people who run a nonprofit fundraise for it but don't also give substantially to it. Most people who are wealthy enough to write big checks to nonprofits start a foundation to give the money, and hire somebody else to run the organizations they fund. I have always felt, coming from the tech industry, that this wasn't effective. Many of the most successful companies of our time now are tech companies. And you often see the entrepreneurs who created those tech start-ups become successful and start a nonprofit, but then they don't themselves run it. And the nonprofits don't end up having the greatness of the actual tech companies. Given my success as a technologist, I knew I could take this same path. But I felt that actually spending my time on the nonprofit as well as my money, and hiring software engineers and the best and the brightest talent from the tech industry to solve this problem for the world, would be a greater contribution. So now Code.org is the number one place I put my money, and it's also where I invest my time and talent. I think this will really help Code.org have an impact.

A Talent-Focused Model

At Code.org, we focus on one end goal: every school in the United States teaching computer science to a diverse student population. We line everything up to achieve that, especially the talent we hire. For example, our staff is now at 50 people, and we interviewed 1,000 to get the right and the best 50. We have engineers that came from Amazon or Microsoft or Dropbox or Google. That's not normal for nonprofits. Even our administrative staff is so skilled that they write the HTML code for our website. As an investor, I have always felt that amazing teams deliver amazing results, and I think that should be true in nonprofits as well as for-profits.

Culturally, we are not an education nonprofit that happens to do a little bit of technology stuff. We are through-and-through a tech company, and how we do what we do is very different than most nonprofits. Most nonprofits don't have a 15-person engineering team, but for us, we see the need for this team because we are investing in our end goal. Our engineering team boosts and amplifies everything we do—from curricula to political advocacy to recruiting teachers—by constructing automated systems to go to scale. For example, we are currently training 2,000 teachers

(continued)

141

(continued)

a month. It's a human-capital-intensive thing to train teachers through in-person trainings, but we're operating at a larger scale than most teacher education institutions in the country because we are using technology to do it.

So Code.org is a different model for a nonprofit, and we are starting to see evidence that this model will have a greater impact. Some education nonprofits in the United States have an expensive contribution-to-cost ratio. For example, it takes $1,000 per student for one educational nonprofit I know of to have an impact, whereas with Code.org, it costs $0.56 to impact one student.

This impact we are having is so phenomenal compared to other places I've donated to in the past. The evidence of our impact just further reinforces my desire to give most of my money here as well as my time and talent. I put my money into Code.org not only because it's my own nonprofit but because I see the impact and results we get in the United States are so much higher than at other U.S. nonprofits and because I believe in the model and team we have developed.

Changing the System

The system-wide approach taken by Code.org is essential, I think. When I started this work, my brother gave me extremely valuable advice. Initially, I was thinking I could create a school or a summer camp or a club in my neighborhood, see how it goes, and expand from there. That's how most nonprofits start. They start in their local community, find a solution that works, and then talk about replication. But my brother, making a tech analogy, said, "If Steve Jobs were looking at this, he would start by thinking about what the world is going to look like 20 or 30 years from now, and then he would plot a line from here to there." That completely changed my view of what the pieces are that need to be in place to achieve our goal. As a result, we don't run any local schools; instead, we think about the entire school system on a national level, and we take a very different approach about how to change the education system because of this broader view.

At Code.org, we go beyond both the classic approaches of "giving a man a fish" and "teaching him how to fish." Rather, we teach the schools how to teach the students how to fish. That's why we have the double benefit of scalability because we do not need to pay the costs every day of what it takes to run a school. We just pay the cost of what it takes to train the teachers, and then the school system is powering the engine to do the rest of the work. That's why it's so much more efficient and systemic. We focus on creating the talent, not running the institutions—on training the teachers to teach the students so they'll be prepared for the world 20 years from now. The incredible support, sacrifice, and passion of these teachers have been critical to our success. We're not the first movement to try to improve the education system, but we may be the first one that can legitimately claim to be teacher-powered. The support of teachers is what has made Code.org and the computer science movement a real success.

To build a new education system for 20 years from now, it also means reaching out to students, parents, principals, school districts, state governments, and the federal government. There's a role for all of those parties to play to get computer science into the curriculum. You can't put it in there unless everybody is on board. And the policies around these computer science classes matter a great deal also. For example, we know that tech has a diversity problem in that there just aren't a lot of girls or African Americans or Hispanic kids taking computer science courses. We've actually done tests in Maryland that show how we might address this problem. We looked at one district that said a computer science class can count toward graduation requirements and another school district that didn't have that policy, and we compared the number of girls taking the courses. In the district where the class didn't count, 15 percent of the students in the class were girls. In the district where it did count, that number was 50 percent. So a small policy change can dramatically change the gender mix of students taking computer science classes, and a similar growth was apparent

(continued)

143

(continued)

in the ethnic representation in the computer science classes, too. Again, to achieve these results we need all parties on board, so we end up having to work at many levels.

Real Success Is About Impact on the World

I mentioned earlier that I was inspired by Steve Jobs's growth mindset. I'm also impressed by Bill Gates, and he serves as a role model for me in deciding to work so hard in my day-to-day job running Code.org. Like me, Bill Gates contributes his time and talent, as well as his money, to philanthropy. But what has been most incredible for me to see is the amount of drive he puts into it. This is the person who least needs to work in the world, the wealthiest man. He does not need anything. Yet he works extremely hard, full-time, on philanthropy. And his philanthropy is not something where he's just giving money and letting the rest of it take care of itself. He's giving his personal time and expertise as well and sticking with it and ensuring its impact.

I'm also motivated by Bono. For most musicians or celebrities who give money to charity, the charity is secondary. But for Bono, the music is there to fund the charity. The entire reason that he's continuing to go on tours is to enable his successful charitable work and trying to eradicate AIDS and poverty. This resonates with me because, again, I feel that after I have a certain amount of money, any other money I make is for giving back. For me, any continued investing I do is to make money to donate to Code.org, and of course most of my time is spent on that as well.

I think every human struggles with the question of why am I here? What the hell is the point? For me, what matters is not defined by how much money I make but by how much impact I have on the world and what good I leave in the world that wasn't there before. I want to try to derive happiness from the impact I can have—not from what I get but from what I give, especially my time and talent.

Hadi Partovi clearly believes in talent. He believes in using talent—in the form of trained teachers—as the lever for systemic change in the education system. He believes in teaching the skills necessary for young people to develop the talent needed in today's economy. He believes in hiring the best talent for the tech-inspired nonprofit he founded and runs. And he believes his own talent is the most valuable gift he can give, even compared to the millions of dollars he's invested as a donor.

Hadi is a great illustration of a belief in talent that we heard over and over again across the full spectrum of donors we talked with—from inheritors to first-generation wealth creators. For those coming into their roles as the next gen in established giving families, this belief in talent was often tied to their desire to be seen as more than just a famous last name or a cash machine. For those whose entrepreneurial success had brought them the resources to be big donors, the passion for giving talent was perhaps even more pronounced.

Only a few of the donors take this belief as far as Hadi does, devoting their talent full-time as employees of the groups they fund. But nearly every donor talked in some way about wanting to make use of individual distinctive abilities in his or her giving.

What Does This Mean?

There's an old adage that says "throwing money at a problem" is not a good solution. Doing so is easy but rarely effective. Our world has a growing list of thorny problems, and the next generation of major donors has a staggering amount of money to throw at them. But next gen donors believe that old saying. They believe social change requires human *and* financial capital, and they stand ready and willing to give both.

The reservoir of skills and expertise these donors have to give remains relatively untapped. Anyone concerned about solving social problems or improving nonprofit effectiveness would do well to figure out how to make use of next gen talents as well as their time and treasure. Not just because doing so would mean they give more of the treasure but also because talent can be, in fact, pretty useful. Jenna's story of breathing new life into established organizations and Hadi's story of using talent to have measurable impact on the education system are good evidence of this.

We should also remember that next gen donors are at a point in their lives when they are finding their philanthropic identities. As we will explore, many inheritors are chomping at the bit to go out and "plow their own trail," or to take over the work of improving their families' trails. And we've heard how earners like Hadi believe the same personal qualities that made them so successful so young in life can make them successful as a new breed of engaged and entrepreneurial donors. For both inheritors and earners, their abilities are a bigger part of their identity than their money. This is not surprising, as Gen Xers and Millennials have been raised to know that they are worth more than their wealth. We shouldn't be shocked, then, to hear how much these donors despise being treated like ATMs and, for women in particular, being seen only as fundraisers and party planners rather than as people with experience, training, and competency.

On the other hand, nonprofits and other ventures seeking to solve our difficult social problems need money. Some might even say they need that money—especially the level of money they can get from these donors—much more than they need skills from donors. Nonprofits might even resent having to spend precious staff time and resources to create "meaningful" volunteer opportunities for their biggest donors when they should spend those resources providing service for their needy clients or on advocacy for their policy proposals.

A way through this quandary, without resentment on either side, can be found in the idea of respect from both sides for the other. Organizations can respect their major donors as more than a last name or a bank account. Donors can respect organizations by not "holding a check over their heads" and by listening, not telling. We heard from some donors who recognize this need for humility and a focus on what is best for the organization. Said one, "I don't think that I have the solution to every problem or that if I just had more time I could be really making the organizations way more effective, but I definitely could play a role and could have an impact based on a variety of my skills."

Next gen donors who are so eager to feel appreciated for their talents and to contribute those in meaningful ways run the risk of falling into a position of entitlement and unhelpful privilege. To avoid this, donors need to listen to and respect what organizations say they need donors to do, not just show up with their quiver of specific skills and say, "Find a way for me to use these." This respectful understanding will be easier as donors get closer to the organizations they seek to help. Some donors we talked with were already trying to take this humbler approach, even honing their talent at stuffing envelopes because that is what their partner grantees needed most at the time, knowing they can ramp up to more skills-based help when needed.

On the nonprofit side, we know there are plenty of organizations out there creatively finding ways to utilize the talents of their younger donors.[2] Unfortunately, the evidence suggests this is not exactly a widespread trend. First, while many nonprofits talk the good Millennial talk, espousing the importance of engaging the next generation of leaders, most have not actually brought next gen donors onto their boards or given them skills-based, hands-on volunteer roles. For example, a recent BoardSource study found that only 16 percent of board members nationwide were under 40. The good news is that this number is on the rise.[3]

Even fewer nonprofits have set up new and creative ways to engage next gen donors—those who will be their major donors for the next several decades—in the talent-focused, respectful, and meaningful ways these donors want. We know many nonprofit leaders are aware that they need to do so, as this is a common question we get when speaking to nonprofits about our research. The question they have is how to do it.

Next gen donors like Jenna Segal have a lot of suggestions for these nonprofits looking to engage them better. Beyond bringing next gen donors onto boards in careful ways like she suggests, and beyond the cliché approach of getting a Millennial to set up your Twitter feed, several ideas came out of our interviews and from our own experience in the field. Most obviously, as Jenna noted, nonprofits must be responsive when next gen donors ask to give their time and talent. Don't just put them off; meet with them, hear them out, and ask questions. Consider a small-scale trial of their ideas before rejecting them out of hand, or maybe find a way for them to take the lead in exploring how they can best plug into the organization's work. If their ideas are off-base, better to be candid with them about why you think so instead of ignoring them or offering vague promises of "we'll take a look at that."

Also, rather than just giving next gen donors a symbolic or token seat on the board, put them in the driver's seat on a special task force that is charged with solving some real problem facing the organization and that requires donors to use their skills to make a serious impact. Better yet, given their penchant for engaging with peers (the subject of Chapter 7), give them the freedom to corral the talents of other next gen donors in service of a task. This requires nonprofits to rethink how they go about solving internal problems or developing new programs. It means approaching those tasks in a collaborative way with engaged next gen donors working alongside staff. Reimagining in this way might pay off in more ways than one.

Not all next gen donors need to go "all in" in the way that Hadi Partovi does, actually running the organizations they fund. But finding better ways for organizations to make good use of the talents of next gen donors seems an essential step in addressing our pressing social challenges. At a minimum, doing so will lead next gen donors to give more. At most, it will marshal the expertise of those donors to expand the organization's impact. Ideally, it will do both.

CHAPTER 7

Inspirational Peer Pressure

Time, talent, and treasure. Encouraging people to give that full triad of gifts has long been a common maxim. We know Gen X and Millennial donors consider it essential to give all three in their own ways. But next gen donors believe they have a fourth valuable asset to offer: their peer networks, their connections to fellow philanthropists who have their own assets to give. So moving forward, we need to add one more T to the mantra: time, talent, treasure, and ties.

The next generation, especially Millennials, is seen as more highly networked than any generation in history and fundamentally peer-driven. This is the Facebook Generation, the generation that thinks of "friends" as the extended network they connect with daily around the country or even the world, not just the people they hang out with in person.[1] Their ability to communicate, advocate, and congregate through an online click, a text, or a tweet, has had impressive consequences. It has helped candidates get elected and activists mobilize thousands for movements like Occupy Wall Street. These young Gen Xers and Millennials stand on the leading edges of our networked society.

As one next gen donor reflects, "Being a networker, and being networked, is now seen as something really respected, whereas in the previous generation, it was something that was respected, but people were a little dubious of it. If you were pushing too much and networking too much, you were looked at with disdain, but now it is something heralded. There is a cultural shift in how we view people who are networkers or who are connected."

Another donor tied this cultural shift to the work of social change, saying, "Our generation, in the digital age, we recognize the power of bringing everyone along with us and building movements." In this way, next gen donors' reliance on ties is both personal and strategic, beneficial to their own growth as well as to the causes they support. Their networks fuel their impact.

Transformation Not Transaction

Of course, we all have networks—people we're connected to and people we call when we want their support for something we're working on, be it a cookie sale for Girls Scouts or a walk for multiple sclerosis. But these networked relationships are more powerful and meaningful for the next gen. Understanding these relationships requires that we understand how the next gen thinks about and uses its peer connections as assets.

For one thing, peer relationships help next gen donors build their identity, like Jenna Weinberg will illustrate in the feature below. We found many next gen donors whose key identity formation experiences came from peer giving networks. The donor below describes an experience similar to what we'll hear from Jenna:

> The appeal of giving in a group with peers is to be able to take my family out of it. It was the first time I've had to grapple with, "What do I care about, and how do I talk about that?" The process became more important than the actual gifting. We made our own plan for how we were going to do our giving.

We developed criteria together. I found that knowing myself better, being able to articulate that, and having the experience of acting on it prepared me for when I work with my parents on family philanthropy. It also gives me the experience, validation, some authority, and agency to be able to go back to my parents and say, "I've done this. I have opinions of my own to bring to the table."

For those who are further along in the identity formation journey, next gen peer groups and giving circles can still feel like a place to belong and to find others facing similar opportunities and challenges. One woman we spoke with admitted, "I didn't realize how much I craved talking to people in a similar situation as me." Having significant wealth and access to philanthropic resources made this woman feel isolated, unable to ask the questions she had about identity, values, and effective philanthropy to just anyone for fear they would think she was, at worst, bragging, or, at best, ill-prepared. Finding peers with whom she could talk candidly helped her work through her identity as a donor. A self-made donor concurs, saying his peer giving experiences helped reinforce his identity. "I need those connections with people who can both understand what I'm trying to do and keep me accountable to the values I'm trying to base it in." Another agreed, "I am continually trying to find my peers and set up ways to be in conversation with them on a regular basis so that I continue to forge the path I want to."

Using peers for identity-building purposes and personal support are good examples of how the next generation sees their engagement with peers differently than past donors. While they observe previous generations often treating philanthropic peers primarily as people who can write checks to their causes, like the quid pro quo "you give to my cause, and I'll give to yours" arrangements in typical old boys' networks, next gen donors see their engagement with networks as less transactional and more transformational, both personally and strategically. They are hungry for meaningful connections with peers in similar situations of philanthropic affluence so that they can connect personally, to learn and grow together and be more effective in their giving.

Funding and learning with peers allows next gen donors to strategize together, to assess impact with one another, as well as to pool their expertise and passion in service of the shared cause. "We are not doing this to be in some big club together! It's not for a sense of belonging that we want to be part of a next gen network; it's for a sense of equality and impact. You might be giving a billion to my million, but we both want to achieve the same goal. We are not just doing this to meet once a year and to go to a conference. We are doing this to accomplish long-term change."

In this way, peer ties become another valuable resource that next gen donors feel they have to give. "We value these ties as an asset, just like the time, talent, and treasure. And we are very careful how we use this asset. Nonprofits sometimes assume next gen donors have a network filled with other potential funders that they can tap into. This might be true, but we take great care in how we use that network."

Next gen donors clearly do not want to be too crass in thinking about the value of ties, either to themselves or to nonprofits. A few cautioned against thinking of their peers in transactional ways, including letting money become the central focus of their interactions.

There is a sort of unspoken nonsolicitation clause that we are in a safe space to air these things because we all know we have significant resources. So, yes, a fundraising ask [in a peer group] can be powerful, but if I am going to make it, I better really need it or see the alignment with the other person's funding. And I'll say, "Look, you know normally I wouldn't do this, but this is so well-aligned with what you do that you should know it exists."

But peer networks can become insulating if participants lose sight of the fact that their work together is meant for a larger purpose and takes place in a social context. One donor was quite blunt about this caution, noting that in general, "Today we ignore the people who live right around the corner from us and instead have these global virtual networks. I don't think that's progress."

Valuing our ties to one another in our extended families and across the globe is certainly not a next gen idea. Kin groups and tribes have been the essential networks holding societies together since the beginning of time. However, the way in which the current next generation connects with, relies on, and taps into their peer networks seems different. If properly harnessed, next gen peer networks can be game-changing for the organizations these donors support.

Jenna Weinberg embodies this new way of using and benefiting from her peer ties. Still in her mid-20s, Jenna currently serves as the chair of the grants committee of the Nathan and Lillian Weinberg Foundation, a supporting foundation of The Associated: Jewish Community Federation of Baltimore, which she stewards with her siblings and cousins. The donor-advised fund was set up by her great-uncle, Harry Weinberg, who established a handful of philanthropic funds in the name of each of his siblings; this one is in honor of Jenna's grandparents. Otherwise known as "Honolulu Harry" from having earned much of his fortune from pineapple groves in Hawaii, Jenna's great-uncle left the majority of his estate to the Harry and Jeanette Weinberg Foundation, one of the largest private charitable foundations in the United States, assisting low-income and vulnerable individuals and families.

Jenna Weinberg

Every Friday night growing up in Baltimore, like in many Jewish homes around the world, my family had Shabbat dinner together. In addition to the standard rituals of lighting candles, blessing the wine, and eating challah, my family added an extra tradition: giving *tzedakah* (Hebrew for "justice" or "righteousness," but often used to mean "charity"). Each person had a quarter by her or his place setting. We would take turns going around the table and placing the coin in the tzedakah box. Each person was also required to share a *mitzvah* ("good deed") they had done over the course of the week. This positive action was something that was expected of me weekly. And not only was I expected to be positively engaged with the world around me, I was expected to recount the deed, reflect on it, and take pride in it. For me, philanthropy was never just about the money but also the actions that go along with it.

Today, as a trustee of a family foundation, I find there is a tension between what the founders focused on and what I would choose to give to if I were the founder. The philanthropic values that I inherited are still the basis of our funding decisions, but as I have come to develop my own approach to giving, I've realized I might choose to act on those values differently than my parents or grandparents did. I believe that just as Judaism has evolved and changed to survive, so, too, should our lens on philanthropy and how we give.

Philanthropy Is the Change I Want to Make in the World

So how did my thinking about philanthropy and my relationship to it evolve? After my junior year of college, I participated in a retreat called Grand Street, a program of 21/64, which provides a peer network and tools for Jewish next gen donors who are or will one day be involved in their family's philanthropy. This retreat was life-changing. It empowered me to ask my parents the questions about this inherited legacy that I had never previously known how to ask.

Coming to terms with my inheritance, beyond the dollars, was an empowering process of self-exploration that was enhanced by doing so with my peers in Grand Street. Through Grand Street, I learned about Slingshot. The idea for Slingshot emerged over a decade ago at one of the first Grand Street retreats. Participants in that retreat felt disconnected from the organizations their parents supported and were looking for new ways to engage in Jewish philanthropy. The result was the creation of the *Slingshot Resource Guide*—a Zagat-style guide that highlights the most innovative and impactful Jewish organizations in North America.

Soon after, this group of young donors created a collaborative giving circle called the Slingshot Fund, which I joined after moving to New York when I graduated from college. The Slingshot Fund is comprised of Jewish funders in their 20s and 30s, who pool their contributions in order to leverage those dollars to make larger gifts. Only organizations featured in the guide are eligible for funding.

Participating in the Slingshot Fund gave me a network of peers who were interested in funding Jewish innovation, exposed me to dozens of Jewish organizations that were relevant to me, encouraged me to grapple with my Jewish and philanthropic values, and empowered me to advocate for the organizations I believe in. It helped me realize that check-writing isn't what philanthropy means to me; rather, philanthropy is thinking about the change I want to make in the world and using everything I have to try to accomplish that change.

After participating in the Fund for two years and feeling the impact of this experience, it was only natural for me to join Slingshot's board of directors when asked. Beyond the fact that Slingshot has allocated more than $3 million to small, under-funded, innovative organizations across the country, it has also created real, meaningful opportunities for the donors involved to contribute in other ways aligned with the organization's

(continued)

(continued)

mission. Being more hands-on and engaged in the organization's governance, decision-making, and operational work has been critical for me.

Since I've always felt that philanthropy isn't just about writing a check and patting myself on the back, this opportunity to serve Slingshot with my other resources felt right to me. When Slingshot's founding executive director decided to leave the organization after five years for a new career opportunity, fellow board members asked if I'd step off the board temporarily in order to step in as the interim director. I was glad I could help the organization at such an integral moment in its growth. Now that I am back on the board with our new executive in place, I have even more to contribute since I understand the organization in more intimate ways than perhaps any other board member. Supported by my peers on the board and using my professional background in working with nonprofits, I feel like I affected organizational change with my skills and networks and not just by using my financial resources.

The Power of Peers

A major influence on my evolution to this view of philanthropy has been my engagement with philanthropic peers. I learned first-hand the value of leveraging support for the causes I believe in by participating in collective giving experiences. The two peer giving groups I've been involved in—the Slingshot Fund and HEKDESH: Dorot Alumni Giving Circle—have also both challenged me to look at giving in new ways.

The Slingshot Fund (as mentioned earlier) is a peer group of inheritors. Each person, usually around 10 to 12 of us in each funding cycle, contributes $7,500, and then we collectively decide how to allocate that pool of funds. This is different from previous generations' models of collective giving, where you outsource your vote to the professionals running the group. What I like about the Slingshot model is that my peers' strategic views can inform my own decisions, and I can look to my peers for opinions about the organizations we are vetting. Getting that candid feedback from a trusted peer is invaluable.

The beauty of this sort of collective giving model is that my peers and I ask questions or share information that force each other to look at an organization in a new way. I have at times completely changed my feeling about a grant proposal because of something a peer shared. Or other times, a peer would make the time to visit an organization because they knew that visiting in person makes a material difference compared to talking over the phone, and their report back has been very meaningful. Doing due diligence together with peers, or going on site visits together, also adds new complexity to my thinking about giving in general. I always walk away from my conversations with peers with more sophisticated thinking about how organizations work and how change is made.

Collective giving has also helped me meet new people who are coming into financial means and will be giving throughout their lifetimes. Getting to know all of these people at an early stage in their philanthropic journeys, and seeing how their priorities and interests develop, not only makes it easier for us to partner in the future but also gives me peers to help me reflect on my own journey.

Gaining Leverage

The second peer giving fund I'm involved with is called HEKDESH. The name HEKDESH comes from the Hebrew word *hekdesh*, which is rooted in the word *kadosh*, meaning "holy." Since medieval times and up through contemporary Israel, hekdesh has referred to a communal fund from which charitable gifts are made.

The HEKDESH giving circle is made up of alumni, and spouses/partners of alumni, of the Dorot Fellowship in Israel, a program focused on leadership development through the lens of emotional intelligence and on becoming active players in social change. For the 2016 funding cycle, HEKDESH had approximately 80 members, who gave a minimum gift of $180

(continued)

159

(continued)

each, allowing us to allocate over $20,000. Since its inception, HEKDESH has given over $80,000 to support vulnerable populations across the globe.

One of the things I love about HEKDESH is that it makes giving accessible to my peers at almost any giving level. I also like that I can leverage my gift to bring even more support to those organizations I really believe in. For example, in the 2016 funding cycle, one of the organizations that I nominated for funding was selected as a HEKDESH grantee. So my $180 contribution turned into a grant of over $4,000 for that organization. Then, when the executive director of that grantee organization came to town, I hosted a group of 10 HEKDESH members to learn more about the organization and develop a deeper relationship with their work.

I find that HEKDESH members are very much in line with my philanthropic priorities. They want to give to the same issues that matter most to me: social justice and human rights in Israel and around the world. And they, too, see it as valuable to grapple with those issues through a Jewish lens. Lately, our board has been thinking a lot about how we as a community can respond to emergency funding situations when we only make grants once a year and are required to give to registered 501(c)(3)s. For example, with the start of the Black Lives Matter movement, we had no structures to figure out how we might give to that movement as a group, and we didn't know which nonprofits we could support that would directly help the activists on the ground. But having a group of peers who were considering how to support this movement and could discuss doing so individually, financially or otherwise, was tremendous.

Finding My Voice

These giving circles have pushed me to grapple with how I want to talk about my interests, how to delve into the problems I'm most concerned about, and how I think changes in the world can really come about. I think the process has, at times, been even more important for me than the actual check-writing.

Discovering my voice by going through the funding process with peers has also prepared me for doing so with members of my family. From having to articulate and advocate for what I care about to coming up with compromises, I've developed skills in those peer processes that now allow me to be much more effective in funding conversations with my parents, siblings, and cousins. My experiences have also given me validation and authority in my family since I'm now seen as more of an expert in the grantmaking process.

As a result of the questions I learned how to ask in Grand Street, my parents, aunts, and uncles decided to pass down to my siblings, cousins, and me the responsibility of allocating funds from one of our family's philanthropic funds—one that was named in honor of my grandparents and set up as a supporting foundation at The Associated: Jewish Community Federation of Baltimore. With this opportunity, I've been able to put the tools I learned in my giving circle experiences to use navigating funding decisions with my family and allocating much-needed resources.

I've seen a tendency for some other inheritors to say, "I'll make my own money and build my career now, and I'll save this philanthropy stuff for later." But I'm interested in the field of philanthropy even while we are finishing school and starting jobs and families. And I think because of this my siblings and cousins have joined me in carving out time for philanthropy now. Frankly, it's been an incredible way for us to get to know each other on a different level. We were always close, but we didn't make time to discuss the issues that matter most to each of us before.

Philanthropy has given our generation of the family a new platform to explore what we care about as well as our relationships with one another. For example, per the mandate of the foundation, we are directed to give to Jewish organizations. Yet many of my siblings and cousins don't feel like Jewish giving overlaps with their own interests. So our foundation professional shared the *Slingshot Guide* with everyone, asking each to choose five organizations that stood out to them. We then compiled the list to see the array of

(continued)

161

(continued)

organizations selected. This opened up the opportunity to explore more deeply what each of us cares about and how that fits into our foundation's giving. And so the Jewish giving we do together now goes more smoothly and has more meaning for each of us.

Our foundation's philanthropy is of course about allocating funds, but it's also a training ground for us, a method of getting to know each other and learning to work together. In this way, I see the collective process of my siblings and cousins as similar to the collective processes I experience in peer giving circles. The practice of working with my peers in the Slingshot Fund and at HEKDESH has prepared me for this other philanthropy work I get to do. And now this work with my siblings and cousins is preparing me for what's next with my family and my giving, whatever that may be.

Jenna's story illustrates the ways in which ties are critical for next gen donors, from the next gen peer network that helped her come to terms with her philanthropic identity to the peer giving circles whose members helped her learn, grow, and become more strategic as a donor.

Filling the Learning Gap

Not only do next gen donors want to offer their peer connections as a resource to organizations they support, but they also greatly value these ties for helping them become better donors. Next gen donors see that through their connections, they learn how to use their other resources of time, talent, and treasure more effectively. Many of the donors we talked with pointed to their peers as a key source of learning how to be more effective donors, especially when they had few other opportunities for the experiential learning that we know (from Chapter 5) they find so helpful.[2]

Next gen donors who lament the lack of access to philanthropic education appreciate that learning from peers can fill this gap while also letting them get involved in giving experiences right away. Many inheritors are waiting for their families to welcome them into the family foundations and to provide opportunities for learning and giving, which in many cases could take years to happen. Earners, too, have to search the Internet or comb through the offerings of philanthropic infrastructure and resource groups to find the help they seek as they decide what to become invested and involved in. For both types of donors, locating a next gen network or peer giving circle gives them access to knowledge and know-how. One donor explains how he struggled in his search for help before finding a philanthropic peer group:

> I was 31 when I was starting to get involved, and I thought, "What exactly am I doing?" I don't want to be in the shadow of my parents. I want to have a say, and I want to use this opportunity in a powerful way. I wanted to meet other people who were in the same boat, and I wanted to learn—to meet [other donors] who are doing this in a way that I respected and to meet those who were *not* doing it in a way that I admired and respected to see the distinction. I wanted to create a community around me that I could learn from. Who are the nonprofits that are really driving change here? I hadn't had access before to peers, so I had not realized how many other families were years, even generations, ahead of me, which I could learn from. Other families had created

processes that I could draw from as I created my own; other families had made mistakes that I could avoid; other families could share what worked and what did not. And I could apply some of those "lessons learned" to my giving and my family foundation's practices.

Another next gen donor, who is also a person of color, shared a similar challenge, but he has yet to find the peer group to fill his learning gap. "There's little knowledge of how different families [of color] are giving. We've got to figure out if there's some special knowledge that people of color could benefit from so that we aren't in a vacuum innovating." This donor's need for peer experiences that more closely match his own and for connections for shared learning is palpable.

What next gen donors learn from peers is not just a general sense of how to be a better donor but, as Jenna points out, specific information about potential grantees or about fields in which they might want to give. In fact, next gen donors trust the strategic analysis of their peers *more* than the wisdom of older generations in their own families or foundations. They trust authentic and direct experience with organizations, even if it is not their own personal experience, and so they connect with a plugged-in network of peers who have had their own hands-on experiences to bolster their knowledge. This sort of practical sharing and learning within peer networks is another way next gen donors think about their ties as a valuable asset they bring to the philanthropic table.

A Little Inspiration

Sometimes the value of peer donor networks is less complicated. Before next gen donors know what help they need, sometimes they just need a little direction, a little inspiration. One donor gushed about his first experience connecting with other next gen donors in a group organized by his family's financial institution:

> Going to the next gen program was incredibly inspiring for me. I realized maybe I wasn't as alone as I thought, and maybe there are some risks worth taking here that I should consider going for. I was able to grow my understanding, but I think the biggest part was the empowerment for me that came out of it—allowing me to watch peers, to hear from other people who are making these decisions and living into who they are and doing it bravely and with enthusiasm. *That's* motivating.

Other rising donors were similarly energized by peers and expressed the effects of meeting inspiring peer role models. One donor said, "I felt pushed to think harder and better." Another explained, "Once you get involved in a peer group, there's a lot of momentum behind that. If you want to become a more philanthropic person, spending time with more philanthropic people will just end up doing that."

For next gen inheritors, particularly those who feel like they are toeing the line of their family's traditional grantmaking approach, having access to innovative ideas through peer donor networks—and seeing what others have accomplished with those ideas—can be especially inspiring. A next gen woman who works with her family foundation explained it this way:

> Because most of my work tends to be more traditional— given that it is within the larger foundation—it is amazing to hear about Tanzania and a pioneering microfinance model that others have been working on. It is like peer pressure but more about inspirational peer pressure, because after I hear a

peer who has lived in Tanzania for the last eight months and has managed to affect X amount of change with this really incredible model that they are helping to pioneer, I leave with an urgent sense of, *I need to get going and do something as well.* I learn from others, but key is the inspiration from all of the incredible work that everyone is doing and at such young ages.

Some donors even worried about the lack of giving by wealthy peers who were not in a peer group that could inspire them, as they saw specific examples of behavior that changed when their peers did engage with each other. One complained about how "there is a tremendous amount of wealth being created" in the high-tech industries "but they don't do as much as they could, or they are waiting to become a billionaire before they give significant funds away." He contrasts this with high-tech entrepreneurs who *are* engaged in peer giving processes, donating more and being more engaged donors. "I have been pleased to see that a lot of those individuals in [a] peer group stepped up and really joined boards or took grantmaking opportunities quite seriously and engaged with recipient organizations."

This inspirational peer pressure is probably the biggest reason next gen donors insist that their peer networks are a highly valuable asset for philanthropy. They can not only give their own time, talent, and treasure but also inspire their peers to do so as well.

Peer Giving Is Strategic Giving

In Chapter 3, we saw that next gen donors identified "recommending a cause or organization to others" as one of the top five most important components of philanthropic strategy. Of course, this priority shows again how much these donors trust each other's recommendations, but it also suggests that the next gen considers sharing recommendations with peers—and even making decisions or giving with those peers—a part of more strategic giving.

One longtime member of a giving circle described why the giving decisions she makes with her peers are more strategic than those she makes alone: "Giving is so much better when there are 20 other people around the table. And on the conference call, then, you have to be strategic. You don't have a choice. You have to present an objective reason as to why an organization should get your grant, as opposed to the next organization on your pile. So the communal and conversational aspect of it has forced me to do what I don't have to do when I am by myself."

Giving circles that involve pooled funds as well as pooled human capital and joint engagement in the giving processes further exemplify how collective giving can be strategic giving. Members read proposals and conduct site visits together. They analyze together how their collective funds can make the most impact on an issue or a system, not just on an organization. In short, they use their ties to combine their time and talents, not just their treasure. A good example of this innovative sort of peer giving process is the Maverick Collective, a philanthropic and advocacy initiative started by the nonprofit Population Services International and designed to build a peer group of engaged next gen women looking to end extreme poverty in their lifetimes. The Maverick Collective leverages not just the money but the expertise, skills, and talents of the next gen women in the group and uses these combined assets to enhance each grantees' success.

What Does This Mean?

Donors throughout the history of giving have been influenced by other donors.[3] But next gen donors are taking this peer influence well beyond the quid pro quo approach that they saw widely practiced by previous generations of big donors. For Gen Xers and Millennials, peers influence not just *where* they give or *how much* but also *how* and *how effectively*. Peers are a primary source of learning, inspiration, and strategic advice, and some donors prefer to give with their peers rather than alone.

Some might say the advent of social networking or peer reviews on products leads next gen donors to seek this kind of peer input in every aspect of their lives—so why not in their grantmaking? However, these donors are also responding to the paucity of other sources of learning in the philanthropic field.[4] There is no road map for being a funder, and most donors don't know where to find the support they need and want. Plenty of philanthropic infrastructure groups serve donors, but many next gen donors feel those institutions are geared to support the existing donor base of Baby Boomers and older givers. The next gen doesn't see a place for itself in these infrastructure groups, causing these donors to turn their focus more intensely to finding or starting their own peer networks and sources of learning. Similarly, these organizations themselves worry that their membership rolls have few next gen donors in the pipeline, and they are uncertain how to recruit the next gen.

A few organizations in this field—including our own—have been trying to meet this need, but we are only addressing a small portion of the demand. The 21/64 team has developed educational programming such as its Next Gen Donor Retreats and Training series, peer learning networks like Grand Street and Ripe for Change, giving circles such as Natan and Slingshot, and other resources geared to new and next gen donors as well as their families and the advisors supporting them. The Dorothy A. Johnson Center for Philanthropy offers The Grantmaking School trainings and the LearnPhilanthropy online portal of learning resources. A few graduate degrees and certifications also focus on giving and grantmaking, and programming and donor education materials are available from several other organizations.[5] But much more is needed.

In our experience at 21/64 running next gen peer groups and giving circles, we have seen both the benefits and challenges of peer giving played out in ways that mirror many of the statements quoted in this chapter. Some next gen donors can't get past the idea of transactional giving and in the end agree to give a grant to each member's favorite organization. But we have found that, in the majority of cases, next gen donors have not only a personal experience but also an educational one in their group giving. And when they do, their individual grantmaking becomes bigger and better because they now know how and what they want to fund. The group's collective giving, too, becomes more strategic because of the "collective genius" that arises through the collaborative grantmaking.[6]

For some nonprofits and advisory firms considering setting up next gen peer groups to meet this clear demand, we can imagine it may feel like a lot of effort to retool a method of engagement when older donors and clients are fine with the current setup. Others may be skeptical about whether these cohort groups are really needed. However, we like to remember that the Baby Boomers—the leaders of nonprofits now—often spent at least a decade serving on committees before stepping into leadership roles. Similarly, next gen peer cohorts give relatively young donors an opportunity to craft their philanthropic identities alongside their peers, building in checks and balances for the hubris of those starting out who may think they know everything but are hungry for strategy to make them better donors. If nonprofits can offer their newer and younger donors the chance to learn and grow *together* within their organizations, they may find themselves with a rising group of donors who are loyal philanthropists for a long time.

On the flip side, nonprofit organizations should caution themselves against seeing next gen donors and their networks as nothing more than trees to shake. Nonprofit professionals can no longer assume that making an emotional ask will be enough to inspire Generation Impact. Next gen donors expect strategic advice from their peers. Therefore, nonprofits that rely on their board members, development committees, and peer-to-peer fundraising teams need to arm their volunteer solicitors with this new information. In the Impact Revolution, next gen donors expect those who reach out to them, even their peers, to bring an analysis of how an organization is making an impact. Only by finding those next gen donors whose interests genuinely align with an organization's mission and impact will nonprofits succeed in involving more Gen X and Millennial donors.

—◌᠊

We have insisted throughout this book that these next gen donors have the potential to be the biggest, most significant donors ever, in part because they have unprecedented resources to give but also because they insist on maximizing the impact of that giving. But next gen donors insist that if they are to become historically significant donors, it won't be simply because they are amplifying their individual giving by giving more or more effectively; it will also be because they are revolutionizing philanthropy by giving better together. And given that they are the most connected and highly networked generations in history, the amount of good that can be done as they give and learn together is truly exciting.

Sara Ojjeh, a founding member of the Maverick Collective—and a donor featured later in this book—shares our excitement:

> The same way that the Gateses blew the Robber Barons out of the water with their philanthropic giving, I think that this next generation is going to blow the Gates Foundation out of the water with our giving. But for that to happen, I think people need to know that they are not alone standing up on a soapbox. We have to be there together, share a common idea or innovation with others, and commit to having an impact on the environment, or animal welfare, or human rights, or whatever, but we have to rally about it and make a difference by doing it together.

PART THREE

Respectful Revolutionaries

CHAPTER 8

Living Values Seamlessly

In Parts 1 and 2, we focused on how next gen donors want to revolutionize philanthropy to prioritize impact and innovation, retool strategy, and go all in with their every asset—time, talent, treasure, and ties. We learned that they don't necessarily want to change *what* causes or issues major donors support so much as *how* they support those causes.

In Part 3, we turn to the questions of *why* emerging next gen donors give and especially *who* they are and what makes them tick. What we learned might surprise you.

Values, Not Valuables

If you follow pop culture, you might label wealthy Millennials and Gen Xers as "self-centered" or "entitled." We all see stories about the decadence of the "Rich Kids of Instagram." But if you listen to next gen donors like John R. Seydel and Justin Rockefeller—who are highlighted in this chapter—you get a very different picture.

In fact, in our combined 40 years in this field, we have found that most next gen donors are driven primarily by values, not valuables. Regardless of their wealth and privilege, their philanthropy

175

is motivated more by what they believe in and care about than by a desire for praise or other less noble impulses.

Our research for this book has confirmed our experience and assumptions. In surveying major donors ages 21 to 40 about the importance of various reasons for engaging in philanthropy, "supporting a mission or cause that I believe in, and that fits with my personal values" came in first out of 23 choices. Nearly every single next gen donor identified that reason for giving as "very important." The second-highest-ranked reason—"fulfilling my duty as a person of privilege to give back to society"—similarly reflects their values orientation, as does "helping the less fortunate and the disadvantaged," which also ranked highly. At the bottom of the list? "Receiving some sort of sincere recognition or thanks," "having the chance to attend a social event," and "receiving some sort of tangible benefit" (like event tickets).

In-depth interviews added dimension to this data. Next gen donors talked a lot about the moral responsibilities that come with wealth and about actions informed by values. "You can be comfortable, but there is a lot of need in the world, and you have the ability to help people. It is a privilege, but there is the responsibility that goes with that." This same next gen donor recalls being told, "Yes, our family has money and we are lucky, and you should never flaunt that." A self-made donor we interviewed emphasized values over valuables as well:

> I don't feel like I'm shortchanging myself or I'm suffering due to my giving money away. I live an extremely comfortable life, and I give 50 percent of my income. And I know there are other people who could do the same. I'm uniquely positioned to get my peers in the tech sector more engaged in giving. There are a lot of people who have money and a lot of people who actually have pretty good values, so I think there's a lot of

room for people to be giving more. It feels like an opportunity partly because it's not like I'm twisting people's arms. I think that if you give people the chance to figure out what it is they want to do and remove the barriers—maybe give them a little push to try it out—I think it grows from there.

The responsibility that most next gen donors feel regarding their wealth is not just a responsibility to avoid ostentation; it is a motivating desire to do good. "Philanthropy matters. It is a part of how you engage with the world. It is a part of being a responsible member of a community. It is part of being an adult." The profound way in which these individuals are driven by values, and live out their values in all the choices they make, is one of the hallmarks of next gen donors.

Origins, Where the Values Come From

Giving to express values of some sort is a common motive conveyed by older major donors as well, as is the desire to give out of a sense of obligation as a person of privilege.[1] In fact, most next gen donors say they learned the value of giving from their parents and grandparents. We actually heard this from both those with inherited wealth and those with self-made wealth, from young techies to entrepreneurial trailblazers.

One self-made earner asserts, "Our parents have modeled for us, my wife and I, this significance of giving back—giving back to the community, thinking about others, thinking about the world around us, and being proactive forces for good." Another alludes to her family's strong values: "It was ingrained in us that those who have a lot must give a lot; if you have, you must also give back." And this donor has no doubts about where his philanthropic values come from, "I would say that, without question, my obligation and duty to do this came from my parents and the childhood I had. They were working on boards when I was young. They were giving money away before I could talk. That is what we do."

Michele Pollack, a vice president at Goldman Sachs, describes in a recent media profile how her grandparents' experiences as Holocaust survivors inform her engagement as a funder and volunteer leader with the nonprofit Selfhelp, which provides a range of community-based services to seniors and vulnerable New Yorkers in a way that Michele feels embodies the values of determination, grit, and dignity she learned from her grandmother, "Bubby."[2]

Despite being children of the Information Age bombarded with social media all day, and despite their passion for fomenting an Impact Revolution in philanthropic practice, next gen donors typically follow their family's lead when it comes to the origins of their value system. They might disagree with older generations on the *how* of giving, but they don't disagree on the *why,* because they learned why from their parents and grandparents. In fact, 89.4 percent of the total population of next gen donors we surveyed said their giving was influenced by their parents, and 62.6 percent said their grandparents. This transmission of philanthropic values within families is often closely connected to the most significant family stories. Take the next gen donor below who shares a classic American success story with philanthropy at its core:

> We actually have a letter that accompanied my great-uncle when he came to the United States by himself at age 15. The letter says, "If you should be so lucky as to make a great fortune in your new country, always remember that comes with responsibility and is connected with turning it back around and being a part of a community." It puts it in this

sort of moral context. It is not your money but money you are a steward of, and it is your obligation, your spiritual and moral obligation, to turn that back around.

John R. Seydel also feels he inherited his values from his family, including a profound commitment to environmental sustainability. John R. is the grandson of Ted Turner, founder of CNN—the world's first live 24-hour global news network—and the United Nations Foundation, established with a billion-dollar grant to promote a more peaceful, more prosperous, and more just world. Below, John R. describes how he is driven by the values he learned from his parents and grandparents and how they demonstrated those lessons both in what they said and how they live.

John Rutherford Seydel III

I'm from Atlanta, born and raised, and I hail from two great families: the Turners and the Seydels. People are more focused on and know more about the Turner side because my grandpa is Ted Turner and, perhaps, too, because when I was growing up he was married to my grandma, Jane Fonda.[3] She's not blood, but she was there in the emergency room when I was born, and we are still close. I am the oldest of 14 grandchildren on that side. On the Seydel side, Pat Mitchell married into our family, and she became another excellent grandmother and role model in my life, as well as my Grandfather Scott and Grandpa Ted.[4] I was raised by good people with great morals. They see a world in which all humans are connected as one species.

My parents have been an even bigger influence on my life. My mom is on 12 different boards and is always busy because she cares about her children's future. It makes her so fired up, and she

(continued)

179

(continued)

always wants to do something about it. Similarly, when I'm at home sleeping in until 8:30 AM, my dad always says, "Enough sleeping in. Let's go! You've got to make something with your life." My parents are driven by passion and have established that model for me, but they have allowed me to choose my own passions, find my own identity. They're there to care for me, to catch me when I fall, to support and motivate me, and they have let me find my own interests.

Their support has been particularly important to me because I feel like, when you're born into a family that has high stature and name recognition, it is really easy for kids to get a big ego or to play around too much. Instead, my parents always kept me grounded. Being exposed to different places around the world, especially developing countries such as Kenya, Tanzania, and Jordan, opened my eyes to the reality outside of U.S. borders. It helped me to see how lucky and fortunate I am—and those of us in the developed world all are—to be in this position.

From *Captain Planet* to Boots on the Ground

Those experiences also nurtured in me my primary passion, which has grown within me since I was a kid. I want to try and save our environment. Growing up, I watched the cartoon *Captain Planet*, where the main character espoused values of sustainability, and I started to think about our long-term viability as a species. We all live in the same place, and if we degrade it, especially as the population rises, it creates major global issues.

In high school I started traveling with my parents and grandparents to visit our ranches and different landholdings, many that have been placed into permanent conservation. Being able to see places in nature and appreciate them nurtured my environmental passion. In fact, I think to truly understand how people are destroying nature, the first thing you have to do is to appreciate the beauty and the vastness of nature. Seeing and appreciating nature, as well as the escalating destruction of it, led me to want to take action to do something about it.

It has also been very helpful for me to be involved in the work of the Turner Foundation starting at a very young age. Founded by my grandpa, and also led by my mom and her four siblings, the Turner Foundation invests in protecting and restoring the natural world. For example, the foundation invests in national and priority state-level efforts for wildlife and habitat conservation such as in the Florida Panhandle, the Sky Islands of New Mexico, the Greater Yellowstone Ecosystem, and southcentral/southeastern Alaska. My mom has been taking me with her to meetings since I was 10 years old. Then, when I turned 16, I became an associate trustee and was invited to attend foundation board meetings in my own right and attend events by the nonprofits we support, so I see our grantees' work firsthand.

The idea of exposure through travel also plays out on the philanthropic side, as Grandpa has taken all of us on educational retreats, where the family comes together in a developing nation to learn about environmental sustainability issues. It is so powerful to see the beauty of what we are trying to protect, to visit grantees and see the actual programs, boots on the ground. We are trying to be an active part of fixing problems, not just giving money to some far-off places. Those retreats are also the one time we get to come together as a family and see each other all in one place—and I think that's been really effective, too, especially in the way that my cousins and I interact with one another as the next gen of this family legacy.

In the end, I believe good philanthropy is guided by values like compassion and love. I think they are two of the most powerful emotional traits that all humans have, no matter our background. I think we are starting to see a turning point, where more people realize how acting out of compassion can make our world a better and more equal and safe place for everyone—no matter what economic background, no matter what race, no matter what gender. If we can appeal to those two core emotions, those two values—compassion and love—we can be better philanthropists and be more fulfilled. At least I know I feel that way.

John R. deeply respects his predecessors and the values they passed down to him—values like hard work, risk-taking, sustainability, and care for people and the earth. His grandparents and parents exposed him to people and places that helped him internalize the family's values while also encouraging him to begin to make them his own.

A Delicate Balance

In the next three chapters, we will hear about many ways that these next gen donors are trying to find a delicate balance between the past and the future—in this case, between receiving respected values from the past and beginning to develop their own expressions of values and ways of living them. Like this donor, they seek a balance between respecting and revolutionizing, honoring and becoming, being grateful and forging their own paths: "I think you can hold onto tradition and the core of why the tradition is there and still evolve it. Christmas provides a nice metaphor for this. The traditions of Christmas are the tree, the lights, the presents, the stockings, etc. But how each generation interprets that is open. I think we are living along the family tradition, but our window dressing is maybe a little bit different."

Each generation's unique experiences inform who they are and how they see the world. Therefore, each generation expresses its values—including inherited values—in ways unique to its generational personality.[5] "I think my values stayed the same [as my predecessors'], but my approach has actually completely changed," points out one next gen donor. "My siblings and I learned the sense of charity and the importance of giving back at home yet are applying it around the world in our own ways."

Crafting and expressing this balance between the past and the future is still a work in progress for most. Each emerging adult needs to individuate, to decide which family values to internalize and which to implement differently or leave behind to make room for his or her own. Regardless of our socioeconomic status, we all feel this tension to some degree. We all struggle with how to respect and honor the past that gave us our start while yearning to reenvision a brighter future. But for next gen donors this struggle takes on added weight as they live under the scrutiny of a spotlight. Plus, they know that how they end up resolving this tension will have a great impact on society.

Justin Rockefeller, whom we first heard from in Chapter 4, invested time in learning about his own famous family history by becoming engaged with family institutions, from the Museum of Modern Art (MoMA) and Japan Society to their many charitable foundations. But as we see next, Justin also talks about respecting the family while helping the Rockefeller Brothers Fund to divest of fossil fuels, migrating its endowment to impact investing and creating The ImPact, a pledge and a platform he cofounded to have families commit to impact investing and to share data about investments in this realm. He, too, pays respect to his roots, honoring the family's value of giving through his service on boards, yet he is working to evolve their investments to better reflect a current expression of next gen values.

Justin Rockefeller

I try to align my personal, professional, and philanthropic values in all my work. I like the synergy of it all. With Rockefeller Brothers Fund, Addepar, and The ImPact, I feel I'm maturing in my quest for

(continued)

183

(continued)

this alignment of values. For example, each advances two world-views I hold at my core: 1) greater transparency increases the odds of better decision-making and more prudent capital allocation, and 2) what one does with one's money has moral consequences.

In a way, this also helps align my legacy with who I am as an independent adult. I didn't want to be paralyzed by my last name; I wanted to embrace it as an opportunity. For every potential con of my surname, there are at least 999 benefits. To me it's neither a weight nor a burden; it's an opportunity. My surname is an unfair life advantage for me and undeniably helps open doors. But, of course, it is up to the individual what each of us does once we walk through those doors. I'm conscious that people associate the name "Rockefeller" with both capitalism and philanthropy; impact investing sits very comfortably at their intersection. I can even trace this back to JDR Sr. [John D. Rockefeller Sr., his great-great-grandfather]. He spent the first half of his life primarily focused on making money (while consistently tithing from his first paycheck), and then the last half more focused on giving it away. So I value my legacy, but I find more compelling Jed Emerson's "blended value" approach, in which capitalism concurrently enhances social and environmental progress.[6]

My "Blended Value" Approach

I try to take this blended value approach in my own investments and giving. My wife and I invest for impact in multiple ways, including direct impact investing in companies producing both financial and social returns and incorporating environmental, social, and governance practices into our investment decision-making process. We've also tried to be thoughtful about aligning our values and our charitable dollars by assigning "percentages of passion" to the causes we care about and then aligning those percentages with the dollars we actually give—a more disciplined approach that we adapted from Elizabeth J. McCormack, who has advised many Rockefellers and others about philanthropy. Put simply, it's prioritizing personal giving in the way foundations have done more formally for decades.

Elizabeth finds that there is often a large disconnect between what donors' care about and what they actually give to. Giving only because a friend asks or spending on galas whose cause is of little interest can add up quickly. Instead, Elizabeth suggested we assign hard percentages to the causes we care about and then use this to make our giving decisions. So my wife and I each separately came up with our percentages, and then combined as best we could through compromise—key in any marriage! Then, each year, we have an approximate figure in mind for our giving—which changes from year to year depending on what's going on in our lives and in the markets—and we fill up our buckets of giving in percentages that align with our interests and values.

The system isn't perfect, but we're a lot more comfortable with it than we were with the feel-it-out-along-the-way approach we had been using. We ask ourselves what the most effective organizations are within each category, just as a foundation would (or as an investor would pick best companies after placing weighted sector/industry bets), then allocate accordingly. When we reach capacity in one bucket, if we are asked to give more to that area, we will say, diplomatically, "We've reached capacity for this year, and you are now under consideration for next year."

My thinking has also been informed by Peter Singer, a philosopher whose lectures I audited in college, who espouses that what you do with money has moral consequences. Martin Luther King Jr. noted that government budgets are moral documents. On an individual level, how you make money and what you do with your money has moral consequences, both by commission (what one does with one's money) and omission (what one doesn't do with one's money). If you buy a luxury good for $3,500, you are in your right to do so, but try to remember that one can also *save a life* with that money. Peter's teachings really planted the seeds of impact investing in me and inform my actions to this day.[7] Guilt isn't typically an effective motivator, but I find the philosophical framework essential.

(continued)

185

(continued)

What the Future Holds

Looking to the future, I'm pretty optimistic because, from my experience, Millennials, having survived The Great Recession, naturally link money and moral consequences. They already align their money and their values through their consumer choices and their employment choices. They vote with their wallets, as they want to buy green tech products, for instance. They want to work for companies like Google, Tesla, Zero Mass Water, Long Game Savings, Ethic Inc., and Modern Meadow that are making the world a better place while making money. And as Millennials inherit—as a whole an estimated $59 trillion in the coming decades—or make their own money, their existing practice of aligning values and money will continue, but with ever increasing resources.

Of course, this will mean the financial industry will have to adapt. As more money invested by Millennials enters the impact marketplace, better fund managers will launch impact funds, and better entrepreneurs will launch impact companies because capital follows talent and talent follows capital. To retain and to win business, wealth advisors will need to change how they engage the next gen and follow advice I've heard Sallie Krawcheck offer: Listen to your clients, learn what they care about, and provide solutions for values-aligned investing. If young clients care about something, see if there's a way to match their portfolio with what they care about. If they care about educating kids, talk to them not only about giving to an effective social enterprise but also about investing in education technology companies. They both address the same problem; they are just two different ways to get there.

I've heard many variations on people's definitions of "success." Mostly I've heard ideas revolve around maximizing happiness through strong interpersonal relationships and/or financial security. I'll define my own success based on whether I'm maximizing the positive impact of my life on the lives of others—those I know and those I'll never meet.

Justin's story echoes so much of what we have talked about in this chapter. To start, he is driven by values. While he hails from an American dynasty and presumably could have done anything as a Rockefeller, we see instead that he is working hard, aligning his values with his giving and investing to make an impact in the world.

Living Seamlessly and Managing Up

Justin is absolutely walking his talk. He is illustrating something we have seen in significant numbers among next gen donors: the aim to live seamlessly, to express, as Justin describes, their "personal, professional, and philanthropic values" consistently, and to make sure their behaviors reflect those values.

Mary Galeti, who we met in Chapter 3, describes these personal, professional, and philanthropic values as now being integrated: "It feels more important than maybe it did for previous generations, who saw social life as very social, professional life as professional, and then family life as all about family. We, I think, see those as more integrated into the self. It is all aligned on this trajectory of whatever it is that we are heading to fund and to be as people. If we lived aligned with our values, we will find meaning as well as impact."

Another next gen donor we interviewed concurred with Mary's point that next gen donors want to bring all of themselves, aggregating what they have from all parts of their lives, when they step up as a donor. He actually presented this notion as his personal mission:

> The single, impelling purpose in my life is to maximize the value that I create for the world with the resources that I have. I think about the financial resources that I have, which are all inherited. I think about the relational, intellectual, spiritual, political, and other resources that I have, and I want to align all

of those toward a common purpose. I have a very clear sense of what value my wealth has created for me. It has given me an opportunity to achieve my full potential as a person. This is kind of a cliché line, but I think money is often the most and least important thing you can give.

These next gen donors all speak to a desire to have their values align with their actions, whether as donors, investors, social entrepreneurs, consumers, or parents. A self-made next gen donor we interviewed explained it this way: "I have a desire to do good in the world and to do things to improve the quality of life for other people. It's an intentional theme informing where I want to spend my time, how I take my kids to volunteer, and the impact I want to have on people. Philanthropy is another part of that intention." Another put it more simply, saying, "Philanthropy is not just something that you do; it is very much a part of who you are."

Some of the donors we spoke with not only want to live seamlessly but also take the initiative to manage up, encouraging more careful values alignment within their families and advisors. "As much as we may have heard from our parents or investment advisors while we were growing up, that 'you make money with this hand, you give away with the other hand,' I think that is being challenged by my generation." How older generations respond to next gen donors managing up will play out over the next decades, but a shared sense of values seems to be the best place to ease the tension of change across generations, even if how those values get implemented starts to look different.

What Does This Mean?

Many older generations of Americans may view values-aligned decision-making as a privilege or a luxury. They often come from a place where just being able to choose a profession counts as a luxury. Many of them took jobs or learned trades because it was the best or only way to provide for their families. The idea of grappling with how to give away one's wealth might seem decadent. But members of the next generation—across all economic levels—don't see wants and needs as mutually exclusive. In a study of college-educated, full-time-employed Millennials from 29 countries, 60 percent choose jobs that had a "sense of purpose"; and among businesses where Millennials say there is a strong sense of purpose, there is significantly higher reporting of financial success and employee satisfaction.[8] Generation Impact wants to live in what Aaron Hurst calls a "purpose economy," one "where value lies in establishing purpose for employees and customers—through serving needs greater than their own, enabling personal growth and building community."[9]

Next gen major donors share this desire for values-driven choices in all parts of their lives. Victoria Rogers in Chapter 5 is a good example of a Millennial who aligns her deeply held belief in accessible art with her many gifts of time, talent, treasure, and ties. Justin Rockefeller similarly notes how Millennials, whether donors or not, "already align their money and their values through their consumer choices and their employment choices," and assumes they want to align their giving and investing as well.

Of course, the consequences of how these high-capacity members of the next gen choose to act on this desire for purpose are far-reaching and great. The choices they make will likely have outsized impacts for all of us and all we care about. As such, we need to pay close attention to the values next gen donors want to enact through their giving and how they want to express these values.

In short, if you want to engage effectively with the next generation, you need to start by engaging them around values, as values drive the seamless way in which they want to live. Ask questions about their values rather than selling your nonprofit's mission or your advisory firm's services. Begin conversations around values, not around contributions or sales.

At 21/64, Sharna's team sees firsthand how next gen donors' values drive their decision-making. To help donors articulate their driving values, 21/64 created a simple but powerful deck of Motivational Values Cards, assembled by listening to the words next gen donors use to describe their motivation values. By sorting the deck, donors can quickly reflect on what's most important to them at any time. Sharna and her team urge nonprofit fundraisers, advisors, parents, and others who work with next gen donors to start by asking them to clarify what they value most. Nonprofits can determine whether a prospect's values align with their mission before investing too much time in cultivating someone who won't be a fit. Advisors can offer values exercises as a helpful tool when clients are writing statements of intent to accompany the philanthropic vehicles they are forming. And for families and giving circles, having a common language around values, even agreeing upon a few core values, enables individuals in a group to more easily and effectively make decisions together.

Taking a few minutes out of busy schedules to articulate values can seem a waste of time to some high-powered donors. Similarly, as fundraisers feel pressure to make an ask in the few minutes they have with donors, or as advisors push to review quarterly investment returns with clients, the groundwork around values often gets brushed aside. This can hinder relationships with next gen donors, especially as they want to clarify who they are and what they value in order to make decisions in alignment with their values. If we don't "go slow to go fast," we risk undermining the very outcomes that next gen donors want to achieve.

For those working not only with next gen donors but also with multigenerational families who give, beginning with values becomes even more critical to the success of any work the family will do together. Without helping families to articulate and prioritize their collective underlying values, families and those who interact with them are often left navigating conflicts between one generation that wants to fund, say, scholarships in the local community versus the next gen donors who want to fund microcredit loans globally. But if next gen donors and their elders realize that the next gen first learned its values from parents and grandparents, these underlying values can serve as a bridge across the generations that helps them find a way through these sorts of differences in philanthropic interests. Remember, the fact that next gen donors want their values to drive how and why they give presents the greatest potential to benefit us all in this Golden Age of Giving.

CHAPTER 9

On the Shoulders
of Giants

Revolutionaries aren't known for their deep respect for legacy. The whole point of revolutions is typically to overthrow the ideals and institutions of the past.

But next gen donors are approaching their Impact Revolution in ways that don't quite fit the radical mold. They want to transform the future of giving, yes, but they also have an admiration for those who contributed to social change before them. In fact, the primary challenge facing many of the donors we talked with is reconciling this respect for the past with their avid desire to improve the future.

One thread connecting the past and the future is the concept of *legacy*. Next gen donors see legacy not as an anchor holding them back so much as an engine pushing them forward. They embody the famous image that Isaac Newton gave to describe his innovations: "If I have seen further, it is by standing on the shoulders of giants."[1]

The Importance of the Family Narrative

For many, legacy is rooted in a master narrative communicated from one generation to the next. Whether we hail from wealth or not, hearing our families' stories offers us a platform to feel we are part of something bigger. It invites us to write our own chapter in what feels like an overarching history. Our study of next gen donors has convinced us that conveying the family narrative—especially in a candid way—influences how much a next gen family member will want to become a giver instead of a taker, the causes he or she will donate to, and maybe even some of the organizations he or she will support.

Psychologists Marshall Duke and Robyn Fivush of Emory University have articulated the significance of family narratives on next generation family members from many backgrounds. Using a "Do You Know?" scale, Duke and Fivush asked children to answer 20 questions about their family history. They found that those who knew more about the stories of their parents and grandparents demonstrated higher self-esteem, had a stronger sense of control over their lives, and believed their families functioned more successfully.[2]

We, too, have seen the importance of passing on family narratives. Yet we often find that families are afraid to share details of their stories that may not seem pretty or positive, for fear of undermining what next gen family members conclude about their forebears. However, Duke and Fivush's research shows that sharing the highs *and* lows of one's story actually has beneficial outcomes. They distinguish between presenting an "ascending narrative" (rags to riches), a "descending narrative" (riches to rags), and an "oscillating narrative" (weathering ups and downs over time and coming out stronger). Duke and Fivush feel this third narrative leads children to develop an "intergenerational self," where family members are aware they belong to something bigger than themselves. In other words, families who share their oscillating narrative with their next generations foster resilience.[3] Similarly, anyone who connects with a larger narrative—a religion, political party, or social movement, for instance—can feel empowered by being part of that collective effort.

For next gen donors who are inheritors, the issue of narrative is even more important because most inheritors keenly feel that their potential to make an outsized impact on the world is leveraged from the legacy of their predecessors. "I have to start from a place of deep respect and humility of why I get to be here. So it still hits me, 'Wow, I get to participate in this through no doing of my own,' and so at the most basic level, it is a total honor to be able to be in this [philanthropic] world at all." As another inheritor put it, "I do what I do because my grandfather started with nothing, grew up in the Great Depression, and was a war veteran. [He] was very successful and lucky and built up this very successful business, but always said, 'Don't forget where you came from' [and] 'Take care of those less fortunate than you are.'"

While some next gen donors feel the family narrative motivates them to give, others are more explicit about honoring their legacy by supporting particular types of organizations. Says one, "My grandparents were Holocaust survivors, so I first started to give to the U.S. Holocaust Museum in Washington, D.C., as part of my wedding. I feel like I have to continue to pass on their stories and teach people about what happened during the Holocaust so that I can ensure that it doesn't happen again."

We heard the theme of legacy underscored when we interviewed next gen donor Alexander ("Alex") Soros. Alex is the son of financier George Soros, one of the most successful investors in history—and, at the time of this publication, one of the 30 wealthiest people in the world. Alex feels he is honoring his parents—particularly his father, an outspoken survivor of Nazi-occupied Hungary—by continuing the family narrative of Jewish identity and advocating for others who may find themselves "stateless," as his father once did.

Alexander Soros

I'm getting my PhD in history now from the great public university of Cal-Berkeley. I try to understand our story and our past through studying the history to which my family is so closely connected. My father is George Soros. He's considered a person of history, a "financial god" in many a circle. And he's given birth to what is now the second-largest foundation in the world, the Open Society Foundation, which is where I participate actively and where my father still focuses the majority of his time.

My father's instincts have always been grounded in his own personal history, and he spoke to me as I was growing up about who he was and how his identity informs his philanthropy. The conversation that ultimately changed my life—and the first time I remember bonding with my father—was when he told me of his experience going into hiding in Budapest during the Holocaust. I was 8 or 9 at the time. In that moment, a man who so many people saw as a hero became human. He spoke of the year when the Germans rounded up the Jews living in Budapest for extermination, which he has acknowledged as the formative experience of his life. My relationship with my father would be quite different if we hadn't had this exchange.

The Formative Years, and Being a Minority

Like other Jews who survived the war by hiding in Hungary, my father has had a complicated relationship with his Jewish identity. Over time, he came to publicly embrace his identity, and his marriage to my mother was an important step in this process. Eventually my father's Jewish identity became a facet of his public persona that his success and fame would amplify.

As I was growing up, my father's and my Jewish identity was one of the commonalities upon which we built a relationship. I was the first Soros to become a bar mitzvah in America, and my decision to do so was linked to my father's public reclamation of his Jewish identity. I know that one of the proudest moments in his life and mine was when I had my bar mitzvah, a Jewish coming-of-age ceremony.

I am most proud of my father for never forgetting what happened to him and what could have happened to him. He was rendered stateless and could have died as a consequence of the Nazis' Final Solution, yet he has resolved to fight for those doomed to a similar fate, regardless of the wealth and security he has attained.

Growing up, I knew it was sheer luck that I had even been born. Here I was, living in the lap of luxury, in one of the most accommodating countries and eras for Jews in history, and yet I always felt like a minority, like a Jew, and developed an affinity for other minority groups who were victims of persecution.

Family Stories Imprinted on Me

I remember being in Santo Domingo with my father and the former president of the Dominican Republic, who was making excuses for his country's deplorable treatment of those who were either at risk of or had become stateless. My father wouldn't back down. "I was stateless," he said. "I know how that feels."

Similarly, a friend of mine working at the United Nations recently asked me why my father cares so much about the Rohingya, a small Muslim minority in Myanmar who are stateless. My response was easy: "He was once a Rohingya himself." When my father saw Sarajevo under siege in the 1990s, he gave a huge humanitarian gift because he saw similarities between the situation there and the situation in Budapest earlier in the century. So while many see him as emotionless, based on my experience as his son, I have no choice but to see him differently—as a passionate, committed, values-driven philanthropist.

I have also come to learn how my grandfather shaped much of my father's outlook. My grandfather moved to America in 1956, but before that he was responsible for getting my father and other members of the family, as well as numerous other Jews, into hiding

(continued)

197

(continued)

to survive World War II. Nevertheless, much of our family never made it out alive. I never met my grandfather, but his outlook on life has lived on in me through my father, and I feel a close affinity to him. After the war he wrote down our family's account, and his own reflections from it, in his memoirs entitled, *Masquerade*. I recall my father giving me the transcript when I was a teenager and the stories being almost a complete replica of the stories my father had been telling me throughout. Sometimes when I feel disoriented or need inspiration I look to this book and his narrative. Out of all the things he wrote, the lines that have struck a lasting chord with me were these:

> The atrocities of the Japanese government made *me*
> ashamed; the measures taken against South African blacks
> were offenses against *me*. It was as though I felt responsibility
> for the whole world. The residue of this feeling stays with me
> today here in America. It is what makes me give up my seat
> for the old black lady in the overcrowded subway, when she
> looks tired; and it fills my eyes with tears when someone tells
> me a story of some spontaneous manifestation of generosity.[4]

The feeling of affinity this quote describes has lived on in my father's philanthropy, and it has definitely shaped my own!

Of course, there is also the influence of my mother, who was instrumental in starting what today are called the Open Society Foundations (OSF), or Soros Foundations, in various parts of the world. I can't overstate her influence on me. Growing up a Jew in the United States, she was linked to the stories of the New Deal, the Great Society, and the civil rights movement. She taught me to aspire to make something of myself while at the same time giving back to society. My mother taught me to be philanthropic, civic-minded, politically involved, and accomplished in my own right. Her and my father's values in this area are not all that different; these values were shared and still are, despite the fact that they are no longer together.

Proud to Be a Steward of Legacy

Around the time of my bar mitzvah, my parents opened the foundations in Central and Eastern Europe, where my father was often attacked as a Jew during the war. My father based his philanthropic mission around Karl Popper's idea of an "open society." Popper and my father have many things in common: Both are Jews from a similar time and place (former Habsburg dominions in Central Europe at threat of statelessness); they both witnessed totalitarianism; and they both have an affinity for cosmopolitanism and the ideology that all human beings belong to a single community with a shared morality.

I grew up with the foundations as they were being incubated, and I see OSF not only as a part of my family but also as a part of my family's legacy. Most of our vacations coincided with visits to existing or newly formed foundations and NGOs [non-governmental organizations] around the world. I have been shaped by many of the OSF-linked people I met along the way, and I feel as though I also want to carry on their legacies and pass along the lessons they taught me. As a member of the OSF Global Board of Directors, my work within the foundations now takes up a large amount of my time. And my father counts on me to be of service in certain areas, especially those areas in which he feels our family will be involved past his lifetime.

Now that I have had the opportunity to witness with my own eyes how my father's legacy makes him the sort of philanthropist he is, I am proud to also be a part of this legacy myself. As I've explained, for my father being stateless and not having citizenship, was a traumatic experience he can personally relate to, and that is now something he fights to keep others from experiencing. More than anything else, that is what we work to achieve through our philanthropy.

I'm most proud of my father for doing all of this because he doesn't *need* to do it. He could very easily take his wealth and be comfortable, or just fight for his own safety in various ways. Instead,

(continued)

(continued)

he devotes his effort and time, which are valuable commodities, to this work. That is something that I am proud of and also something that I want to keep the torch lit on, something I want to keep doing.

A Legacy Applied

With my own philanthropy, it wasn't a question of *if*; it was a question of *when*. Why wait? I knew I was going to do it, to set up a foundation, so why wait until I was older? There are problems going on in the world now; why not get started with my own giving now? My father said, "This is your money; you can do whatever you want with it, but that's the amount of money you're receiving." His saying that obviously makes me feel the need to be responsible with it.

So then I began to think about how I wanted to do that. My father and I have this ongoing discussion about the difference between philanthropists and activists. He is definitely more of an activist. For example, I remember one time somebody came to ask for money for a hospital in the Congo, and my father's response was, "You know, you are putting a Band-Aid on a wound. I would rather solve the larger problem there, which has political implications." But this would require more than just giving money. You get more reward, obviously, in giving your time and fighting for issues, whether it's working with local governments or on international governance, than just writing a check for a hospital.

In the last year, I've encountered myself becoming what I would describe as more of an advocate than a philanthropist. I find I want to fight for those things in the world that I want to see change. And I look at donations, whether foundation grants or political donations, as instruments for the type of change I seek to make or commitments to the convictions I have. Therefore, I have encouraged my grantees that are seeking to become more politically active to count on me as a 501(c)(4) donor, since it is harder to raise money for that sort of political organization than it is for the more traditional 501(c)(3).

This is partly because of my legacy and partly because of my studies in history. I worry that, throughout history, trying to avoid politics has often been a predicate for totalitarianism. I won't get a tax deduction if I give to a 501(c)(4) political organization, but the consequences of a lot of people not being willing to support political change has, from my own study of history, not been good.

As it is, I believe foundations and philanthropists get too much credit for their giving, which ultimately is a gift they are allowed from the IRS. For example, I was asked to speak to a group of donors in Brazil about American foundations and incentivizing philanthropy there—the assumption being that Brazilian foundations were not as robust and civically engaged as American foundations and were more risk-averse in comparison, too. I first needed to learn about the Brazilian tax code and discovered that it doesn't incentivize philanthropic giving. I didn't want to come across as a proponent of American exceptionalism or a blind champion of philanthropy, so I encouraged the audience of Brazilian donors to see the change they could advocate for in their own tax policy, and I conjectured that by building in incentives like tax deductions, they might catalyze more philanthropy. That said, I didn't want to provide them with a solution; instead, I wanted to point them to the tools they had themselves if they wanted to utilize them.

I'm also not interested in being known as a philanthropist, being part of the philanthropy industry. There was a literary scholar who did a study looking at the rhetoric of the World Bank in the 1950s versus today, asking, "What has changed?" Well, a few things have changed—for one, the number of times the World Bank cites the World Bank. In the 1950s the World Bank talked about actual things like ending poverty, building roads, dams, etc. Since then, the World Bank has talked a lot more about themselves, and they've also created new words, which this scholar calls "bank talk." This creates an inherent problem. In order for the World Bank to reach its goals, like ending poverty, they're asking people to end their careers by succeeding at their jobs. But this is harder when you talk mostly about yourself instead of the external problems. Similarly, in philanthropy, we

(continued)

(continued)

have what you might call "NGO talk." It's easier to focus on self than on solving problems. So organizations like the World Bank or big foundations exist in perpetuity rather than asking people to end their own careers by ending poverty or succeeding at solving societal problems.

Risk, Impact, and Affecting Change

A lot of the greatest things that OSF has been able to achieve—and hopefully the Alexander Soros Foundation will, too—have been because of a willingness to take risks and chances on both people and our own reputations, to act boldly, and to see the way things go. When it comes to things like aid or development, a lot of people say, "Oh, the Gates Foundation does that." Or, "Open Society Foundations does that. So we don't need to do that." But this is a misunderstanding of the role of philanthropy. A New York City nonprofit director once said something to me such as, "I could ask your father for X amount of money, but in the end, New York taxpayers have much more money than your father does." It's the truth. As collective citizens, the idea that a couple of progressive wealthy people are dealing with societal issues alone is a problem.

So how can we affect change? How can the philanthropic sector solve problems? We now live in an age of governance and procedure, but that's all very new. If there is a right way to have a foundation, I'm agnostic toward it.

If asked by other next gen donors what to fund or how to fund, I would say, "Find out what your idea is, find an ideology, locate your convictions." I would ask, "What are your personal stories? What are the things you want to change? What is the reason?" If you have convictions, this will make what you are doing much more rewarding, and it will give you a better understanding of what it is you are trying to accomplish. As I've said, my own convictions are linked to personal history and to our family legacy. I'm proud of that, and I intend to keep doing whatever I can to affect change.

Learning Your Past to Shape Your Future

Alex's identity and ideology are built on his family's history and clearly influence his philanthropy and the way he approaches making a difference in the world. Hearing the actual stories and discovering the man behind the icon gave Alex a family narrative he could connect to and find himself in. His grandfather's narrative, furthermore, is a guiding light when Alex needs inspiration, providing him with an intergenerational self and a strong legacy upon which to build.

In addition to this theme, Alex raises some provocative questions that other next gen donors are asking as well: Are foundations and philanthropists already getting too much credit for their giving? How will next gen donors use political giving to affect democracy? How can we avoid the perception that "big philanthropy will take care of it all," and instead encourage everyone to embrace their social responsibilities to give within their means?

To do his part, in 2012 Alex set up the Alexander Soros Foundation, with many of the same values as his parents. It will fund issues complementary to the mission of the Open Society Foundations but in a way that suits Alex's vision for carrying his legacy forward. Similarly, in Chapter 6, we heard self-made donor Hadi Partovi extol his father's commitment to creating an educational system in Iran amidst the overturn of the political system, inspiring Hadi's own commitment to creating a computer science education movement in the United States.

Whether we are earners or inheritors, wealthy or of modest means, the stories of our parents and grandparents very often have a profound effect on who we become in the world. However, their choices don't have to become our journeys. We can comprehend the significant influence that legacy has on our lives and also make our own choices within the different contexts in which we live. Next gen donors have deep respect for those upon whose shoulders they stand, but they also want to see further: "For me, knowing the history, knowing the story, inspires what I do next, even if it's evolved and adapted in different ways. It's knowing the history that allows me to pick and choose and decide what resonates going forward."

Taking Stewardship to the Next Level

The notion of stewardship has a long history, starting in ancient Greece, where it referred to the person charged with the care of a household and entrusted with other valuables. Over time, it took on a religious meaning—humans are responsible to care for the world that God created and entrusted to them; in recent years it has been used to justify environmental sustainability, the idea being that we are stewards of the earth and must preserve it for future generations.[5]

But next gen donors want to take stewardship to the next level. They do not merely want to honor family legacy by preserving it and passing it along to future generations. They want to *improve* their legacies to have even more impact. In other words, they are carrying a torch not only out of respect for their predecessors but also to illuminate new paths for progress.

Some talked about the pressure they feel to take philanthropy to the next level, especially when the family narrative is already so impressive. "Because your family has done so much in so many areas, you feel like, if we are really going to add something to the legacy, you need to do better than just be a caretaker. You need to do something that is really different and new." Others grapple with the question "How can *I* make a difference?" This donor articulates a sentiment we heard from many of her peers: "[I'm] paying respect to the opportunities that I had, paying respect to the philanthropy that I learned, but taking that and evolving it into something that will be more uniquely my own."

Whether they see it as an opportunity or a responsibility, potential or pressure, significant numbers of next gen donors feel that stewarding the legacy of their predecessors means adding to an already impressive narrative—and, specifically, adding something "different and new." As one explained, "I do value the foundation, the legacy, the communal component of us doing things together. But I think we can have a bigger impact than we're having. I would like us to be riskier; I'd like us to use our connections and networks, all of the tools in the toolbox, more than we do."

We can see here another impetus behind the deep desire of next gen donors for impact, innovation, and new adventures in philanthropy. It is a way for them to take their legacies to the next level. Once again, we can predict a somewhat messy and chaotic—yet exciting—time ahead as next gen donors stretch their wings. This drive to take legacy to the next level can lead to powerful results. We've seen this already with Victoria Rogers, building on her father's initial inspiration to give to your passions by finding new ways of bringing to life the creative projects she loves, and with Jenna Segal, who revives respected existing institutions with relevant new programmatic ideas.

The contributions of America's great entrepreneurs and philanthropists can be awe-inspiring, but just imagine thinking that one's own accomplishments would be measured against such feats. John R. Seydel could easily have let being Ted Turner's grandson define his identity, crumbling under the weight of that magnitude. Instead, he has embarked on a journey, encouraged by his parents and grandparents, of self-discovery, of learning about the world outside his privileged upbringing, and, perhaps most important, finding and then cultivating his own passion for giving and ability to affect change.

John Rutherford Seydel III

People have always said to me, "You must be thrilled that your grandpa created CNN. He created this media empire, and his team won the World Series." However, I was really too young to even appreciate all that, as I was only starting to mature when he accomplished those wins. Then things took a turn for him when I was 12 or 13, and it began the third phase of his life, which has by far had the biggest influence on me. In this phase, my grandpa has been focused on making the world a better place, making people's lives better. He wants to show that you don't have to wait until you die to give; rather, it's better to make change and make a positive impact on people's lives now, when you are alive. It seems to me that's a pretty good way to feel fulfilled.

Clearly my grandfather's legacy is huge. I have big shoes to fill. This third phase of his life—his philanthropic phase—has been the most important, and his spirituality has really given him a tremendous humanitarian perspective and sense of fulfillment, more than making billions of dollars did for him; it certainly has been more influential to the way I think.

My Own Choices

I believe it is extremely important to look at what your parents and grandparents value, and what makes them fulfilled, on your way to figuring out who you want to be. I often think about how Grandpa Ted raced and lost in thousands of sailing races, and yet, learned from all of them, before that one race when he won the America's Cup. Similarly, my dad preaches to me every day that something you've tried is only a true failure if you don't learn from it. So I'm willing to take the risks to create my own legacy and, in doing so, to learn from my mistakes and my potential failures how to become a better person and make a bigger impact. Obviously, I also want to be able to do my own thing, whether it's fixing political infrastructure or having an impact through a social entrepreneurial venture.

So I'm trying to apply what Grandpa Ted has taught me, and what my parents have taught me, and then add my own creative aspect to it to find new solutions.

For example, one of my long-term goals is to be a politician. It would be my dream to be a senator and represent the values of my generation in the local and national political discussion. In college, I majored in political science with a minor in business and communications. I hope to use that training to try to fix the political infrastructure by using technology, which has simplified our life so much in every other aspect. One way to do this is to amplify people's voices using social media. I started building a web-based platform called Revolution Nation that helps simplify and customize politics according to what you are passionate about. The platform will help you hold your politicians accountable when they are making decisions on issues you care about.

Balance Takes Many Forms

John R. appears at ease talking about stewarding his legacy while finding his own passions. But for some next gen donors, the tension between maintaining family legacy and writing their own chapters is palpable.

One way rising donors can ease that tension is by being crystal clear that their first (though not only) role is to maintain the existing mission and the original donor's intent, even supporting legacy organizations funded by their predecessors. As this donor notes, "I have always felt an intense responsibility to 'the family.' The stewardship of the family is going to allow you to do everything else, and so you take good care of the family, and the family takes good care of you." Another next gen donor concurs, "To us it was very clear that that is what we should be doing, that this is *his* legacy, and there is this feeling that this should honor his legacy and his interests. We shouldn't confuse that with our own interests."

Others find ways to respect legacy while also revolutionizing philanthropy, funding some legacy organizations out of a sense of duty or obligation while making room to fund their own interests. "I think you have to get creative with it and figure out how that innovation and that personal connection can fit within the legacy to engage the next generation."

Most try to strike a balance. Alex Soros serves on the board of the Open Society Foundations as well as funds some of his own interests under the auspices of his own foundation. John R. serves on the board of the Turner Foundation while creating his own app. Katherine Lorenz, who is president of a foundation her grandparents established and is featured in Chapter 10 has managed to find a balance between stewarding the family legacy and helping the next generation realize its own impact, too:

> As president of a family foundation with multiple generations on the board, I see my role as trying to balance three goals: to make an impact, to help the family stay together, and to carry on the legacy established by my grandparents. One way I believe I can help lead the foundation is by encouraging us to invest in high-impact philanthropy, having the most bang for our philanthropic buck. But equally important is having this be a valuable experience for the family—that the foundation brings us together around issues we are all passionate about. I think if we are successful in meeting these first two goals, seeing how one informs the other, then we will inevitably accomplish the third and leave a positive and lasting legacy for my grandparents.

Others, like self-made entrepreneurs, are freer to become the philanthropists they want to be. Yet even they feel the pressure to write a new kind of chapter in their family history, as they have acquired more financial resources than previous generations ever experienced. Many are starting to communicate the importance of philanthropy to their own children: "I would like for [my children] to see me and to learn about getting involved in a more hands-on way, whether it's board roles or volunteering. I want my kids to understand that there's a universe beyond them that they need to contribute to."

Another donor understands that she and her husband may be the initiators of a philanthropic legacy that could last for decades beyond themselves: "To what extent will we pass on this experience [to our children] as we get more familiar with it? How much do we want philanthropy to be part of their lives, and how much will they take to it? What if, for all we know, they actually really end up being the most engaged and innovative thinkers in all of this?"

What Does This Mean?

In our experience working with and studying family foundations and the next gen, we've seen siblings and cousins struggle with how to implement their parents' or grandparents' wishes if those aren't written down or otherwise captured in specific detail. Rather than leaving the next generation to guess, we encourage elders to tell their stories and communicate their legacies *during their lifetimes* in a very direct way. Talking about your family stories gives you the chance to be intentional about what you convey and gives your next generation family members the chance to ask questions about what you mean. After you're gone, it's too late, and children are left to interpret for themselves.

Moreover, most next gen donors actually want to have an open discussion with their elders about how to implement—and hopefully evolve—their wishes. Such clarity can be grounding and even affirming for the next gen. It can move them from sadness and ambiguity when someone dies to clarity and self-confidence. We will see a lovely example of this in Chapter 10, when Katherine Lorenz describes how hearing what her grandfather wanted for the family foundation has helped her navigate the road forward.

Frank family conversations about legacy before elders pass let the next generation figure out how to resolve the tension we've described between stewarding the family's legacy and improving upon it. As we've heard, next gen donors often feel the potential to build on their heritage and make an impact on the world in their own right *because* of their family legacies. On the flip side, the conversations can help older family members appreciate members of the next gen as respectful revolutionaries with the best of intentions. All sides can be more satisfied that the family narrative can remain intact even as the story evolves.

Even when a family takes to heart how important it is to communicate legacy to the next generation, that communication isn't always easy to do; it can be hard for family members to talk about what will happen when they die. But tools exist that can help spark the conversations. 21/64 has developed Picture Your Legacy cards to help donors describe their legacies; donors sift through images designed to enable them to articulate what they haven't yet found words to express. Advisors like Susan Turnbull, Eric Weiner, and Elana Zaiman help people write "ethical wills," or legacy letters that capture—beyond financial inheritance—the stories, lessons learned, and messages that people want to leave to their family, friends, and communities.[6] And, of course, there are biographers, videographers, oral historians, and others who help people to convey their family stories.

Open conversations about legacy are not only essential for families; they are also crucial for nonprofits that want to ask next gen donors to continue a predecessor's support of their organization. This is particularly true when families have supported key institutions in our society that may be at risk. Without direction from parents and grandparents, especially about those organizations they hold most dear, next gen donors do not always know how to handle requests for support, and organizations can suffer the consequences.

It behooves the nonprofit to ask major donors before they pass to speak with their children about their wishes. Even if the next gen donors decide they will not continue these legacy gifts, the earlier a nonprofit knows about that possibility, the better. For example, while 21/64 was working with an institution on building relationships with next gen donors, the organization's leader described a troubling problem. He had sheepishly admitted that a major donor who had funded 10 percent of the group's annual budget had recently passed away, and the leader didn't have a relationship with the donor's next of kin. He shrugged, embarrassed by his failure and chagrined by the gravity of the situation. He wasn't sure this donor's son would continue to support the nonprofit, leaving him with a huge funding gap to fill.

This executive is not alone in his predicament. Just as some family members don't want to talk about their mortality, nonprofit executives are often reticent to raise that reality with their donors. However, proactive practitioners will realize they need to discuss legacy with their donors during donors' lifetimes. They need to ask to meet the next of kin and maybe even suggest endowing gifts if donors don't want to burden their children with that obligation. Smart nonprofit professionals should pitch the opportunity to have these important conversations, facilitated by them, a trusted advisor, as a value-add for their donors.

Similarly, advisors to wealthy individuals will likely find that their clients are interested in talking not only about their financial legacies but also about their philanthropic legacies. Most, in fact, are more interested in talking about engaging their next generations than they are in talking about their tax planning.[7] Advisors would do well to learn how to help families have not just what Scott and Todd Fithian called "below the line" conversations about the mechanics and laws of estate planning, but also "above the line" conversations about their values, legacies, and ideas for the future.[8] The Fithians learned that clients want a space to discuss their personal and philanthropic legacies with others in the family. Professionals should strive to become trusted advisors who offer that space to their clients, both those who want to communicate their hopes and intentions to the next generation and those who are looking for help in carrying those intentions forward while still following their own hopes and dreams. In short, advisors should help their philanthropic clients have transformational, not just transactional, conversations.

―♆

Though we are convinced that next gen donors want to be revolutionary *and* respectful, we shouldn't fool ourselves into thinking these two impulses always mix well. The next gen's powerful commitment to impact and experimentation will sometimes clash with its commitment to legacy. In some dramatic cases, the generational differences will be so great that not even the most compelling version of the family narrative can help the next gen see a path forward that still honors the past. The next gen might want to actively disavow any controversial history—how the money was made, for instance. In other cases, the approach suggested by legacy might be producing such meager results that the next gen cannot find a way to continue it without compromising the dominant desire for impact.

But on the whole, our research has shown us many more examples of next gen donors who are earnestly and eagerly searching for ways to honor their elders' legacies *and* adapt their giving to have maximum impact. We talked to plenty of donors, like Alex Soros and John R. Seydel, who consider making an impact in the future to be the best way they can steward their legacy. What worries us more are the many families who do not have the open, constructive conversations about legacy that allow next gen donors to take this productive approach, encouraging and guiding them to craft their own philanthropic identities and to reach their potential as the philanthropists of tomorrow that we need them to be.

CHAPTER 10

Fielding a Multigenerational Team

Historically, family enterprises, be they businesses or foundations, have treated succession like a relay race, preparing for when the patriarch or matriarch retires or passes away, and hands the proverbial baton off to the next generation. Similarly, in nonprofits, plans for leadership succession have traditionally focused on how the executive director or board of directors—those who perhaps founded and funded the entity for decades—would someday hand over the reins. These transitions could be emotionally as well as practically difficult, but they were inevitable and often couldn't happen soon enough for the generation waiting in the wings.

But the image of passing a baton doesn't fit the reality of today's philanthropic world, and it isn't one next gen donors find all that helpful. Generations increasingly find themselves working as a team, together versus sequentially. Just as any baseball manager wouldn't field a team of all pitchers, a philanthropic enterprise or nonprofit needs players with diverse skills and experiences on the field at the same time.

Next gen donors aren't waiting for their elders to pass away, retire, or even create a succession plan; instead, they are assuming that every generation brings assets to the work of solving our greatest societal ills. Generation Impact is ready to take the field *alongside* older generations, not in place of them nor from the sidelines.

A New Multigenerational Landscape

Many of us harbor a mental image of major philanthropists as Gilded Age barons—men like Andrew Carnegie or Julius Rosenwald, who amassed fortunes and then retired into a life of philanthropy, devoting the sunsets of their lives to finding personal fulfillment by making meaningful contributions to society. Carnegie lived until he was 84, and while he declared his intention to be philanthropic early in life, he only focused diligently on giving for about the last couple decades of his life. This was by design.[1] Rosenwald (who founded Sears, Roebuck and Co.) lived until he was almost 70 and is rightfully celebrated for his remarkable efforts to support education for African American children in the American South in the early twentieth century. His philanthropic accomplishments came mostly in the last 20 years of his life.[2]

Compare this approach to that of the well-known major donors of today, who Daniel Lurie noted in Chapter 2 are giving earlier in their lives: "[W]e have never seen people this wealthy at this young of an age before. The Carnegies were wealthy much later in life. Back then, no one was a billionaire in their 20s; it took time for people to build their fortunes, whereas now, especially here in Silicon Valley, we have seen billion-dollar fortunes built in a 5-to-10-year span. We're living in the new gold rush."

More men and women are becoming enormously wealthy at much younger ages, and these next gen donors clearly understand that they can (and maybe should) be engaged in giving throughout their lives. This means they are giving at the *same time* as older donors, not waiting until those donors step aside.

In addition, the normal lifespan in the United States is much longer today than in the past. Average life span rose from 47.3 in 1900 to 76.8 in 2000.[3] In fact, as members of the post-Millennial "Gen Z" (born between 1995 and 2015) begin to turn 21, there are now five distinct generations operating as adults in our society today, and having four or even five generations in a family alive at the same time is not unheard of.[4] So as people live longer—*much* longer—more generations are finding themselves actively engaged in giving simultaneously, whether within the same family or as donors to the same cause.

This makes for a fundamentally different philanthropic landscape. Families and institutions have to shift from planning for vertical succession down the generations to finding ways for multiple generations of adults to be involved simultaneously. Those in late adulthood who might have imagined themselves retiring into their philanthropy are finding themselves funding alongside their children and even their grandchildren. One donor described this valuable cross-generational learning in his family:

> We really talked about, "What do we want this [family foundation] to be? What's the change we want to see in the world?" And we started focusing and asked our advisors to bring us examples of who's doing good work in this program area. It wasn't going to be about any one of our individual interests. It was going to be something that we did together. Everybody felt like, "Wow! We could really move the needle on something here." We could pick an issue and actually do something—together.

Many inheritors, like Katherine Lorenz, are experiencing three or more generations involved in their family foundations simultaneously. Katherine's grandparents, Cynthia and George Mitchell, were active givers in their later years, contributing to charitable causes, naming institutions, and communicating their wishes until their health no longer permitted. Rather than waiting for her grandparents' passing to get involved in the family foundation, Katherine and her family members engaged three generations simultaneously in strategic giving. Then, when her grandfather passed away, the family was ready with a plan.

This new reality requires structural changes in foundation and nonprofit governance to accommodate multiple generations leading at the same time, cultural changes in how stakeholders interact, and changes in the way grantseekers interact with family foundations. From Katherine's example, we can learn how giving will evolve in this new multigenerational Golden Age of Giving, replacing the traditional notions of Gilded Age philanthropy.

Know-How and Know-Who

But why would elders bring in the next generation in the first place? In the traditional view, they did so only for the next gen to carry out their legacies—to finish what they had started. But next gen donors see themselves as more than heirs apparent. They feel they have unique assets to bring to the playing field. They believe in the power of multigenerational teams and are driven by impact. They are courageous enough to take risks and deploy new tools or strategies, and they are willing to bring their full selves to the table—their "know-how" *and* their "know-who." One donor describes it this way:

> Being young and entering this field has been incredible. On the one hand, I have been adopted by so many mentors and have been able to ask questions like, "How do I do X, because

I don't see it? I read a book, but the book doesn't really tell me how." My mentors will then talk it through with me. But then, on the other hand, I'm delighted to find that I can in return offer my insights as a next gen in this field, like when an older colleague asks, "Our family's third generation is coming on. How do we engage them? Tell me about 'The Facebook'!"

Another donor reflected on both the differences that arise when multiple generations are involved and how these differences can be productive in the end. She started off saying, "My family has taught me everything I know about giving and how to give." But she immediately qualified that statement: "I approach it very differently and, of course, bring different things to the table as a young person with a fresh perspective." She then tried to explain how both statements can be true. "I find that my own practice—my 'road map' to giving—is based upon what they have taught me. Even the things that I choose to do differently are based upon what I did not like about the things that they did."

Even if the value of participation is sorted out, the on-ramp to engagement is often vague. "Anything that the foundation does is done on behalf of us and the family, but we don't actually have a voice in what it does. I am almost 27, and I don't know if there is an intention to bring us on into that foundation." Or, as another said, "A lot of the [other young donors] whom I have spoken to, they don't have a seat at their family foundation table, and they don't know if they're going to have one. They all seem to be struggling with the same kind of [question] 'Where do I fit in?'"

In a way, the question today is not *should* philanthropic families and nonprofits invite the next gen into the work, but can they afford *not* to? Without these unique next gen talents and complementary/contemporary skills, can philanthropic families and nonprofits drive

change fast enough to meet the increasing demands of today's ills by doing what they've always done? The next gen donors we interviewed are skeptical.

This ability to field a team, to bridge the wisdom and experience of the older philanthropists with the risk-taking and creativity of next generation donors, is illustrated in Katherine Lorenz's story below. In her early adulthood, Katherine became not just a next gen trustee but the executive director of her grandparents' significant foundation. In this role, she has led a shift from a hierarchical structure to a multigenerational, multibranch family foundation team that brings collective wisdom to their work in order to have an even greater impact.

Katherine Lorenz

I was born and raised in Austin, Texas. Although I never would have called it "philanthropy" at the time, I realize now that our family's values embodied exactly what it means to be philanthropic. My parents always treated people from all walks of life with respect; we constantly had someone in need living in our home—always an open door.

My grandmother, Cynthia Woods Mitchell, passed away in 2009 after a long, heart-wrenching battle with Alzheimer's disease. My grandfather, George P. Mitchell, passed away in 2013 at age 94. They left behind 10 children, 25 grandchildren, and 7 great-grandchildren.

My grandfather is most known for pioneering the technology that unleashed the shale gas boom—he is often referred to as "the father of fracking." He began working in the oil and gas industry in the 1940s. In the 1970s, Mitchell Energy & Development Corp. went public and then sold to Devon Energy in 2001.

My grandfather was a visionary in every sense of the word. When he thought something was possible, he did not give up until

---

he made it a reality—even in the face of skepticism and contro-versy. I think his determination to extract natural gas from shale exemplified his visionary nature. He knew it should be possible to make the gas flow from shale, and he knew his company—and the world, for that matter—needed this energy source that was an alternative to coal or oil. Like so many areas of his life, he stood up for what he believed and he pursued his vision, even when every-one around him thought he was nuts.

My grandfather was also a huge risk-taker. His wealth came from a series of major bets that turned out right. He was not afraid to say what he thought. And he was not afraid to piss people off in order to do what he thought was right. Those values of doing what you think is right and standing up for what you believe—going out and taking the risk to do it—are very present today in both the family and the foundation. You need the appetite for risk to do high-impact philanthropy like we want to do, that desire to be bold, to take risks, to stand up for what we believe is inherent in our family's nature.

Sustainability and a Sustained Commitment to It

Given the business that my grandfather was in, there was an inter-esting connection between the family's legacy in the energy busi-ness and the world's need to move to a cleaner energy future.

In the late 1960s, my grandfather was inspired by Buckminster Fuller and his ideas about "Spaceship Earth"—that the earth's resources are finite, yet the population is growing, so all of humanity must work together to ensure the health of the planet and the survival of its people. He became passionate about sustainability and had a very clear vision of what sustainability meant to him. For decades, in every interview or conversation, he would say, "If you can't make the world work with 6 billion people, how are you going to make it work with 10 billion? And what are you going to do about it?" That last question, "And what are you going to do about it?", was critical in his thinking, as he

(continued)

221

(continued)

believed each of us has a role to play in ensuring the sustainability of the planet.

My grandfather pursued his role through philanthropy, and he began investing significant philanthropic dollars into sustainability issues. For example, he funded the creation of a conference series focused on getting CEOs of large companies to think about sustainability, and he endowed the National Academies of Science to maintain a permanent focus on sustainability science. He was also very clear with our family that the core focus of the foundation he and my grandmother established was to be sustainability.

While my grandfather is most well known for his work in the oil and gas industry, he was most proud of his work in developing The Woodlands. He founded this community in 1974 north of Houston, Texas, with the idea that it would be a place where people could live in harmony with nature. It now has over 100,000 residents and stands as another piece of our family legacy.

Before he passed away, my grandfather signed the Giving Pledge, making public his and my grandmother's long-held intention to give the majority of their wealth to philanthropic purposes. I was intrigued when Bill and Melinda Gates and Warren Buffett started the Giving Pledge in 2010, urging all billionaires to pledge the majority of their wealth to philanthropy either during their lifetimes or upon their deaths. While my grandparents had made the decision years before, I thought it was really wonderful for them to be able to share this commitment with the world very publicly, hopefully inspiring other families to make similar philanthropic commitments.

Thanks to my grandfather's influence, as a family we have been deeply concerned about and involved in the environment for decades and are also actively fulfilling his mandate regarding the family foundation. To honor my grandparents' legacy, the Cynthia and George Mitchell Foundation is primarily focused on sustainability issues in Texas.

Learning by Doing

Today, I have the privilege of running our family foundation, but frankly this is not where I expected to be when I was starting my career. I went to Davidson College in North Carolina, where I majored in economics, minored in Spanish, and studied abroad in Chile. While in South America, I became intrigued with the world of economic development, particularly around health policy and economic policies, as a way to pull the developing world out of poverty. So, right out of college, I lived in a rural village in Nicaragua for two months in a one-room house with a family of six, with no running water or electricity. It was a town of about 300. They said in an emergency I was supposed to borrow a horse and ride to the highway, which was an hour away. No radio, no phone, living in a poor community for a few months; it was a life-changing experience. I think many people, myself included, go into those situations thinking, "I'm going to teach them how life is lived," and what I ended up realizing is that the people there taught me much, much more than I could teach them. That experience opened my eyes to an entirely different way of life and to how most of the world actually lives.

After a year back in the United States working for development nonprofits, I realized I needed more than just a summer experience in order to more deeply understand rural poverty issues. I moved to Mexico in 2003 for what was supposed to be a yearlong stay and ended up staying for almost six years. I went to Oaxaca, Mexico, with a friend I had met there the summer before to continue what had been a student-led health program in the rural communities. We realized there was a lot more need and more potential for impact, and we needed to formalize an organization and fundraise.

We created Puente a la Salud Comunitaria (Bridge to Community Health) and initially focused on using amaranth, a very high-protein grain native to the region, as a natural way to improve

(continued)

223

(continued)

health in the rural communities. We focused on integrating amaranth into the diets of children who were malnourished or at risk for malnutrition. In the early days, we concentrated on cooking workshops with women, teaching them to integrate amaranth into their daily diet. As the program evolved, we began to expand into family gardens and then larger plots of amaranth, creating economic opportunities for rural families.

My family gave us some seed capital, though I went without a salary most of the time. And I self-funded some of the work in the early days. But I didn't want Puente to be solely dependent on my contributions or those of my family. Puente needed to become a public charity with many funding streams to sustain itself.

There is no better way to learn than by doing—and cofounding and building Puente was the greatest learning opportunity of my life. From navigating the legal issues of founding a nonprofit in Mexico to designing rural health programs to fundraising and managing a staff, I learned what it takes to build an organization from the ground up. To this day, 14 years later, I continue to spend a month or more there each year. I find that connecting with the people of rural Oaxaca helps me stay motivated in my philanthropic work—the people I got to know there and all that I learned in that work continue to inspire and rejuvenate me.

An Unexpected Role

While this was under way, in 2004 our family's foundation back in Texas went through a strategic planning process, which was the first time any of my generation, the "G3," had been invited to participate. Although my aunt ran the foundation for 19 years, most of that time my grandparents made all the critical decisions. Our experience in the strategic planning process was the first time we felt like we participated in a "family foundation" rather than my grandparents' foundation. All G2s (my mom and her siblings) and all G3s (the cousins) over 25 years of age had an equal voice in the process. Fortunately, and amazingly, we discovered how well our values and visions aligned as we planned for the future of the foundation.

Because my grandparents were very open about their desire for the majority of their wealth to go to the foundation upon their passing, we knew that the foundation would grow significantly overnight after they both passed away. But this planning process allowed us to have a dialogue about the future of the foundation while my grandparents were still able to give input rather than try to guess what they would have wanted after they were gone. Even though my grandparents still made the critical decisions for the next several years, we knew it was important to begin to make decisions together as a family and work out the kinks while my grandparents were still alive.

Given my grandfather's passion for and clear direction that the focus of the foundation's work should be sustainability, we knew that was our starting point. But *sustainability* is a broad word that can mean so many different things to different people. Translating that into a grantmaking program that the family could get behind was not quite as straightforward. After organizing multiple educational sessions where the board could learn about sustainability together, we voted to focus our first grantmaking program on clean energy.

We felt it was important to start our giving in an area where we had some expertise and had a unique insight into the issue. As we began to learn more about the challenges and opportunities with clean energy, we learned how closely linked energy is to climate change, one of the most critical areas to address within the broad topic of sustainability. With our roots in Texas, and the fact that Texas is the energy capital of the United States, it made sense to focus our work on clean energy in Texas.

As my generation became more involved in the foundation, I began to develop an interest in how foundations work and make decisions. I signed up for The Philanthropy Workshop (TPW), a

(continued)

225

(continued)

three-week course in strategic philanthropy founded by the Rockefeller Foundation. Through my TPW experience, I had a revelation that if I wanted to have the most impact in the world I should consider not just learning from but also working with other families in philanthropy. I had accumulated this unique experience of having built a nonprofit from the ground up, living in and working with impoverished communities, so I understood the reality of being an executive director of a struggling, shoestring-budget nonprofit. But at the same time, I had the experience of being part of a philanthropic family, and I understood how we were grappling with issues of wealth and legacy. I started thinking of how I could build a career that drew on both of these experiences.

I stepped into a professional role in the foundation world through the Institute for Philanthropy, which was based in London and was the organization that ran TPW. I was hired to open and manage their New York office. This role gave me an amazing opportunity to grow and learn about strategic grantmaking while I helped facilitate TPW and supported many philanthropic families in their quest to make more impact with their giving.

Then, in 2011, after 19 years at the helm of our family foundation, my aunt decided to step down as president. I knew leading our foundation through a big generational transition and scale-up upon the passing of my grandparents would be a challenge, but I also knew it was the most important and meaningful work I would ever do. Given my interest in the field of philanthropy and all that I had learned in my training at TPW, I decided to throw my hat in the ring. I was not alone; there were others who were also interested in the role. I was honored when the board—all family members—voted for me, and I happily accepted.

Multigenerational Demands of the Job

The most critical part of my role as president in the first two years was spending time with my grandfather. I knew it was the most important part of the job, but it turned out to also be the most personally fulfilling, to work with him to build the vision for what the foundation would be for generations to come. I had dinner with him several nights a week. I recorded conversations we had about his dreams for the foundation and his priorities for the family. I spent hours going over interviews he had given outlining his desires for the future. And I took every opportunity to strategize with him how we could build this foundation so it truly embodied the legacy he and my grandmother had dreamed of.

As I began to implement changes, I discovered just how complex leadership transitions can be, particularly in an intergenerational and family setting. For example, I felt strongly we should be more open and transparent, but I came to realize this was a big cultural and generational shift for much of the family. When I was a grantseeker myself, I appreciated foundations that had clear and transparent guidelines about what they gave to, how to apply, and whether or not we might be a fit for a grant. Knowing we were not a fit was as helpful as knowing we were, as there is nothing more frustrating than spending hours applying for a grant you later find out was never even a possibility. However, family foundations tend to be opaque about how they make grant decisions, often in an effort to protect family members by preserving their anonymity. And I knew this concern was critical for some of my own family members. However, one of the first hires I made as president was a communications strategist. Building a robust website where grantees could learn about the foundation and apply online was a priority for me, although not everyone agreed with me on this.

Another generational difference I saw was around impact with our giving. We all care equally about impact; *how* we do that is different from generation to generation. For example, while my grandfather was a true innovator, my grandparents sought to make change by funding tangible things, such as endowments, buildings, even a telescope. My grandfather's giving focused on education and science at large, well-established institutions.

(continued)

227

(continued)

My grandmother's philanthropic passions were around caring for the underserved—helping those in need—and in honor of her, the foundation had been building out a strategy focused on education and poverty institutions in Galveston, a place that was near and dear to both my grandparents' hearts. But as my aunt and I led the foundation during this transition, I realized that we view philanthropic strategy differently from my grandparents. We worry more about the programs *inside* the buildings rather than the bricks on the *outside*. We want to invest in people and build capacity at smaller organizations, and we see advocating for public policy change as an important strategic lever. My grandparents also often focused on individuals, looking at ways to help them navigate a broken system. Our generation looks to fix the broken system so that all individuals have an equal opportunity at success.

However, my grandmother did make very clear that her desire was for the foundation to be a positive force for good in the family. Part of the legacy she wanted to leave was a way for us to stay together as a family and, together *as* a family, to have a meaningful impact on the world. I try to fulfill that legacy as well.

So as president of a family foundation with multiple generations on the board, I see my role as trying to balance three goals: to make an impact, to help the family stay together, and to carry on the legacy established by my grandparents. One way I believe I can help lead the foundation is by encouraging us to invest in high-impact philanthropy, having the most bang for our philanthropic buck. But equally important is having this be a valuable experience for the family—that the foundation brings us together around issues we are all passionate about. I think if we are successful in meeting these first two goals, seeing how one informs the other, then we will inevitably accomplish the third and leave a positive and lasting legacy for my grandparents.

Katherine's story is clearly one of a shift from hierarchical leadership by a patriarch and matriarch to leadership by a multigenerational team. She is convinced this decision is now essential to the future of the foundation, as well as its potential impact.

Katherine's story is echoed by others, like this next gen donor, who feels the shift in his family to a multigenerational family foundation as well:

> I remember this sort of "come to Jesus" meeting where we asked, "What are we going to do?" There was a decision made to involve my generation, which was in part a reflection of, "Oh my God, we need more hands on deck." But it was also a reflection of, "Let's make this a true family foundation." Let's make this not about my grandparents' giving or my dad's schools, but let's make this something we do together. When I think about our family foundation trajectory, that was a very seminal and decisive decision, and somewhat radically different decision than I think other families make—that this will be about us doing something together.

Building Peerage, Not Adding a Kids' Table

The two stories above make this shift to a multigenerational family foundation seem like a relatively smooth transition. In other cases, next gen donors are knocking at the door rather than being invited in, or feeling frustrated at being left at the kids' table. Some elder leaders of foundations and nonprofits seem less than excited about the new multigenerational reality. They approach such change with trepidation or resistance, reluctant to lose their hard-won leadership, worried it will disrupt the good work they have been doing or that they will have to spend too much time negotiating differences or guiding the next gen so it doesn't make mistakes.

Even when an invitation to participate has been extended, working simultaneously with other generations can be tough. One young adult family foundation trustee joked that when he explains to his elders that "I'm just doing what you taught me," they counter with "Wait, we taught you that? No, that's not what we were saying. That's how you took it." He explains what this means: "We kind of took what they were saying and just interpreted it differently than they did. The core principles are the same, but they just don't think of doing it the way that we do." This next gen sees the difference as a positive, adapting family values to current needs of the day, but his elders might not feel the same.

Still, the fact is we are already in the midst of this sea change. For most foundations and nonprofits the germane question now is "How do we navigate this shift to a multigenerational team, and catalyze it for greater impact?"[5]

Steve Treat, a licensed therapist from the Council for Relationships who has counseled high-net-worth families for decades, talks about "achieving peerage."[6] Parents and children, he explains, are used to a power dynamic where the parent is in charge of the child; however, when children come of age and are given philanthropic responsibilities, the parent-child dynamic must shift to one of peers to enable a healthy working relationship. Their relationship must evolve to embrace this new reality, or children can be left feeling infantilized or undermined.

As we saw in Chapters 5 and 6, next gen donors are not fans of being treated as lightweights. They see themselves as part of a Do Something Generation, reared volunteering and even giving before the age of 21. So you can imagine that as these donors get to the age where they can be active members of their family's giving process, or where they can start to be leading donors to nonprofits, frustration can arise if they are not afforded the chance to do so. When we asked next gen donors about how they are involved in their family's philanthropy, 66 percent said they had been invited by their elders to give their opinions on the family's philanthropy, but only 37.1 percent served on their family foundation's primary board and 16.2 percent on a committee. We also heard this frustration bubble up in our interviews. Some next gen donors in giving families talked about being ready to get involved in their family philanthropy long before their elders are ready to fully engage them. "I'm learning about all these amazing things that we could and should be doing. I would bring them to the family, but it is not really my role; I don't want to step on any toes."

For nonprofit professionals who see the next gen strictly as "their donors' children," becoming peers with next gen funders may feel uncomfortable. But if they don't adapt their relationship with next gen donors to one of adult peers, these donors likely won't be around very long. Ultimately, if not offered something substantive, they will see the relationship as condescending or as merely transactional, with nonprofit professionals focused more on their pocketbooks than on seeing them as mature contributors to organizations.

Respecting Generational Personalities

Despite good intentions, not all donors, professionals, and volunteers in the nonprofit world have an easy time learning to work across generations. Just as organizing a holiday dinner for multiple generations of family members can be complicated—satisfying food preferences from steak and potatoes to vegan and gluten-free—so too are groups discovering that philanthropy can bring people together even as it unearths generational differences.

So how can multigenerational groups learn to work well together? When we ask donors what informs their philanthropic decision-making, we often hear similarities across the "generational cohorts" to which each person belongs.[7] While not a hard science, examining the events and conditions that each cohort experienced during its formative years helps one understand the different lens each generation brings to the table. Appreciating different "generational personalities" not only informs how cohorts vote on a decision but helps build awareness and empathy among stakeholders so they can learn *why* they vote that way and build lasting relationships across the generations.

For example, the Traditionalists (born between 1925 and 1945) grew up amid the invention of airplanes, automobiles, and movies, but the lasting imprimatur was from the World Wars, the Depression, segregation, and other experiences that left them feeling cautious yet loyal to people and institutions that gave them opportunities for growth, from the New Deal to the GI Bill. They fund institutions both local and civic in nature, often giving back to where they earned their wealth and to the people whose stories mirror their own.

Boomers (born between 1945 and 1965) grew up in a post–World War II era with an economic boom, mobilized by the civil rights, women's rights, gay rights, and antiwar movements; buoyed by innovations of the birth control pill, the moon landing, and *Brown vs. Board of Education;* and tempered by the explosion of the atomic bomb as well as the assassinations of John F. Kennedy, Martin Luther King Jr., and Robert F. Kennedy. For the most part, they maintained their optimism and continue to invest in causes they hold dear, believing they can affect change in a democracy, and at present they lead the majority of the governmental bodies, nonprofits, and family foundations in the United States.

Born between 1965 and 1980, Gen Xers experienced a very different upbringing, one with changing parenting norms. Women moved into the workforce, leaving many Xers to become "latchkey kids." The "free love" of the Boomers' Woodstock transitioned into the AIDS epidemic to the Xers, and the divorce rate tripled during their upbringing. As such, Xers tend to be cynical about institutions, a healthy skepticism they bring to philanthropic and nonprofit organizations as well. At the same time, the invention of MTV, the personal computer, the Walkman, and Atari video consoles led to independence at early ages. As the smallest generational cohort, virtually unnoticed between the much larger Boomer and Millennial generations, Xers experienced less competition and became adept at responding to challenges in creative ways.[8] In the philanthropic space, they are perhaps best known as social entrepreneurs founding Teach for America, charity: water, Venture for America, Dress for Success, and more.

While Gen Yers (born between 1980 and 1995) don't like the label Millennial, they were named such because they were born in the run-up to the turn of the millennium. Quite distinct from Gen Xers in their formative-year experiences, American Millennials' childhoods were ravaged by Oklahoma City; 9/11; Hurricanes Katrina and Rita; and Columbine, Virginia Tech, and other shootings—events that all took place on American soil. Not only did these sorts of incidents lead to hovering helicopter parents, they fostered in Millennials a deep sense of civic engagement to vote and volunteer motivated by a desire for a world free of danger and a better life for all. The invention of the Internet gave them the tools to connect, communicate, advocate, and contribute at the click of a button, years before their predecessors dreamed they would become involved in social change and charitable giving. Like Boomers, Millennials are a huge generation, so they've grown up facing stiff competition in all parts of their lives. This environment can fuel them to be more aggressive in their philanthropy as well, as this Millennial theorizes: "We are a generation that are all go-getters. To get where we are right now, we had to kick ass in college and get into the best grad school. And then be protégées out of the gate, and storm the gates of where we wanted to work—and get in and rise to the top and then be the next whatever. I am always amazed when people don't take that same attitude to their philanthropy and that same chutzpah."

Generation Z (born between 1995 and 2015) is growing up in a diverse world where an African American family led from the White House and where marriage equality is becoming the norm. The Great Recession led most to become very practical, setting up lemonade stands to earn their own funds and establishing savings accounts early on. Assuming their generation won't financially outpace their predecessors, 60 percent of Gen Z high school graduates claim they'd rather be an entrepreneur than an employee after college.[9] As digital natives, they suffer from FOMO ("fear of missing out"). They prefer the visuals of emojis, Instagram, and Snapchat to calls, e-mails, and texts, and they are DIY-ers ("do-it-yourself-ers"), which means their philanthropic celebrities are on YouTube (think ice bucket challenge) rather than in boardrooms.[10] How they will emerge as philanthropists is yet to be determined, but their conviction that differences among people are normal will likely lead Generation Z to bring compassion and open-mindedness to bear on seemingly intractable problems.

As these generational personalities interact more and more on the philanthropic stage, understanding where they are coming from will help all sides see the benefits that the others bring. One next gen donor describes what it can look like this way: "A lot is achieved when the next generation is able to respect the older generation's wisdom and experience and the older generation is able to respect the next generation's ability to question worlds and deeply think about things, even if they might not have the technical vocabulary of doing it for 30 years."

What Does This Mean?

Bringing new perspectives, revolutionary ideas, and innovative approaches doesn't always lead to multigenerational harmony or greater impact. Especially within existing family foundations and stable nonprofit institutions, next gen donors interrupting the status quo can feel disruptive and lead some to feel they're doing unnecessary extra work to accommodate said new ideas. But next gens are coming whether we want them to or not, so we all have to learn to communicate across generational divides. Otherwise, grantmaking could devolve into feel-good but ineffective giving at best, or misguided efforts brought about by dysfunctional group dynamics at worst.

This notion of how hard it is to shift from a vertical leadership succession plan to a multigenerational leadership team hit home for Sharna when a rabbi told her the story of a Jewish family discussing their adoption of a Chinese baby. The parents were curious as to how their family would evolve. The rabbi replied, "You won't be a Jewish family with a Chinese child. You will become an Asian-Jewish family." As with adopting a child, bringing in a new generation requires the whole system to adapt, and that may feel hard for the stakeholders.

Professionals helping their boards navigate the shift from hierarchical leadership to multigenerational engagement don't always grasp the full implications. Many assume that adding token next gen members to their boards while continuing the status quo is sufficient. In that case, the foundation or nonprofit organization is really still run by the elders, perhaps with a kids' table attached, and never achieves the greater-than-the-sum-of-its-parts success possible when harnessing the talents of all team members. And families and nonprofits that choose status quo for fear of change or difficult transitions soon realize that without melding, their organizational strength will wane.[11]

In today's global Information Age and sharing economy, families and nonprofits that don't look to next gen adults with twenty-first-century skills to join their teams can lose competitive advantage. Family foundations, for example, might overlook nonprofits with cutting-edge methods because existing older trustees don't know how to assess those methods. Similarly, nonprofits that look to replace older donors with someone in their generational cohort will lose out on the talents and ties that engaged next gen donors could bring.

Ultimately, families and nonprofits will need to make a mind-set shift, seeing the value of a diverse set of people and skills as a way to capture and enhance everyone's resources (time, talent, treasure, and ties) rather than a loss of control or status quo. Then becoming a multigenerational operation will require a shift to a multigenerational governance structure, where next gen voices are encouraged and valued and where they can ultimately affect policy or grant-making decisions. Those most successful at making this shift, like the family foundation Katherine Lorenz now runs, celebrate the new types of talents and abilities next gen donors bring *and* help elders feel valued for their wisdom and experience so they don't feel like they have to give up control but can stay and make room for the next gen to bring its unique strengths to the endeavor.

Dr. Jeffrey Solomon, president of the Andrea and Charles Bronfman Philanthropies, likens the on-ramping of next gen donors in a nonprofit to changing a car tire while the car is driving 60 miles an hour. Next generation donors are often adults already—with degrees, careers, and families of their own—who want to bring their ideas and experiences to bear on the organization. This is hard to do when the entity is already cruising along successfully. Nonprofits and families that want to engage next gen donors, he recommends, should set aside time for a board or organizational retreat to orient the new members, discuss the opportunities and challenges at hand, and assign buddies within the organization who will help acclimate the next gen donors to the organization during their first year.

There are consulting groups, of course, who assist groups in different sectors as they navigate becoming a multigenerational entity. BridgeWorks, for instance, focuses on generational trends in the workplace; 21/64, Relative Solutions, and others help next gen donors, families, and advisors manage change as they transition their wealth and philanthropy from generation to generation. Outside facilitators can help nonprofit professionals, families, and board members who struggle with multigenerational engagement communicate about the dynamics productively, making the work of the whole organization more effective.

Engaging multiple generations in meaningful roles with decision-making powers is a hard shift for most families and nonprofits to make. The work to be done is a far cry from simply creating a junior board that has no decision-making authority. To be successful, organizations will need to make space for next gen donors on their main boards, honor longstanding board members with the title of "emeritus" and engage them on specific projects to tap their expertise, and devise meaningful opportunities for donors of all ages to interact. Organizational leaders who can treat next gen donors like peers and build multigenerational decision-making bodies have a greater chance at longevity and relevance.[12] Those families and nonprofits that realize their ability to succeed lies in generations working together will have the best chance of performing as a team, of sustaining their organizations, and, above all, of making an impact.

CHAPTER 11

Next Gen Philanthropic Identity

For next gen donors who have earned their own wealth, discovering that they have financial resources that they didn't have growing up—enough to be philanthropic at a young age—can be a new and disorienting reality. These "immigrants" to wealth, as James Grubman calls them in his book *Strangers in Paradise,* have to acculturate to their new land, learn a new language, and figure out the role they want to play there.[1] Just as immigrants to a new country struggle to assimilate, so do self-made earners—who didn't grow up with wealth—work to claim this new aspect of who they are and how they want to be. If these earners are giving-minded, this struggle includes figuring out what kind of donors they wish to become. It means forming a philanthropic identity.

For those who are inheriting wealth and a philanthropic legacy, the drivers are different, but the basic motivation is the same. Inheritors feel the weight of their predecessors' successes, the privileges afforded them by virtue of winning what Warren Buffett calls the "ovarian lottery," and the endless possibilities of what they could fund. With the world constantly monitoring for signs of their failure or success, these next gen inheritors wrestle with forming philanthropic identities based on their own purposes rather than becoming paralyzed by the successes of their predecessors, their prosperity, or the possibilities available to them.[2] Like earners, they too face the challenge of crafting their distinctive philanthropic identity.

The Importance of Becoming

As a next generation donor herself, *Generation Impact* co-author Sharna Goldseker has experienced this challenge firsthand:

> Growing up in Baltimore with the same last name as one of the city's 10 largest private foundations, I was often asked if I was the daughter of Mr. and Mrs. Goldseker or granddaughter of Morris Goldseker, my great-uncle who established the Goldseker Foundation upon his passing. As I grew, fundraisers began approaching me for gifts, long before I even understood what philanthropy meant. This awakened in me uncomfortable feelings about the privilege I inherited by dint of my birth. When I attempted to earn the right to that legacy, I inquired about becoming involved in nonprofit organizations and serving on committees and boards, but I was told I was too young to engage meaningfully in the nonprofit world. I should "wait until my 30s" or "get married and have children first" was some of the advice I got from development officers. "Come back when my parents stepped off the boards" was the unspoken message I got from others. Those encounters led me to want to find my own identity as a donor and to consider the difference I could make in my own right.

Sharna began interning for different nonprofits in her teens as a way to ascertain what kind of work she wanted to do and support in the nonprofit space. She began attending events and conferences to learn the craft of grantmaking and to develop an awareness of social issues, learn more about how philanthropy could address those issues, and begin to meet her philanthropic peers.

We heard similar stories of proactive, often self-guided learning from the next gen donors we interviewed. This was true for first-generation wealth-earners as well as inheritors, especially as the earners didn't have the option to learn within an established philanthropic family structure. Experiential learning was seen by many as especially powerful. This came through clearly in the survey as well. As we noted in Chapter 5, when we asked next gen donors what shapes their philanthropic learning and development, "personal experience as a donor, volunteer, board member, etc." ranked the highest out of nine possible influences; in fact, 72.3 percent of respondents considered this "very important," and most others viewed it as "somewhat important."

Next gen donors who had structured opportunities to learn—either within their own families or as part of other institutions—often highlighted these as catalyzing their philanthropic identity. Explaining the importance of experience, this woman said, "I served on the grants committee of the community foundation for four years in high school and that really got me engaged, starting at the age of 15, with the philanthropy world." Or think of John R. Seydel's "learning trips" with his grandpa Ted Turner:

> Grandpa has taken all of us on educational retreats, where the family comes together in a developing nation to learn about environmental sustainability issues. It is so powerful to see the beauty of what we are trying to protect, to visit grantees and see the actual programs, boots on the ground. The biggest recommendation I can offer to parents [is] allow your kids to get involved early. Show them what the world is really like

241

outside of your state or outside of American borders. You don't have to wait. You can do this as a family, even if just once a year.

As attorney, activist, and author Bryan Stevenson notes, it takes proximity to people not like us in order to build empathy and catalyze change.[3] And next gen donors seem to concur. Survey respondents listed "personal observations or analysis of the significant need for philanthropy" as highly influential, especially when compared to "something learned in school," which was near the bottom of the list.

Certainly next gen donors seem eager to learn, seeking out opportunities to grow as donors. But what fascinated us most in our exploration of next gen donors is that for many, this process of identity formation is as fulfilling as the results of that process. In short, the *becoming* is as meaningful as the *being*.

Ideally, the becoming process precedes the being, meaning the majority of these Gen X and Millennial donors have the opportunity to form their identities before acting as major donors in their own rights. But this is not always the case given the much earlier ages at which they are beginning to give, and some next gen donors would say they are simultaneously becoming even as they are being. Regardless, these young donors are both intentional and proactive about the becoming process, actively crafting their identities and designing their legacies *now* rather than waiting until they retire to decide who they are as philanthropists and what legacies they want to leave. As this donor explains, "I feel like what happens too many times is that people just have a for-profit career, retire, and then try to reinvent themselves as philanthropists. That is not the best way to do it. I feel like engaging as early as possible, so you can learn and grow like a person does throughout their lives, is [better]."

We found that 51 percent of next gen donors we surveyed began making charitable donations before the age of 20, and another 47 percent between the ages of 21 and 30, demonstrating that they are actively giving even as they wrestle with identity development in emerging adulthood.[4] Add to this the microscope that most next gen donors live under in this social media age, plus the responsibility of the unprecedented dollars and resources they steward, and we can appreciate how the pressures of "becoming" are more significant for this generation of donors than any before. While they aren't asking for sympathy for their burden, they are taking responsibility for growing into the donors they want to become—and feel they ought to be.

Katherine Lorenz, for example, talked about her journey volunteering in a rural community in Nicaragua, founding and growing a nonprofit in Mexico, and learning about strategic philanthropy with a group of peers—all experiences she had far from the trappings of her regular life on the way to assuming the leadership mantle of her family's foundation. Other next gen donors described how they see their early giving as a runway to more significant philanthropy later on. It's as if allocating thousands of dollars annually serves as "practice" for when additional resources come to them. "I spend a lot more time thinking about giving $35,000 away than might be justified, but partly this has been in preparation for the dollars coming into my life in the future. I'm being really thoughtful. That way, as future dollars come, I will be much more prepared."

Just how seriously these Gen Xers and Millennials think about becoming the donors they want to be might be unexpected given the typical assumptions about—and media portrayals of—wealthy young people as entitled or unnecessarily disruptive. Instead, we found that the vast majority of next gen donors we interviewed would become quite animated in talking about this process of becoming. Perhaps this passion is in part a way to fend off any illusions people might hold about them or their wealth. But their eagerness to learn seemed due to their appreciation of just how complicated and critical their journeys were and would be, given their means to effect major change.

The Difficulty of the Launch

Developmental psychologists, from Carl Jung to Erik Erikson and (more recently) Jeffrey Arnett, have long emphasized the importance of the stage when an adolescent becomes an adult, a period where children launch from their parents and define what being their own person means. Psychologist and researcher Meg Jay, however, claims that as a society we're undermining the next generation's ability to launch. In her book *The Defining Decade,* Jay contends that there is no more critical a time than our 20s to build "identity capital." As Jay defines it, "Identity capital is a collection of our personal assets . . . [it] is how we build ourselves—bit by bit, over time."[5] If emerging adults don't experience jobs and relationships that serve as the building blocks of their careers and future marriages/partnerships, they will have to begin building identity capital in their 30s, when it's emotionally, psychologically, biologically, and practically harder to start adulthood.

We believe, as Jay contends, that our society looks at the twentysomething years with rose-colored glasses, as a time when emerging adults can be carefree. As such, we may undervalue the significance of the 20s as a time for identity formation. For example, if families and advisors are not prepared to transfer some financial resources to the next generation so it can practice investing, saving, spending, and giving, they can forget or neglect to grant permission to launch as independent adults who need to learn to manage their resources with confidence. If families, advisors, and nonprofit professionals are fearful of next gen donors' new ideas, they run the risk of leaving them at the kids' table too long, squandering the energy next gen donors are eager to bring to their philanthropic pursuits. While elders might feel they are well founded in their concerns about lending next gen donors the proverbial keys to the car, what we've learned is that having their own set of keys is the very thing that helps them to develop—philanthropically and otherwise.

We heard that for 72.3 percent of next gen donors, learning from their own experience is "very important" to them as the way they want to develop as a donor. And for those who are inheriting a family legacy of giving, "the launch" takes on a particular cast. They want to "plow their own trails," even if those trails have been heavily traversed by the well-known family members who came before. "You need to have that separation," says one donor. "It's a universal experience, being able to develop your own gravitas and responsibility, your own sense of accomplishment, and not necessarily within something that's being given to you or managed for you." Another next gen donor echoes: "I have a really strong drive to create my own legacy, or take what my parents have given and continue on from there and not settle for 'this is what my parents handed me.' Rather, I want to take what they accomplished and continue to move up the ladder." Doing this, the donor continues, would require going through a process "where I could identify and figure out what I valued, what I wanted to do, what I found meaning in. I had to gain my bearings, earn my own identity, and in a way that wasn't on the coattails of my family."

The journeys of these next gen donors resemble those of others entering adulthood, trying to establish their own identities. The big difference is that their launching process has greater consequences for others, as who they become as donors impacts where and how they will give their unprecedented resources. While most well-meaning twentysomethings are grappling with college graduation, finding meaningful and gainful employment, and moving out of their parents' homes, next gen donors do all that *and* see themselves as responsible for both their family legacies and for making a difference in the world.

As we heard in Chapter 7, being in the company of peers during the launch process helps some reconsider and potentially separate from the perspectives of their upbringing and to determine the donors they want to become. The opportunity to reflect on their identities away from their families—or, for earners, alongside other new donors coming into this unique role—gives them room to individuate, to contemplate who they want to be as donors, and to flex their philanthropic muscles in a supportive space.

Several next gen donors we interviewed describe these collective experiences as empowering. Sara Ojjeh, for one, credits her parents with helping her launch alongside her siblings. The four were given philanthropic assets to allocate together, supported by education, a few basic parameters, and a couple of trusted advisors. Her father had helped grow the family business, TAG Group, most widely known for TAG Heuer watches, and had always been philanthropic, though usually in anonymous ways. Sara's early experience propelled her on a journey that has now taken her around the globe and helped her form a clear sense of her own philanthropic identity.

Sara Ojjeh

I was born in Paris to an American mother and a French-Syrian father. When I was 5, my family and I moved from Paris to Geneva, and I spent the rest of my childhood and teens there until I graduated from the International School of Geneva and moved to New York to go to New York University. I'm one of four children and have two wonderful older sisters and an amazing younger brother.

Our parents had always been philanthropic, but always anonymously, and didn't necessarily communicate with us about their philanthropy. My father is the kind of man who at fundraising dinners made the biggest pledge, yet he would invite the organization to follow up with him, choosing to remain anonymous at the event. It was never about the immediate gratification for him but always the end result. My grandfather was a self-made man who built many businesses through his career. He immigrated to France from Syria before WWII broke out and earned money during the war by broadcasting the news on the radio in Arabic. My father went into the family business straight out of graduate school and helped grow TAG Group, mostly known for TAG Heuer watches, among other ventures.

A Chance to Learn

One night when I was about 15, my brother 13, and my sisters 18 and 19, we were sitting at dinner when my father said, "We have a project for the four of you." Both an intriguing and surprising opening line. He continued to explain that my parents had put a sum of money in a bank account—not a structured philanthropic fund, but just a bank account—and wanted us to work together to give away the money in a strategic manner with the help of a new group of philanthropic advisors that had just started in Geneva. It was paramount for our parents that we recognize how fortunate we are and how to give effectively. In order to find structure for

(continued)

(continued)

this endeavor, it was crucial to have philanthropic advisors help us shape and organize our giving.

At the time, I rolled my eyes and felt immediately over-whelmed. At 15, I was already consumed with studying for the SATs, starting my international baccalaureate, focusing on college applications, and I thought, "Are you kidding me?" I barely had time to myself. Little did I know that this project would shape my life's path.

My parents had established four ground rules for us. First, they wanted to teach us the importance of learning to work together as equals, regardless of our age differences and gender. In particular, my parents really wanted us to be able to say no to each other. And what happens if it's a 50–50 split when we vote—how does that work? How do we navigate these things? They conveyed to us that inevitably in other areas of life (presumably financially and otherwise), we were going to have to learn to work together and respect each other as peers, not just as siblings.

Second, and most important, we had to remain anonymous. Third, we had to complete the giving within four years. This was to ensure that we would prioritize our giving in addition to the other things we had going on individually, as well as learn the value of setting deadlines. Plus, it was to help us understand the different and sustainable changes we could make in a specific time frame.

Last, in those four years, 50 percent of the annual funds had to go to a project that my parents supported in neighboring France, which has a large immigrant community and often needed emergency grants, such as scholarships or vocational training funds. Within this specific community, issues of poverty, racial tension, gender-based violence, and religion were all present, which allowed us to interact with various needs in one area. But more important, this was to teach us that we didn't need to go far from home to find people in need.

We started working with the team at Wise Philanthropy Advisors in early 2006 and became more focused on our goals thanks to their guidance. Their process of organizing us was really smart because we are four strong-willed, independent individuals, and Wise took the time to interview us individually to see what made us tick and where we have the most common threads.

What that came down to was an emphasis on education. My grandfather used to say to my dad, "In life you can lose everything, but nobody can take away your education," and that value was engrained in us from a young age. We focused on education—starting with smaller grants and then building up as we grew more comfortable and engaged.

We also wanted to fund projects where we were going to see the results of our investments in the long-term. Our goals were never to show off a plaque of recognition but to know that, whatever the project may be, it was going to be sustainable and help that community for years to come. That was always the baseline for us. Our advisors—"The Wise Guys," as we nicknamed them—were really good about sending us information in the beginning to get us started in understanding their due diligence process and then following up with us by getting together and discussing progress.

The Freedom to Take Risks

By the end of the third year, we took the reins and brought forward our own potential grantees and projects. Our dad wanted to hear all the details of our grants and was proud of our work, while our mom wanted to be in the action with us, so she started joining us for our learning journeys out in the field. Seeing the work on the ground solidified something for all of us. We speak with great affection when reminiscing about our site visits to meet girls in Cambodia and the infamous night in Tanzania when after a site visit, cockroaches awaited us in bed. These bonding and deeply enriching experiences remain some of our fondest memories as a family. Visiting numerous projects in four continents helped us build a stronger connection as siblings, form a greater understanding of the importance of giving, and a deep appreciation that the

(continued)

(continued)

grantees touched and fulfilled us with more than we ever could have given them. What had begun as a 4-year commitment turned into a 10-year commitment. Little did my parents know at the time that their idea of getting their teenage children to work together actually shifted every single one of our individual life paths.

After a few years in this philanthropic experience, my eldest sister went on to learn Arabic, get her master's in development from the London School of Economics, and then worked at Children's Investment Fund Foundation (CIFF). My second sister ended up shifting from communications to public policy and worked with embassies before getting her teaching degree from Columbia University. I transitioned from public relations to corporate social responsibility and now philanthropy, getting my master's in grantmaking and fundraising from New York University. Recently, I founded my own consulting company, working in an advisory capacity with individuals and family offices on their philanthropic portfolios. My brother has recently graduated from university and is constantly helping us with the financial management aspects of our philanthropy. There is a newfound energy that we have in the way we work together and respect each other as peers, which I think philanthropy allowed us to find and that we probably would not have found otherwise.

I feel like what my parents gave us was freedom. They let us know it was okay to make mistakes and even have grants that could fail. But we had to fail together and learn why we failed in order to apply the lessons as we moved on to other experiences. That ability to fail was a gift they gave us, as much as the initial allocations of funds in the bank account.

We also learned to have that sense of agency in coming to our parents and saying this is the research we conducted, this is what we decided together, and this is what we are funding. The role of Wise was to chaperone and guide us in our journey, which allowed us to feel a sense of freedom from our parents' choices, and yet permitted them to trust our process. Our projects provided independence and an opportunity to learn how to trust. It was something that we could drive and then choose to share with our parents.

By taking chances on projects, I learned to have conviction about the impact I aim to make. I built this confidence in my early 20s around what I wanted to learn and catalyze through funding opportunities. I think it's what gave me the assurance to talk to the CEO of a fashion brand and say, "Hi, I'm 23 years old and would like to share my ideas about starting a corporate social responsibility program with you." And then be able to follow through with those ideas.

Finding My Voice, Adapting My Approach

Shortly after receiving my undergraduate degree in media cultures and communications from New York University, I went to work for Michael Kors, which at the time was growing exponentially. I was familiar with the CEO and did a literal elevator pitch on one Friday afternoon, saying, "I think the company should start doing some good for the world and show that (in air quotes) 'Kors Cares,' to keep up with competitors." He said, "Great. Meet me on Monday and let me know what you've got." The company ended up creating a four-year partnership, which they have just renewed, with the United Nations World Food Programme and built an entire campaign around it called Watch Hunger Stop that provided 100 meals to a child in need for every campaign watch purchased. I credit the success of my time at Michael Kors, and the confidence I had to push boundaries and take risks, to my parents for giving us the opportunity and experience with our philanthropy.

After leaving Michael Kors, I was serendipitously introduced to my lead grantee, Population Services International (PSI), the largest global health organization in the world, with which I have had an incredible journey. In 2013, I became the second Founding Member of Maverick Collective, a community of

(continued)

251

(continued)

strategic philanthropists cofounded by Her Royal Highness Mette Marit of Norway and Melinda Gates, focused on supporting pilot projects in women's and girls' health to end extreme poverty. Through my work with Maverick Collective, I have been able to find my voice as a next gen donor. For the first time, I am leading a philanthropic project on my own, but my siblings and I have communicated about every detail, and I value their opinions and insights. For example, when I got back from Uganda last year, where I was visiting various maternal health clinics, my sisters were texting me, asking me about the long-term goals of the project and how to impact maternal health issues.

We now share this philanthropic experience, so we swap site-visit information like it's gossip. We've done this before; we've done our due diligence together. We have a context and a language for philanthropy that we share. I don't think my parents ever expected that allowing me to practice philanthropy with my siblings would lead me to pursue a career in the field and get a master's in it. It gave me the foundation I needed to have the confidence to do what I'm doing now.

Over time, I think my values have stayed the same, but my approach has completely changed. My motto is that "Charity starts at home, but philanthropy starts with partnership." I believe that charity is the one-on-one connection. It is, "How can I help my neighbor?" With my work as a birth doula, I aim to help one mother at a time in my own community, and that is my one-on-one connection. But with my philanthropic peers as well as nonprofit partners, I am able to grow philanthropic efforts and affect systemic change.

I think that my parents taught us a lot of things, but I recognize for myself that to be not just any philanthropist, but an effective philanthropist, you have to have the right partners. If next gen philanthropy is going to work, we need to partner together, as a generation, to tackle the world's most pressing issues. Part of catalyzing my peers is having to come forward and use my name with pride, stepping outside of my anonymous-philanthropy comfort zone. I feel like there is a stigma of being a kid who comes from wealth, and that most who grow up with some wealth feel a little guilt associated with the privilege we have. I thought that if I stepped forward and I said this is who I am, and you can assume what you want about where I come from—well, I'm okay with that because, more important, this is what I'm doing with my voice and assets. I want to inspire and encourage other people to do the same, stand up and be comfortable with making change. If you have the *ability* to make a difference, you have the *responsibility* to do so.

I believe in sustainable change and in making an impact close to and far away from home. My values remain the same, but my approach is louder. If there are more dollars going to girls' and women's health because other next gens heard my story, then it is worth it, even if I lose a little bit of my privacy. I'm okay with that. I think *that* is the real shift—to lend my voice for the sake of sustainable change.

A Generational Identity

Next gen donors are breaking away from the traditional approach to philanthropy of writing checks and attending galas. We want to do it differently. I think it's one of the reasons that social media campaigns take off like wildfire. We want to support an initiative that's loud and that we can do all together, and the more the merrier in creating change. We can work within family structures and outside of them, too, to see how we can connect around philanthropy. We are a generation that is both impatient and collaborative, and those combined create a brilliant new platform for philanthropy. Together, we can move the needle further and faster, holding each other accountable for our involvement and action.

I believe that nonprofits are going to have to get creative to respond to the next generation of donors. Recently, while visiting a clinic that serves teenage mothers in a rural area outside of Santo Domingo, the mothers seemed embarrassed that foreigners

(continued)

(continued)

just walked in with the director of the program to observe them, and rightly so. I excused myself from the group and sat in the waiting room with these young mothers informally, using my best Spanish to speak with them and hear their stories, listen to their voices. That's what I want to do, connect with the women, learn from their struggles and experiences, and build a greater understanding of their needs and how to address them.

With this in mind, I've started thinking about how to be a more strategic funder; to understand the difference between being emotional and being effective. You can't go into the field and say, "I want to take every baby home, or to give every person who asks five dollars." That is not realistic and you have to learn that rationale for yourself. Nobody can teach it to you unless you go, see, feel, and understand. Most important, you have to ask how you can be most effective and helpful, not assume you know the solutions to their issues.

For my twenty-first birthday I asked for donations instead of gifts and raised about $50,000 that my parents matched. My siblings and I ended up working to distribute it together, tapping into each other's strengths to make the decisions. We decided to give the funds to Pencils of Promise at a time when the organization was just a few years old and a grant of this size was incredibly significant. Their first proposal was to build four schools and name one school after each sibling, which did not resonate with us at all. Instead we asked, "Where is the most need?" They said in teacher training and additional infrastructure such as building toilets, and then the decision was quickly made. They can get people to build schools just by lifting their paddle at their annual gala, but to get somebody to invest in the people on the ground, the teachers and students, is much harder. This is where the partnerships in philanthropy make the greatest difference.

Of course, you still need philanthropists who are just going to write checks and trust that someone is doing the work properly. But especially as a next gen donor, if you want to break the mold of traditional philanthropy and understand how you're going to be most effective, you have to experience it firsthand. You have to understand why it is important not to only build a school structure but to build the toilets to go with it to keep girls in school, and invest in the teacher training programs as well. Understanding how everything in these communities is interconnected and dependent is the key to their sustainability.

I model this in my partnership with PSI, too. When approached to fund a pilot project in maternal health, I knew I didn't have the wherewithal to conduct the research and due diligence to the extent that they can. So I asked them where the biggest need for maternal health exists today, and they said Uganda. All right, then, Uganda it is. I think that donors have to trust NGOs [non-governmental organizations] and give them the agency they need to help you meet your donor goals and create the sustainable and life-changing differences.

Similarly, it's the responsibility of advisors and perhaps the organization as well to say, "Okay, you want to build a school and you want your name on it, but could you also work with another family where together you could build a school and also cover the necessary infrastructure?" Then there's a partnership among the donors and with the organization. Partnership is not only between donor and organization, but also between various donors with shared goals.

The Significance of the Journey

What can other families do to catalyze this kind of philanthropic education for their kids? Not all parents have the same vision that mine did, who allowed us to learn by experience—like we did when we made a not-so-effective-grant early on—and even permitted us to learn by failing a few times. Yet I think there are many ways that make sense, depending on their ages. When you're young, you're interested in charity, so explore the human experience, like volunteering locally. Then, by the time that child is a teenager, his

(continued)

255

(continued)

or her interests may have evolved into working on drug prevention or sex trafficking, and there is an ability to talk with parents and advisors, and discuss and compare projects, and consider your motivations to connect emotionally and effectively.

Then, I would say, in your late teens and 20s, there is an opportunity to find peers, to find partners, so next gen donors can work together; perhaps partnering with siblings, like I did, or finding the right peer network or couple of families that want to fund a project together. Part of an advisor's role is to encourage parents to start that conversation with their children and to find the right partners to help those kids grow in that capacity. If and when children are ready to work with their family foundations or other vehicles, maybe invite them to manage and allocate 1 percent of the 5 percent payout of the foundation. Give them some responsibility and autonomy. Allow the next generation in your family to have some agency, and let them do their own research and figure out their own philanthropic paths. While they may fail, they are guaranteed to learn from it.

The impressive learning journey that Sara and her siblings were afforded may be more elaborate than most families will permit. But the significance of the deliberate education at a critical time in a young adult's life is the key takeaway. The permission to have this learning experience not only helped her solidify her philanthropic identity but also helped her launch into the world with confidence, clarity, and discernment—a priceless life experience. While Sara's journey hasn't been linear, her active reflection on her emerging identity has led her to have a strong sense of who she is and what she wants to accomplish as a donor.

Breaking Norms: Next Gen Is Now Gen

While many next gen donors are still in the "becoming" phase of forming their identities as major philanthropists, some would argue that the next generation should be called the "Now Generation," given their ability to start giving at a young age. American philanthropists of the past would typically have grown their earnings during what Erik Erikson called their "generative" years—age 40 to 64—after which time, in their "maturity" stage, individuals would tend to feel financially secure enough, reflecting on a life well lived, to set aside funds for future generations as well as contributing to society.[6] One of the hallmarks of next gen donors, as we've said—and a chief indicator of how they are breaking the mold—is their determination to make a difference *now*. Rather than assume they can wait to engage with next gen donors in 20 years, parents, advisors, and nonprofit professionals are realizing, like the Ojjeh parents, that the next gen is coming of age with the resources and inclination to fund now.

Next gen donors express a sense not only of opportunity but also of urgency, which shows up in their desire to make their families' philanthropy more effective and in how they press their advisors to be more proactive in their recommendations for what and how they can fund. While families, advisors, and nonprofits may experience this urgency as hubris, this take-charge attitude is more a recognition of how the next gen perceives society's problems: vast and urgent. As we heard in Chapter 9 from Alex Soros, many rising donors simply ask, "Why wait?" One donor said, "I feel it is very important to give back now, not wait until later to start doing something significant." Another describes how she pushed her family to give more than the legally required minimum payout of 5 percent of foundation assets each year because she believed the grantees needed it:

257

The family foundation my parents set up when we were kids was very informal. We were told we were on the board. It was just the four of us in the family meeting at the end of every year, as dictated by tax policy, to determine, "Well, where's the 5 percent going to go?" But once I was in my 20s I said, "Wait a minute. As a family, we have way more that we could be doing. I'll go first. I will take all the assets that are under my control and I will start thinking about an aggressive giving plan for pretty much all of that."

Generation Impact is eager to give now even if initial efforts result in failure—failure that can be very public if they are part of a wealthy family. One donor echoed what we heard Sara say about the benefit of making mistakes in order to learn from them: "I think that we only learn from our experiences, and we learn best from our failures, so we have to go out there and have the experiences on our own, learn from our own actions, learn from our own mistakes, and hopefully those are done in ways and at a level that isn't catastrophic."

If you are a parent and your kids are ever afraid to make a mistake for fear of what you will think, imagine what it's like to be a child from a prominent wealthy family whose every move is of public interest. At least at a younger age the mistakes are proportionate and the opportunity for resilience likely; the funds and the stakes will only increase over time.

What Does This Mean?

When you began this book, you might have imagined that trust fund inheritors and young tech billionaires would while away the hours traveling to Art Basel or swimming in the surf in Ibiza.

Instead we heard Hannah Quimby describe driving around Maine to learn about the issues on the ground. Sara Ojjeh raised money to give to Pencils for Promise to fund toilets and teacher training. And Victoria Rogers volunteered for years at the Sue Duncan Children's Center in the South Side of Chicago. As we've shown, Hannah, Sara, and Victoria are more the next gen donor rule than the exception. Their exploration of their own identities at an early age, in concert with their philanthropic learning journeys, resulted in a strong sense of identity for each.

The next gen donors we've met here are merely crafting their distinctive identities, something all individuals struggle with as they move from adolescence to adulthood. Yet they are doing so laden with responsibility, both to their predecessors and to humanity, knowing that their philanthropic choices have the potential to hurt or help society to staggering degrees. Fair or not, the identity journeys of next gen donors are likely to have a bigger impact on our world than the journeys of most others. That is why we look closely at those journeys here, and why we are heartened that these donors take their journeys so seriously.

Of course, real people, causes, and organizations will feel the consequences of choices these still-learning donors will make. Both donors themselves and those who help them should remain vigilant about avoiding catastrophic mistakes—even those occurring in the pursuit of learning.

As parents, teachers, advisors, and mentors to the rising generation—whether of wealth and philanthropy or not—we can help the next generation prepare for its imminent responsibilities.[7] As this stage of identity formation is so critical, we need to start building the self-confidence and behaviors to foster it. Given the research findings that more than half of these next gen donors began giving before age 21, we have more freedom than we think to start addressing these issues early.

Next gen donors clearly want support for their identity journeys, and there are resources to help them, from peer groups to learning platforms to individual advisors to books.[8] Nonprofit professionals can also be helpful partners to next gen donors in their identity journeys. Sara tells us, "I believe that nonprofits are going to have to get creative to respond to the next generation of donors." We agree. As we have argued throughout this book, nonprofits will have to be open-minded about ways to engage next gen donors, taking their ideas seriously and giving them the opportunities for the hands-on, meaningful experiences that they so passionately want. Nonprofits that do so can reap tremendous benefits while providing the next gen with the learning experiences they crave.

Advisors can help facilitate this self-actualization process for next gen donors too. If doing so altruistically isn't motivation enough, research shows that after a client's first parent passes away, only 45 percent of next gen wealth-holders stay with their parents' advisors, and after the second parent passes away, only 2 percent remain.[9] Advisors will have to build direct relationships with the next generation in order to retain their business in years to come. Advisory firms could retrain personnel to operate in a multigenerational context, assign generationally matched staff to clients of different generations, and develop new tools for marketing, technology products, and relationship management to meet the worldview of younger clients.

Advisors and nonprofit professionals might also consider the role they can play in encouraging patriarchs and matriarchs to successfully launch their children by making them aware of some of the conferences, peer groups, resources, and consultants who can assist them in this work. We realize older donors and clients are today's bread-and-butter, and advisors and nonprofits want to focus on them; however, next gen donors will be tomorrow's lifeline, and a little time devoted to them now could yield tenfold tomorrow.

For families, ironically, this task of supporting children, grandchildren, nieces, and nephews may be the most challenging. It can be hard for older generations to move beyond the memories of the vulnerable child—with skinned knees and fifth birthdays. But research consistently shows that those parents who work hard to instill values in their children—who expose them to a world beyond their own and ensure them that their family has weathered challenges successfully—*those* are the parents who grow goodness in their children. Take this next gen donor:

> My parents took us to the slums of Kenya to visit a microfinance project they funded, to the mud hut in which my grandpa lived growing up. They even shipped me off to work on an Amazon deforestation project when I was 12 for seven days, a duration I recall because I marked the days by the number of PowerBars I brought to eat each day. Today, I look back with appreciation that my father had said to me, "You were born on third base. You didn't hit a triple." Growing up in Silicon Valley, I was in a bubble and needed to see how others lived. It affected me profoundly.

—⁀꙳

We find this trend toward giving at earlier stages of life, coupled with an identity journey, to be an exciting development for the field, largely because the needs are great and additional dollars will make a difference, but also because people in their 20s and 30s are more willing to take risks and suspend disbelief, making room to imagine a future that is better not just for themselves but for all of us. Given their youth, their platforms of privilege, and their desire to take their legacies to the next level, they are also more likely to find new and innovative ways to make an impact than we can even conceive of today. We look forward to seeing how the world evolves because of the next gen donors in Generation Impact, who are launching, learning, experimenting, growing, and giving. We are hopeful.

CHAPTER 12

Conclusion: Making the Most of the Golden Age of Giving

This book began with a somewhat audacious claim: Major Gen X and Millennial donors will be the most significant philanthropists ever.

Not only will these next gen donors have unprecedented resources to give, but they are giving and will continue to give in game-changing new ways. They are leading an Impact Revolution in philanthropy, which will be the hallmark of a new Golden Age of Giving—certainly in the United States, and perhaps across the globe.

This view of the next generation is surprising in part because it clashes with the images we often get of wealthy people in their 20s and 30s now: living in a materialistic bubble, sheltered first by helicopter parents and later by elite private institutions, obsessing over the next start-up to fund or gala to attend. Philanthropy for them, we're often told, is simply a luxury good they acquire to show off, a vanity project to build their brands.

While plenty of jet-setters fit this stereotype, especially given the current economic climate of explosive wealth creation and concentration, those are not the next gen donors we've met in our research and in this book. Instead, we've spent time with social entrepreneurs like Daniel Lurie, working closely with community partners to identify and invest in better ways to fight poverty; rising philanthropic leaders like Jenna Weinberg, learning with peers while earnestly stewarding and advancing a cherished legacy of giving; and passionate global donors like Sara Ojjeh, building close relationships with people in need and the nonprofits serving them.

Troubling social problems persist on the global, national, and local levels. And the biggest donors can have a disproportionate impact on those issues by investing in research and strategy, experimenting with promising innovations, and funding advocacy to change unjust or ineffective systems. Their role is magnified even more in these politically turbulent and uncertain times, when policymaking is in a stalemate and divisiveness inhibits much progress. We need engaged major donors perhaps now more than ever.

Not every reader will agree with our cautiously hopeful depiction of the next gen donors in Generation Impact. Their brash eagerness and willingness to experiment might elicit skepticism or outright resistance from stalwart philanthropic traditionalists. Their fervent desire for closer engagement with organizations—engagement that makes use of their time and talent as well as their considerable treasure and social ties—might seem a recipe for disaster. What nonprofit wants to coddle overly intrusive donors? As such, we've tried to not only disclose what we have learned about these earnest next gen donors but also give a sober assessment of their limitations and challenges. And we have offered guidance to nonprofit professionals, giving families, advisors, and next gen donors themselves about how to work together, avoiding potential pitfalls in the world of major giving.

Two things we hope we can all agree on are that the next generation of big donors will have a huge impact on our collective future and that we need to learn more about them, specifically what kind of philanthropists they are becoming. Conveying their plans in their own voices has been the chief goal of this book.

The Coming Revolution

Like previous generations of major donors, Gen Xers and Millennials feel a responsibility to give and want their giving to make a difference on a diverse array of causes. Unlike previous generations, they prioritize impact above all else, and they are willing to revolutionize philanthropy to get better results.

This drive for impact means next gen donors feel they have no choice but to make changes to philanthropic strategy and to take risks that could lead to new results. As one put it, "We need a different MO [modus operandi] here. This one isn't working." Next gen donors from philanthropic families are ready to work alongside their parents and grandparents on a multigenerational team, but they, and first-generation donors, *will* go it alone if they have to. They will even be "unreasonable"—to use Scott Belsky's word—if having more impact requires that.

Their vision, though, is to be both revolutionary *and* respectful. They want revolution not for revolution's sake but for impact's sake. Next gen donors acknowledge what they have learned from previous generations and want to be good stewards of legacy. They see their philanthropic innovations as honoring what donors in the past have accomplished by taking giving to the next level. They credit parents and grandparents with teaching them positive values around giving and want to instill and inhabit those values seamlessly across all parts of their lives. In fact, this search to find the right balance of the past and future, of respect and revolution, is the central identity challenge facing Generation Impact.

We know next gen donors themselves are eager to launch the revolution *now*. To us, this means there are big transformations on the immediate horizon, and the pace of change will steadily increase in the next few years, with some areas shifting faster than others.

In the short term, we expect to see many donors launch trial experiments to test out new innovations—like more next gen giving circles and funding collaboratives, new social responsibility screens introduced for foundation endowments, and use of sector-blending giving vehicles by individual donors to maximize their options. Other changes will take much longer, like nonprofits retooling their donor engagement strategies to bring donors more meaningfully into their everyday work and families sharing full decision-making power across generations. But even these complex and long-term changes are starting to happen, as the next gen donor stories in this book have illustrated. Hannah Quimby is starting to fundamentally change funder-grantee relationships in her home state of Maine. Katherine Lorenz has guided her family foundation to become a working multigenerational team.

The pacing of the revolution is one area where we noted a difference between first-generation *earners* and next generation *inheritors*. While both groups want to revolutionize philanthropy in similar strategic ways—to be more innovative and hands-on, to give and learn more with peers—they differ in their capacity to implement those changes right away. Earners can implement their ideal philanthropic strategy more rapidly, while inheritors usually face the added complication of working through established family structures. Earners can blaze their own trails, while inheritors often have to protect the trails as well as forge ahead.

All next gen donors, however, face the challenge of actually implementing their revolutionary visions, which will not be easy in a field full of large institutions, diverse stakeholders, and entrenched practices. There is no small amount of trepidation among nonprofits, especially about rapid changes that might negatively affect the people they serve or the crucial social outcomes their mission aspires to achieve. This means the Impact Revolution could take longer than next gen donors would like, which could in turn leave them frustrated. But if their focus is impact and they're committed to being engaged, we expect they will stick around to see their changes take full effect.

Will the Golden Age Really Be Golden?

As we discovered in Chapter 1, the next generation of major donors will have more money to give than any previous generation, which is the first requirement for a new Golden Age. The historic wealth concentration we are experiencing in the United States, plus the $59 trillion wealth transfer—most of it occurring among a relatively small group of high-net-worth families—ensures this. And remember, American families with $1 million or more in net worth account for 50 percent of the total amount of charitable contributions, even though they are only 7 percent of the total population—and this concentration of wealth and big giving is likely to increase.[1] But this economic reality, even compounded by the fact that next gen donors want to give throughout their lives rather than only after they retire, doesn't alone guarantee a Golden Age of Giving. These vast resources also need to be given with care.

Next gen donors will likely ruffle a few feathers as they become the donors they aspire to be. Their push to change giving is motivated by good intentions and values, but as we've said (and

267

history has shown), revolutions are messy. To ensure the impact is both genuine and positive, we must try to facilitate healthy and respectful relationships between next gen donors and nonprofits, and between next gen donors and their own families as well as advisors. And we must help ensure that resources end up where they are most needed. But adapting will be well worth the hassle if next gen donors can help move the needle on persistent, complex problems. That possibility alone is enough for us to believe Generation Impact warrants the chance to try to revolutionize giving.

—⸙—

We are resolutely optimistic, but nonetheless we've tried to identify potential shifts as next gen donors enter the playing field. For one, large organizations, intermediaries, and other organizations that have a harder time showing the direct impact of gifts will struggle to attract next gen donors. The same holds for organizations in which opportunities for skills-based engagement by donors are harder to find. Adjusting will require time, effort, and a willingness to reallocate staff and other resources. The upside is that if organizations *can* adapt, engaging next gen donors in the hands-on, meaningful ways they crave, those donors will be both bigger and better donors over a longer period of time.

The Impact Revolution will also blur the boundaries between the for-profit and nonprofit sectors, as next gen donors avidly embrace market solutions to social problems. Of course, there are times when market solutions *can* solve a problem in a more sustainable way—like building a factory to employ locals to make and sell mosquito nets instead of distributing the nets as an act of charity. Next gen social investors are right to be excited about these cases. And we applaud how devoted they are to aligning their capital investments with their social goals, using their economic power to pressure businesses to become more socially responsible, and funneling the increasingly concentrated wealth in our society toward ethical companies and the highest-performing nonprofits. Yet there are times when business solutions can lead to mission creep for nonprofits, and business metrics are not always appropriate to measure the achievement of social goals. We expect that such tensions will continue to arise in new and difficult ways as next gen donors blur the boundaries more and more.

Also, we should never forget that next gen donors, no matter how earnest, will have tremendous power in this Golden Age. Like all donors, they will operate outside of the formal strictures of democratic accountability—free to give, or not to give, to what they want, when they want.[2] We can't vote away their power if they fail. This is why we are strongly encouraged by how frequently and fervently current next gen donors told us they want to be helpful, even humble partners with the groups they support. Whether they maintain this approach will determine whether they are leading a revolution with healthy power dynamics or not. The fact that next gen donors believe so deeply in transparency is encouraging, if they are willing to apply that belief to their own giving and avoid the secrecy of many big donors of the past. Their intense interest in peer engagement can also help—as peers check each other on strategy, they can also balance each other on the misuse of power.

We should note that few next gen donors talked much about how they want to work with government (or not) to help solve social problems—though some did see philanthropy as an experimental realm, where they have the freedom to design innovations that government can then "take to scale." However, as next gen donors ramp up their giving, it will be essential for them to have a clear grasp of how their investments integrate with government efforts on the same causes. This is especially the case in a time of major uncertainty and disagreement about the proper role of government. We suspect if our interviews occurred after the 2016 election there would have been much more discussion of this issue.

Finally, we need to remember that the active donors that we have described in this book are not the only members of the Gen X and Millennial Generations who will eventually become major donors. The concentration and transfer of wealth suggests there will be plenty more on the rise, and they will have plenty of money to give. How can we be sure these not-yet-active next gen donors will be equally forward-thinking, conscientious, and focused on impact?[3]

Here, too, we have some reason for cautious optimism. The current next gen donors we talked with for this book are the pioneers of their generation and are already outspoken proponents of a next gen approach to giving. We believe, based in part on what we've already seen, that their peers will follow their lead and look to learn from their experiences, especially in a generation that is so highly networked. We also know that research has identified distinct "generational personalities," which will likely influence new next gen donors. Still, some of the newer next gen donors will likely come from more diverse social and ethnic groups than current donors, bringing fresh ideas and practices to next gen giving. And as giving continues to expand outside the United States, what next gen donors "look like" will become more complex. Future research should certainly focus on these newer next gen donors.

—❧—

This is a crucial moment in history. Next gen donors are actively taking over big giving in ways that we think will transform philanthropy. Many readers of this book will be supporting these donors along their journeys, as parents, grandparents, siblings, cousins, friends, advisors, grantees, partners, and peers. We hope all we've learned about next gen donors in this book can inform that work, helping both the donors and those engaged with them to take best advantage of their historic opportunity.

Below we summarize the advice offered throughout the book—first, the lessons for nonprofit professionals, families and family staff, and advisors; second, the lessons for next gen donors themselves.

Seek Transformation Not Transaction

Next gen donors are seeking transformation—in themselves, in their interactions with organizations and peers, and in the issues and causes they care about. Nonprofit professionals, family members, advisors, and other staff can help the next gen achieve these transformations and can also benefit in the process. This is because transformation involves trust, genuine partnerships, and long-term, meaningful results—things that will be good for all of us.

Engage next gen donors around their values, not their valuables. Ask them about their values and talk through how those might align with your mission. Help them verbalize and prioritize. Remember, next gen donors want to align all their life choices with their values in seamless ways. Don't be surprised when they make those connections.

Show them the impact your work is having. Help next gen donors see the concrete difference their giving makes—not just the line on the thermometer that will rise a notch with their donation—even if doing so means making a big problem feel smaller and more approachable. Work together with next gen donors to define and clarify what "impact" means for all parties.

271

Welcome the new, even the risky. Take their ideas seriously, both about how to transform strategy and about new tools that hold promise for greater impact. If they give you a gift but also give you an idea, consider whether the idea has merit and longevity. They know not everything will work out—or work out right now—but as Jenna Segal pointed out, the worst thing a nonprofit can do is tell a next gen donor, "We'll take a look at that," and then never follow through. The same can be said for families.

Be open, honest, and probably more transparent than you might like. Next gen donors want to have close and candid relationships, especially with nonprofits. They want to understand the organization "warts and all." Be careful not to make this merely communication *to* these donors; make it conversation *with* them. The relationship should be two-way, not carefully curated and formalized.

Find ways for rising donors to "go all in." Don't just treat them like an ATM or a party planner. They want meaningful engagement with nonprofits and in their families—opportunities that aren't manufactured or put on but that lead to serving an organization. They want to do work that makes a difference, work that takes advantage of the skills and expertise they have to offer, and work that is genuinely needed. So find ways for them to roll up their sleeves and take on real issues that lead to transformation within them and for the organization. Respect them by looking for ways you can grow together.

Embrace their peer orientation and act as a connector. Next gen donors love learning and giving with peers, but they might not know how to find those peers. If an advisor or nonprofit can connect them to like donors, they will appreciate that as significant value added. Also help them find ways to move beyond the transactional "quid pro quo" engagement with peers to a transformational engagement that inspires, educates, and helps them become more strategic. Invite them to tackle a problem with their peers, not just raise money from them.

Help them find their place in the family story. Next gen donors, particularly inheritors, often say they want to be good stewards of their family's legacy, but this often means improving the legacy beyond what they've inherited. Finding their places in narratives that are larger than themselves will help give them more self-confidence, clarity, and sense of control, which are necessary to take this next step. You can be a resource to them as they figure this out.

Appreciate and take advantage of generational differences. Next gen donors believe that every generation brings assets to the work of solving our greatest societal ills. They are ready to take the field alongside other generations, not in place of them. Find ways to make use of the distinct skills of different generations and then call attention to the benefits this brings. Facilitate cross-generational conversations about legacy, strategy, risk, and other aspects of giving. Seek to build peerage among generations. Don't relegate them to the kids' table, because they won't tolerate that for very long and will go elsewhere.

Be a source of learning and experience. These rising donors take their identities and learning journeys seriously and are eager for help along the way. They especially want opportunities to learn from experience, to learn from grantees about what is really needed, and to learn about what is new and innovative in the field. There are too few learning sources in this field geared to new and next gen donors; if you can be one of those sources, they will appreciate you even more.

Help them launch. Give them the power and permission to find their own voices. Help them become the donors they want to be and that we all need them to be.

Use Your Power for Good

Next gen donors, you have incredible power—not just as people with money to give but as the hope for the future of the groups you support, perhaps even for the world. It might not always feel this way, especially to those of you who are just coming into your own as donors, but know that you have power—in your financial resources, in your family legacies, in your networks, even in your youth. But with this power comes responsibility. As you work to find the best way to use your power for good, you might ask yourself, as Bill and Melinda Gates suggested in their annual letter to the field in 2016, "What is your superpower?"[4] Here are the themes that came up in our research to consider as you take the lead in effecting change for the better.

Recognize that you can't innovate your way out of every problem. Sometimes the tried-and-true is still the best solution. When you do have a great new strategic idea or new tool for impact, give your partners—especially older organizations—time to adjust to that new idea and even adapt to implement it. Welcome their questions and try learning about the new tools together. Then celebrate the greater impact your innovation brings.

Listen more than tell. You are asking organizations to respect you as a whole person, as more than a bank account. You want them to open up to you, and to engage you in ways that will cost them time, effort, and even money. Rely on their expertise about the field they've studied and sweated in for years. As you develop respectful, close relationships, you will learn how best to work together and how to speak candidly. Such trust-building takes time. Note that this same nurturing of mutual respect and trust is essential within families. There, even more, try to listen more than you tell—or at least listen *before* you tell.

Prioritize learning, but not at the cost of impact. Look proactively for ways to develop skills, experience, and wisdom, but don't let your own learning curve push impact to the side. There will be times when you confront a trade-off between advancing your learning and achieving the impact you and others want. Choose impact, and you will be surprised how much you learn along the way. If you want to experiment with a new tool to learn how it works, be sure this isn't costing the organization more than helping it. Most important: Remember that failure is a great learning tool but also that it has real consequences for people in need. Don't be afraid to fail, but assess the risk of potential failure carefully so you know if the learning will be worth it.

Be resilient. Don't bail on an organization or on your family if you don't see impact right away or feel you aren't being engaged properly. Many types of impact take a long time to achieve and can be hard to identify. Dig deep, look closely, and ask questions. Your Impact Revolution might be frustrating for the families and organizations that will need to adapt, and it might get frustrating for you to wait on structural and cultural shifts that you think should be self-evident and quick. But don't lose hope. The world needs your energy, drive, persistence, risk-taking, and ability to see a different future. We are all counting on you to bring about the change you want to see in the world.

275

The Next Gen Is the Now Gen

After years of research and other work with next gen donors, our best advice is this: Don't wait! Gen X and Millennial major donors are eager to jumpstart their Impact Revolution—to get their hands dirty and take their seats at the philanthropic table. They might not be the biggest donors to our favorite causes this year, or even for 5 or 10 years to come, but eventually they will be, and then they will give more than any previous generation as they dominate major giving for decades to come. Those organizations, professionals, families, and advisors that can figure out how best to engage next gen donors *now* will gain loyal and active supporters for a very long time.

More broadly, we all need to realize that a revolution is coming, and we need to make the most of it. Learning more about the eager and well-meaning leaders of Generation Impact is a crucial first step in our journey. We hope this book helps us all to make a lasting impact on the world.

APPENDIX

Methods and Data

The candid reflections and insights in this book come from individuals in their 20s and 30s with a capacity for high-level giving now or in the future, many of whom have never before shared their thoughts on philanthropy. Data from these donors comes from an online survey and in-depth, semistructured interviews, and our analysis of this data is based on our combined 40 years of experience in the philanthropic field.

Despite their power to control big giving and a range of social causes for decades to come, there has been surprisingly little research—good or bad—on Gen X and Millennial major donors. We know a bit about giving and philanthropic attitudes among rising generational cohorts overall but less specifically about those people within the cohorts who have the capacity for major giving. And we have some good data on high-net-worth donors in general, but this data is rarely parsed and analyzed in depth by age cohorts.

Because of this, our project was designed from the beginning to be more inductive than deductive, more about asking exploratory and open-ended questions than about testing hypotheses. We also had a distinctly applied orientation, knowing that we wanted our findings to be of direct help to both this population of next gen donors and those who work closely with them. These aspects of our approach influenced our research questions, methods, data collection, analysis, and presentation of the results.

This book builds on a research report published in 2013, which included the survey findings and a subset of interviews but not much discussion of the implications of our findings about next gen donors.[1] This book adds new stories (including the 13 featured donors) and a considerable amount of new data, identifies in greater depth the most significant patterns in what they told us, and highlights implications and advice targeted to specific audiences, from families to wealth advisors to nonprofit professionals and fundraisers.

We sincerely hope this exploratory, generative investigation can now inform additional research on this incredibly important population. We indicate some questions and areas for future research below.

Data Collection and Analysis

The research began in 2011 with an initial literature review, focused on topics such as generational identities and philanthropic preferences, trends and challenges in multigenerational family philanthropy, and giving by high-net-worth donors. This review helped clarify the focus of the study and informed the specific questions for these donors.

Using our relationships with partner organizations across the country, as well as our own organizational lists, in early 2012 we invited potential participants to take our survey and then screened responses to be sure each respondent met our age and financial requirements. The threshold for sufficient financial capacity for high-level giving included both individual and family measures. Respondents had to meet *at least one* of the following requirements:

- Personal net worth of $500,000 or more

- Personal income of $100,000 or more

- Annual personal giving of $5,000 or more

- Annual family giving of $10,000 or more

- Endowed family philanthropic assets of $500,000 or more

A significant majority of respondents qualified on more than one of these criteria, and many far exceeded these minimum levels.

After screening on these criteria, as well as eliminating significantly incomplete responses, our final survey sample included 310 valid respondents, although many specific questions received fewer answers because of attrition or skipped questions. All responses were recorded anonymously.

We designed the survey instrument to get detailed information and open-ended reflections from each respondent. The survey gathered information about each donor's "personal" philanthropy (the giving and volunteering of their immediate household, including spouse or partner and children) and their "family's" philanthropy (the giving and volunteering of extended family, including family giving vehicles such as a family foundation). Questions focused on each donor's range of philanthropic activities, preferred strategies and causes, reasons for giving, sources of information and learning, and demographic details.

We identified interview candidates through our network of project partners, numerous colleagues in the field, and our own networks.[2] In the end, we interviewed a total of 75 individual donors.[3] Interviews were done mostly in person or via Skype (three were conducted only by phone), and lasted from 1 to 2 ½ hours. The interviews were recorded and either fully or partially transcribed.

Interviewees were assured of confidentiality and anonymity, which is why all quotes are given anonymously—except those from the 13 featured donors. Any potentially identifiable information in quotations was removed or anonymized. Quotations, from either the interviews or open-ended survey replies, have been only slightly edited for readability and grammar.

The interviews were conducted on a "guided conversation" model. They probed further into the core research topics listed for the survey above but also asked for more detailed explanations, for examples and stories, and for specific advice these donors would offer to those who want to engage them better.[4]

We asked 13 of the 75 individuals interviewed for this project to become featured, named donors in the book, sharing pieces of their personal story and their reflections on giving in their own words. While all the donors we interviewed were fascinating in some way, the donors we selected to feature had both compelling stories and a particular fit with one or more of the core themes in the book. After gaining their permission, we provided an initial draft of their feature based on portions of their interview transcript. They edited the drafts, sometimes extensively, adding new details and examples. After additional editing stages, the words presented now in the book as each donor's first-person account—and any other quotes we provide in the book from these named donors—have been approved by each donor.

Excel and SPSS statistical software were used to generate frequencies and cross-tabulations of the survey data and to conduct Chi-square significance tests. A portion of the interview transcripts were coded using NVivo qualitative research software, primarily in the first phase of the research as a way to codify and confirm emergent themes and patterns.

Our analysis of all the data, and our interpretation of the most significant patterns in what these donors told us, is based in part on what we've learned during our decades of experience studying and working to improve philanthropy. We also draw implications for what the numerous findings mean for those who engage next gen donors professionally or in their families and for all of us who care about the causes and benefit from the organizations these donors support.

Note that the full set of 75 interviews provides the bulk of the data cited in this book. Only a few of the specific numbers from the survey data are cited here, though some of the quotations in the book came from open-ended questions from the survey—and of course many of the patterns and themes we explore here emerged initially in our analysis of the survey.[5]

Characteristics of the Sample

Some of the next gen donors we describe throughout this book have last names that nearly every U.S. citizen will recognize; others have little or no public profile as donors, despite devoting a high percentage of their earnings, and much of their free time, to philanthropic passions. We surveyed and talked to first-generation wealth creators as well as inheritors; among the latter were widely varying degrees and types of engagement in broader family giving processes. Some are next gen members of families with massive global foundations; others hail from families with small foundations giving only in specific regions.

The donors examined in this book give through giving circles, through their own donor-advised funds, and through many other vehicles and charitable activities such as online, in-kind, and event giving. Some focus as much on making impacts with their investments as their gifts. Most of the donors serve as volunteers in some capacity and have since early in their lives. Some are both donors and professionals working in the philanthropic field—running their families' foundations, working for philanthropy support organizations, and so on. Others prefer that their friends and neighbors don't know how big a donor they or their family are and will be in the future.

We worked hard to contact a large and diverse sample of this generally hard-to-reach population. In selecting the samples for both the survey and interviews, intentional efforts were made to increase diversity along several key dimensions, including age, gender, race or ethnicity, and geographic distribution. We also actively sought to include many donors who were themselves first-generation wealth creators, even though these are harder to identify because they are less likely to be connected to a known giving institution (like a multigenerational family foundation).

Table A.1 summarizes the demographic and other personal characteristics of the sample of next gen donors in the survey and interviews.[6]

On the whole, the next gen donors referenced in this book are highly educated and employed full-time. The majority are married but without children, and two-thirds are women. Their income, wealth, and levels of giving and endowed charitable assets (either personal or family) place them in the top tiers of socioeconomic status and philanthropic contributions in the United States. They clearly have significant capacity for major giving now and in the future.

The age range we focused on (21 to 40) includes, roughly, the younger half of the Gen X Generation and the older half of the Millennial Generation. We zeroed in on that age range because that is the time in next gen donors' lives when they are settling into their roles as major donors—when they are taking a more formal

Table A.1 Demographic and Other Characteristics of Survey and Interview Samples

	Survey	Interviews
Gender	*n = 224*	*n = 65*
Female	63.8%	63.1%
Male	36.2	36.9
Age	*n = 310*	*n = 64*
21–25	13.5	7.8
26–30	31.0	35.9
31–35	31.9	17.2
36–40	23.5	35.9
Older than 40	0.0	3.1
Race/Ethnicity	*n = 225*	*n = 64*
Caucasian	95.6	89.1
African American/Black	0.9	4.7
Latino(a)/Hispanic	0.4	1.6
Asian American	2.2	7.8
Arab American	0.0	1.6
Native American or Alaska Native	0.4	0.0
Native Hawaiian or Other Pacific Islander	0.9	0.0
Mixed Racial/Ethnic Heritage	1.8	6.3
Other	2.7	3.1
Education	*n = 227*	*n = 65*
Professional Degree or Doctoral Degree	8.8	10.8
Master's Degree	45.4	36.9
Bachelor's Degree	44.5	52.3
Associate's Degree	0.4	0.0
High School Degree/GED	0.9	0.0
Marital/Partnership Status	*n = 226*	*n = 64*
Married or long-term partnership	60.6	54.7
Single, never married or partnership	34.5	37.5
Single, divorced	4.0	1.6
Separated	0.4	1.6
Other	0.4	4.7
Children 18 or Under in Household	*n = 227*	*n = 63*
0	61.2	76.2
1 to 3	38.8	23.8

(continued)

Table A.1   *(continued)*

	Survey	Interviews
Residence	*n = 194*	*n = 63*
Northeast	31.4	35.0
Great Lakes/Midwest	20.7	12.7
South/South Atlantic	23.2	15.9
Pacific/Mountain	24.8	36.5
Employment Status	*n = 227*	*n = 64*
Full-time (40 hours a week or more)	61.2	54.7
Part-time (fewer than 40 hours a week)	13.2	6.3
Self-employed	8.8	25.0
Student, not also employed	8.4	9.4
Stay-at-home parent, not also employed	5.3	3.1
Other	3.1	1.6
Political Affiliation	*n = 225*	*n = 63*
Extremely Liberal	12.4	20.6
Liberal	42.7	52.4
Moderate/Independent	27.6	23.8
Conservative	13.8	3.2
Extremely Conservative	1.8	0.0
Don't know	1.8	0.0
Religious Affiliation	*n = 225*	*n = 63*
Christian	34.7	22.2
Jewish	32.0	28.6
Buddhist	1.3	3.2
Hindu	0.0	1.6
Agnostic	12.0	15.9
Atheist	4.9	14.3
Unaffiliated	12.0	9.5
Other	3.1	4.8
Religious Attendance	*n = 224*	*n = 63*
More than once a week	2.2	0.0
Once a week	13.8	4.8
Once a month	25.0	17.5
Once a year	10.3	12.7
Less than once a year	4.5	4.8
Only on holy days	24.1	33.3
Never	20.1	27.0

Table A.1   *(continued)*

	Survey	Interviews
Generation of Wealth	*n = 307*	*n = 38*
I am the primary wealth creator	7.2	15.8
Other family members in my generation	2.0	2.6
My parents' generation	41.0	34.2
My grandparents' generation	34.9	18.4
My great-grandparents' generation	12.1	15.8
Generations before my great-grandparents	2.3	10.5
Don't know	0.7	2.6
Personal Annual Income	*n = 272*	*n = 61*
$50,000 or less	23.5	9.8
$50,000–$100,000	21.3	21.3
$100,000–$500,000	47.8	54.1
$500,000–$1 million	4.8	6.6
More than $1 million	2.6	8.2
Personal Net Worth	*n = 274*	*n = 61*
$100,000 or less	17.9	8.2
$100,000–$500,000	24.8	6.6
$500,000–$1 million	14.6	14.8
$1 million–$10 million	34.3	42.6
More than $10 million	8.4	27.9
Personal Annual Giving	*n = 310*	*n = 62*
Not currently giving personal money	2.6	0.0
$1,000 or less	29.0	8.1
$1,000–$5,000	26.2	16.1
$5,000–$10,000	15.1	17.8
$10,000–$50,000	19.4	29.0
$50,000–$100,000	3.5	6.5
More than $100,000	4.2	22.6
Family Annual Giving	*n = 303*	*n = 60*
$10,000 or less	12.5	3.3
$10,000–$50,000	16.9	10.0
$50,000–$250,000	15.9	18.3
$250,000–$1 million	27.8	16.7
$1 million–$5 million	10.9	31.7
More than $5 million	12.2	13.3
Don't know	4.0	6.7

(continued)

Table A.1   *(continued)*

	Survey	Interviews
Family Endowed Philanthropic Assets	*n = 303*	*n = 60*
$500,000 or less	16.5	10.0
$500,000–$5 million	16.8	13.3
$5 million–$25 million	15.5	21.7
$25 million–$100 million	14.2	23.3
$100 million–$500 million	5.3	8.3
More than $500 million	1.3	3.3
Don't know	30.4	20.0

role in their family's foundation, for example, or starting to think about how they want to give the wealth they are creating in their burgeoning careers or inheriting as part of the wealth transfer. Note that the ages summarized in Table A.1 reflect the respondents' ages at the time they took the survey or sat for an interview.[7]

This research was deliberately limited to next gen high-capacity donors based in the United States, although it did include donors from across the country and many individuals with global families and global philanthropic interests. We hope this study can prompt additional research on next gen donors in other countries, and the growing number of major donors who transcend national boundaries in both their giving and their living.[8]

The sample for both the survey and the interviews included many donors who self-identified as liberal/progressive or moderate in political orientation, and very few who said they were conservative. This is due, in part, to the fact that these generational cohorts, overall, skew more liberal and progressive than previous generations.[9] There are also several established next gen donor networks on the progressive end of the spectrum but fewer on the conservative end. We tried to increase the number of political conservatives in the interview sample, but were unable to connect extensively with donors from that community. Although we did find that the political conservatives we interviewed were not notably different on key elements of the next gen approach to giving, we hope future research can investigate these questions further.

There are also significantly more Jews in our sample of next gen donors than in the general U.S. population, perhaps because of Sharna's history and ties to the Jewish philanthropic community. The upside of this experience is that we were able to get more next gen donors overall to participate in the study and speak candidly about their philanthropy. Regardless, the oversample is not as dramatic as it might seem given that Jews are a higher percentage of the high-net-worth population in the United States than in the general population.[10]

The number of nonwhite next gen donors in our samples is also considerably smaller than in the general population. This is due to the much smaller percentage of the high-net-worth population in the United States that is nonwhite, especially African American and Latino(a)/Hispanic. In fact, our interview sample includes a *higher* percentage of donors from some of those non-white race/ethnic categories (and those of mixed heritage) than is found among high-net-worth individuals overall.[11] Again, we made special efforts to reach out through networks to identify next gen donors from diverse racial and ethnic categories.

Current Limitations and Future Research

As an exploratory, cross-sectional study on a difficult-to-reach population, this study has certain limitations, ones we hope any research that builds on this study can overcome. For one thing, this study primarily examined what next gen donors think and say about their philanthropic approach and action rather than on a direct observation of their activity. We include self-reported measures of their behavior instead of just analyzing their attitudes or beliefs about hypothetical behavior. We report our findings here through the lens of a combined 40 plus years of experiences observing and working with next gen donors, and have confidence in our assessment; that said, we know not everything research subjects say is reflected in what they do, so future research that focuses on close observations of next gen donor behavior will be important.

Similarly, while we identify instances when our findings about the philanthropic preferences and approach of next gen donors are similar or different to previous research on older donors, many of the differences between generations discussed in this book are based on what the next gen donors say they *perceive* as clear differences. It is important to remember that their parents and grandparents—and other major donors from previous generations—would likely not agree with all of the next gen donors' assessments of differences. Future research that examines perceptions of the next gen by older generations would be interesting, as well as additional research that compares similar data on philanthropic practices and philosophies as expressed by each generation.

Another challenge for a study like this is: How do we know if the approach that next gen donors favor now will be the same across their lifetimes? Which of the findings in this book are due to a distinctive generational perspective on giving by Gen Xers or Millennials, and which are merely what any emerging donors of this age prefer? How much of what we report in this book is a cohort effect, and how much is a life cycle effect? To be sure, this book provides a picture of next gen donors at a specific point in time and at one point in their developments. But even taken in the most limited sense, we think this book is useful as a snapshot of next gen donors as they are today, in this crucial moment when they are becoming more engaged in giving.

We also have some reason to believe the findings here are more than temporary features. We know that research (cited earlier) has identified distinct generational personalities that endure across each generation's lifetimes and that developmental psychology tells us the character traits and preferences we form in our emerging adult years will form the core of our personalities over the life course. This means we can expect that many aspects of the next gen donors presented here will persist as they age. However, we also hope these questions can be answered in future longitudinal studies that track these donors as they age and take on more and more responsibility in philanthropic circles. This book can be useful, then, as a benchmark because these donors are the first group of philanthropists in history to be giving so much at such young ages, so we can now track their attitudes and actions over the course of their lives. As the most significant philanthropists ever, we hope they will be studied for a long time.

Finally, as noted in the conclusion, our sample of next gen donors includes some selection bias. The donors included in this study are those who are currently active—some much more than others, of course—in philanthropy, enough to at least be in the process of forming a philanthropic identity and a set of ideas and plans about their giving. We cannot claim, then, that they are fully representative of the full population of Gen X or Millennial individuals who will eventually become major donors. There are surely many others in this age group who have yet to begin their philanthropic journeys. As an initial, inductive, generative study of an understudied and exclusive population, we accept a certain amount of selection bias as unavoidable. And as described earlier, the sample we study here will be leaders of the larger cohort as it emerges, so there is a research purpose to focusing closely on them in this initial examination. The next gen donors in this book are blazing the next gen's path for the future of giving, and as their peers begin to join them they will not only be influenced by similar generational dynamics but will also look to their already active peers for guidance and inspiration. Again, only further research on the broad range of next gen donors will help us know whether the clear trends we've explored in this book continue as the next gen takes over big giving in the United States.

NOTES

Chapter 1: Introduction

1. For more examples like these, see Joel L. Fleishman, J. Scott Kohler, and Steven Schindler, *Casebook for The Foundation: A Great American Secret* (New York: Public Affairs Books, 2007).
2. See Waldemar A. Nielsen, *Golden Donors: A New Anatomy of the Great Foundations* (New York: Routledge, 2001).
3. Sean Parker, "Philanthropy for Hackers," *The Wall Street Journal*, June 26, 2015. Sean Parker, age 37 at the time of writing, is the founder of Napster, former president of Facebook, and a tech entrepreneur and investor.
4. For example, see John J. Havens and Paul G. Schervish, *A Golden Age of Philanthropy Still Beckons: National Wealth Transfer and Potential for Philanthropy Technical Report* (Boston College Center on Wealth and Philanthropy, 2014); Leslie R. Crutchfield, John V. Kanna, and Mark R. Kramer, *Do More Than Give: The Six Practices of Donors Who Change the World* (San Francisco: Jossey-Bass, 2011); Leslie Lenkowsky, "Big Philanthropy," *The Wilson Quarterly 31*(1) (2007): 47–51; Peter Singer, "What Should a Billionaire Give—and What Should You?," *The New York Times Magazine*, December 17, 2006.
5. Emmanuel Saez and Gabriel Zucman, "Wealth and Inequality in the United States Since 1913: Evidence from Capitalized Income Tax Data" (working paper 20625, National Bureau of Economic Research, Washington, D.C., 2014).
6. Chuck Collins and Josh Hoxie, *Billionaire Bonanza Report: The Forbes 400 and the Rest of Us* (Washington, D.C.: Institute for Policy Studies, 2015). Deborah Hardoon, *An Economy for the 99%* (Oxford, U.K.: Oxfam International, 2017). See also Credit Suisse, *Global Wealth Databook 2016* (Zurich: Credit Suisse AG Research Institute, 2016).
7. Saez and Zucman, "Wealth and Inequality."

8. Lawrence Mishel and Alyssa Davis, *Top CEOs Make 300 Times More than Typical Workers* (issue brief #399, Economic Policy Institute, Washington, D.C., 2015).

9. Based on data published annually in *Forbes* magazine. For historical data, see "Number of Billionaires in the United States from 1987 to 2012," http://www.statista.com/statistics/220093/number-of-billionaires-in-the-united-states/.

10. *The 2016 U.S. Trust Study of High Net Worth Philanthropy* (U.S. Trust and Indiana University Lilly Family School of Philanthropy, 2016). John J. Havens, Mary A. O'Herlihy, and Paul G. Schervish, "Charitable Giving: How Much, By Whom, To What, and How?," in *The Nonprofit Sector: A Research Handbook,* ed. Walter W. Powell and Richard Steinberg, 2nd ed. (New Haven, CT: Yale University Press, 2006).

11. Havens and Schervish, *Golden Age.* Note that the $59 trillion figure does not include the full value of assets transferred during the family members' lifetimes, so the total transfer is likely to be higher. Also, this estimate is based on fairly conservative economic projections for the coming decades. Much more wealth could be transferred, in the end.

12. This complex picture of the Gen X and Millennial generational personalities emerges from the considerable cultural commentary and limited scholarly research on these generations. See, for instance, Paul Taylor, *The Next America: Boomers, Millennials and the Looming Generational Showdown* (New York: PublicAffairs, 2014); Jean Twenge, *Generation Me: Why Today's Young Americans Are More Confident, Assertive, Entitled—And More Miserable Than Ever Before,* Revised and Updated Edition (New York: Atria, 2014); Neil Howe, "Generation X: Once Extreme, Now Exhausted," *Forbes,* August 27, 2014; Joel Stein, "Millennials: The Me Me Me Generation," *Time,* May 20, 2013; Christine Henseler, ed., *Generation X Goes Global: Mapping a Youth Culture in Motion* (New York: Routledge, 2012); Paul Taylor and Scott Keeter, eds., *Millennials: Confident. Connected. Open to Change,* (Pew Research Center, 2010); Bernard Rosen, *Masks and Mirrors: Generation X and the Chameleon Personality* (Westport, CT: Praeger, 2001); Neil Howe and William Strauss, *Millennials Rising: The Next Great Generation* (New York: Vintage Books, 2000).

13. There is some emerging evidence that, on the whole, Gen Xers and Millennials are giving slightly less than previous generations at the same time in their lives. But this finding is for people of all levels of wealth in these generations, not those at the top end. Interestingly, this finding also seems to be true for men only, not women. See Women's Philanthropy Institute, *WomenGive16* (Indiana University Lilly Family School of Philanthropy, 2016). As the Appendix shows, two-thirds of our survey and interview samples were women.

14. Our focus in this book is on the next gen donors who are most active and reflective about their giving at this stage in their lives. See Chapter 12 and the Appendix for the implications—positive and negative—of this limitation of our study.
15. This book builds on our widely cited 2013 report: 21/64 and Dorothy A. Johnson Center for Philanthropy, *Next Gen Donors: Respecting Legacy, Revolutionizing Philanthropy* (2013); it's available at nextgendonors.org. The report was discussed in articles, blogs, and op-eds published in the *New York Times, Forbes, Chronicle of Philanthropy, Stanford Social Innovation Review, Huffington Post, Alliance,* and elsewhere. For summaries we wrote at the time, see Sharna Goldseker and Michael Moody, "Young Wealthy Donors Bring Taste for Risk, Hands-On Involvement to Philanthropy," *Chronicle of Philanthropy*, May 19, 2013, and Amy Clarke et al., "What do the next generation of major donors want?," *Alliance 18*(4) (December 2013).

Chapter 2: Show Me the Impact

1. Mark Zuckerberg, age 33 at the time of this writing, is the chairman, chief executive, and cofounder of Facebook. As of 2016, his net worth was well over $50 billion. His wife, Dr. Priscilla Chan, is a pediatrician and former high school teacher. Their other philanthropic initiatives have included $100 million to reform the Newark (NJ) public schools, $120 million to San Francisco Bay Area public schools, and nearly $1 billion worth of Facebook stock to the Silicon Valley Community Foundation.
2. See the Chan Zuckerberg Initiative homepage: chanzuckerberg.com.
3. See www.goodventures.org and www.openphilanthropy.org. As Ms. Tuna put it in an interview, "The charities that are the most aggressive and best at marketing aren't necessarily the ones doing the most good." Quoted in Vindu Goel, "Philanthropy in Silicon Valley: Big Bets on Big Ideas," *New York Times,* November 4, 2016, p. F7.
4. Parker, "Philanthropy for Hackers" (see Chap. 1, n. 3).
5. Quote from the website of the Parker Foundation: parker.org/about.
6. See *The 2016 U.S. Trust Study; Cause, Influence, and the Next Generation Workforce: The 2015 Millennial Impact Report* (Achieve, Inc., 2015) (see Chap. 1, n. 10); K. M. Rosqueta, K. Noonan, and M. Shark, "I'm Not Rockefeller: Implications for Major Foundations Seeking to Engage Ultra-High-Net-Worth Donors," *The Foundation Review 3*(4) (2011): 96–109; A. Goldberg, K. Pittelman, and Resource Generation, *Creating Change through Family Philanthropy: The Next Generation* (Brooklyn, NY: Soft Skull Press, 2006); Paul G. Schervish, "Today's wealth holder and tomorrow's giving: The new dynamics of wealth and philanthropy," *Journal of Gift Planning* 9 (2005): 15–37; F. Ostrower, *Why the Wealthy Give:*

The Culture of Elite Philanthropy (Princeton, NJ: Princeton University Press, 1995).

7. P. Slovic et al., "Psychic numbing and mass atrocity," in *The Behavioral Foundations of Public Policy,* ed. E. Shafir (Princeton, NJ: Princeton University Press), 126–142.

8. Perhaps this is why aid organizations often highlight a single individual story of suffering—"Help the little girl who lost her home"—rather than offer overwhelming statistics—"Help the 3 million people affected by the hurricane." *New York Times* columnist Nicholas Kristof makes this argument in N. D. Kristof and S. WuDunn, *A Path Appears: Transforming Lives, Creating Opportunity* (New York: Alfred A. Knopf, 2015), 191–195.

9. See S. Colby, N. Stone, and P. Cartarr, "Zeroing in on Impact: In an Era of Declining Resources, Nonprofits Need to Clarify Their Intended Impact," *Stanford Social Innovation Review* (Fall 2004), http://centreonphilanthropy .com/files/kb_articles/1251128244Zeroing%20in%20on%20Impact.pdf.

10. This question of perpetuity versus "spending down" did not come up in our interviews much, but when it did it was often when a next gen donor was arguing passionately for spending down in order to have maximum impact now rather than later. Still, 10.1 percent of donors in our survey said they had plans for a bequest or were using a gift annuity or other planned giving vehicle.

11. This debate has become an especially hot one in the nonprofit world recently. See Paul Shoemaker, "Reconstructing Philanthropy from the Outside In," *Stanford Social Innovation Review* (February 2015); Dan Pallotta, *Uncharitable: How Restraints on Nonprofits Undermine Their Potential* (Lebanon, NH: Tufts University Press, 2008); and the website for the Overhead Myth campaign (overheadmyth.com).

12. U. Gneezy, E. Keenan, and A. Gneezy, "Behavioral economics: Avoiding overhead aversion in charity," *Science* (October 31, 2014).

Chapter 3: Changing Strategies for a New Golden Age

1. Those in our survey who said their causes were different were much more likely to also say they were not very involved in their family's giving.

2. See Paul Brest, "Strategic Philanthropy and Its Discontents," *Stanford Social Innovation Review* (April 2015); Crutchfield, Kanna, and Kramer, *Do More Than Give*; Patricia Patrizi and Elizabeth Heid Thompson, "Beyond the Veneer of Strategic Philanthropy," *The Foundation Review* 2 (2011): 52–60; Thomas J. Tierney and Joel L. Fleishman, *Give Smart: Philanthropy That Gets Results* (New York: Public Affairs Books, 2011); Peter Frumkin, *Strategic Giving: The Art and Science of Philanthropy* (Chicago: University of Chicago Press, 2006).

3. The survey defined "family" giving as the giving vehicles used by the donor's extended family—most commonly a family foundation created by a previous generation. "Personal" giving was giving by the next gen donor, his or her spouse/partner, and children.

4. See Olivier Zunz, *Philanthropy in America: A History* (Princeton, NJ: Princeton University Press, 2012); Peter Dobkin Hall, "A Historical Overview of Philanthropy, Voluntary Associations, and Nonprofit Organizations in the United States, 1600–2000," in *The Nonprofit Sector: A Research Handbook,* ed. Walter W. Powell and Richard Steinberg, 2nd ed (New Haven, CT: Yale University Press, 2006).

5. While next gen donors are clearly more focused than previous generations on giving to racial justice and social justice/civil rights causes—including, as the next chapter shows, giving for movement organizing—this was still not a common response when we asked them about their primary philanthropic passions. Even the donors of color we spoke with tended to talk more about changing strategies and innovating new tools than about shifting the funding landscape toward greater funding for racial or social justice. They do want this shift, it was just not as salient in their comments as the desire to change giving strategies.

6. See Taylor, *Next America*, pp. 8, 30, and 119 (see Chap. 1, n. 12); Taylor and Keeter, *Millennials*; L. Kaufman, "Selling green: What managers and marketers need to know about consumer environmental attitudes," *Environmental Quality Management 8*(4) (1999): 11–20.

7. Peter Diamandis, *Abundance: The Future Is Better Than You Think* (New York: Free Press, 2012).

8. Some studies have shown that while donors say information is important to them, they do not necessarily actually retrieve and use that information when making giving decisions. See Hope Consulting, *Money for Good II* (San Francisco: Hope Consulting, 2011).

Chapter 4: Why Not Innovate?

1. Pavithra Mohan, "Here's Why the Chan Zuckerberg Initiative is an LLC, According to Zuck," *Fast Company* (December 3, 2015). See also Megan O'Neil, "Chan Responds to Questions About Plans for Facebook Fortune," *Chronicle of Philanthropy*, December 22, 2015; Benjamin Soskis, "Will Zuckerberg and Chan's $45bn Pledge Change Philanthropy?," *The Guardian*, December 2, 2015.

2. "Double-bottom-line" businesses or social enterprises are ones that prioritize and measure their social impacts alongside their financial profits. "Triple-bottom-line" adds environmental impacts as a third factor that businesses seeks to maximize.

3. This mindset also shows up in the interest of younger generations in finding careers where they can "do good while doing well." See Achieve, Inc., *Cause, Influence*; (see Chap. 2, n. 6); J. M. Twenge et al., "Generational differences in work values: Leisure and extrinsic values increasing, social and intrinsic values decreasing," *Journal of Management 36*(5) (2010): 1117–1142.

4. Other critics argue for treating the 5 percent more as a floor than a ceiling for grant-making, and even argue for "spending down" endowments by upping grant levels to meet today's urgent needs. Some next gen donors we spoke with were strong advocates of this approach, and some argued against foundations existing "in perpetuity." But this viewpoint was not as widely popular as the belief that *whatever* funds are in an endowment must be invested with social impact in mind.

5. See Antony Bugg-Levine and Jed Emerson, *Impact Investing: Transforming How We Make Money While Making a Difference* (San Francisco: Jossey-Bass, 2011).

6. This approach has appeal to other generations of wealthy individuals, some of whom have embraced so-called "philanthrocapitalism." See Matthew Bishop and Michael Green, *Philanthrocapitalism: How the Rich Can Save the World* (New York: Bloomsbury Press, 2008).

7. A B Corp is a for-profit entity that is certified as meeting "rigorous standards of social and environmental performance, accountability, and transparency" (see bcorporation.net). Some states also allow companies to legally register as "Benefit Corporations" or "L3Cs" (Low-profit Limited Liability Corporations). On the appeal of these to Millennials, see Chris Miller, "Millennials and Hybrid Legal Structures Are Here to Stay," *Stanford Social Innovation Review* (July 2016).

8. Patagonia website November 2016. Patagonia has been a certified B Corp since December 2011.

9. The distinction between a 501(c)(3) and 501(c)(4) organization is one made by the IRS code for tax-exempt entities. Most traditional nonprofits are (c)(3), which means they are tax-exempt and can receive tax-deductible donations, but are very limited in the amount of lobbying they can do. A (c)(4) organization is also tax-exempt, but contributors cannot deduct their donations; in turn, (c)(4)s can engage in more substantial lobbying and even some election-related activities. Neither type of organization can endorse candidates, though.

10. Rockefeller Sr., with his close advisor Frederick Taylor Gates, developed ways to give more efficiently and effectively—part of an approach historians have come to call "scientific philanthropy." He also, along with the likes of Andrew Carnegie, encouraged fellow philanthropists to do the same. See John D. Rockefeller, "Some Random Reminiscences of Men and Events," *The World's Work* (October 1908).

11. ESG is an abbreviation for "environmental, social, and governance"—three common factors by which investments are judged to determine their ethical impact and social responsibility.

12. More information at: theimpact.org

13. Our findings about the vehicles used by the next gen match those found in other research studies conducted on giving by Gen Xers and Millennials overall: See Achieve, Inc., *Cause, Influence*; (see Chap. 2, n. 6); Mark Rovner, *The Charitable Habits of Generations Y, X, Baby Boomers, and Matures* (Blackbaud, 2013). Note that the major shift in philanthropy toward using donor-advised funds (DAFs) rather than foundations wasn't something that next gen donors talked much about. They were more concerned with whether *any* vehicle allowed them to be more strategic and more closely engaged. But some donors who were part of multigenerational family foundations liked having a personal DAF as it gave them this opportunity to give in their own way. Among our survey respondents, 20 percent had a personal DAF, and 42 percent said their families had a DAF.

14. Goel, "Philanthropy in Silicon Valley" (see Chap. 2, n. 3).

15. A recent report in the field noted that Millennials were already significantly more likely than Boomers to incorporate new trends into their giving and investing. The report even labeled them the "Impact Generation" because of their concern for having impact with all their assets. See *The Future of Philanthropy: Where Individual Giving is Going* (Fidelity Charitable, 2016). See also Achieve, Inc., *Cause, Influence*; (see Chap. 2, n. 6).

16. For example, Mark Zuckerberg's first major foray into big giving, a $100 million grant to improve public education in Newark, New Jersey, was prominently criticized for failing to achieve its ambitious goals and failing to help school children in need. For his part, Mr. Zuckerberg acknowledges they didn't achieve the impact they wanted, but points to some successes in Newark, and emphasizes what he learned that will now help him in his future (even larger) investments in education and other areas. See Dale Russakoff, *The Prize: Who's in Charge of America's Schools?* (Boston: Houghton Mifflin Harcourt, 2015); Benjamin Herold, "Zuckerberg Talks Personalized Learning, Philanthropy, and Lessons From Newark," *EdWeek 35*(23) (2016): 1, 11.

17. Christian Seelos and Johanna Mair, "Innovation is Not the Holy Grail," *Stanford Social Innovation Review* (Fall 2012).

18. See Angela M. Eikenberry, "Refusing the Market: A Democratic Discourse for Voluntary and Nonprofit Organizations," *Nonprofit and Voluntary Sector Quarterly 38*(4) (2009): 582–596; Patricia Mooney Nickel and Angela M. Eikenberry, "A Critique of the Discourse of Marketized Philanthropy," *American Behavioral Scientist* 52 (2009): 974–989.

19. Veronica Dagher, "To Woo Millennials, Financial Advisers Turn to Their Charitable Side," *Wall Street Journal*, June 5, 2017.

Chapter 5: The "Do Something" Generation

1. See S. E. Helms, "Involuntary Volunteering: The Impact of Mandated Service in Public Schools," *Economics of Education Review* 36 (2013): 295–310; and *Volunteer Growth in America: A Review of Trends Since 1974,* (Washington D.C.: Corporation for National and Community Service, December 2006).
2. For other studies that show this penchant for giving time among Millennials overall, see Kara D. Saratovsky and Derrick Feldmann, *Cause for Change: The Why and How of Nonprofit Millennial Engagement* (San Francisco: Jossey-Bass, 2013); and Center on Philanthropy at Indiana University, "Charitable Giving and the Millennial Generation," *Giving USA Spotlight* 2 (2010): 1–12.
3. Nonprofits looking to engage next gen donors effectively as volunteers as part of a fundraising strategy can find practical tips and tools in Emily Davis, *Fundraising and the Next Generation* (Hoboken, NJ: Wiley, 2012).

Chapter 6: More Than an ATM

1. We should point out that, when used effectively, a youth advisory committee or junior board can be a powerful tool for engaging next gen donors into the core work of a nonprofit, or to get the next gen involved in a family foundation in powerful ways. See Kevin Laskowski, Annie Hernandez, and Katie Marcus Reker, "Igniting the Spark: Creating Effective Next Generation Boards," (*Passages Issue Brief,* National Center for Family Philanthropy, June 2013).
2. For examples as well as suggestions for nonprofits, see Derrick Feldmann and Emily Yu, "Millennials and the Social Sector: What's Next?," *Stanford Social Innovation Review* (June 18, 2014); Saratovsky and Feldmann, *Cause for Change.*
3. BoardSource, *Leading with Intent: A National Index of Nonprofit Board Practices* (Washington, D.C.: BoardSource, 2015).

Chapter 7: Inspirational Peer Pressure

1. See Christine Barton, Jeff Fromm, and Chris Egan, *The Millennial Consumer: Debunking Stereotypes* (Boston: Boston Consulting Group, 2012); Taylor and Keeter, *Millennials* (see Chap. 3, n. 6).
2. For additional evidence of this, see Saratovsky and Feldmann, *Cause for Change*; Davis, *Fundraising*; Stephanie M. Lerner, "Next-Generation Philanthropy: Examining a Next-Generation Jewish Philanthropy Network," *The Foundation Review* 3(4) (2011): 82–95; and for evidence outside the United States, see Charities Aid Foundation, *The Future Stars of*

Philanthropy: How the Next Generation Can Shape a Bright Future (London: Charities Aid Foundation, 2013).

3. See Zunz, *Philanthropy in America* (see Chap. 3, n. 4); Hall, "Historical Overview" (see Chap. 3, n. 4); Ostrower, *Why the Wealthy* (see Chap. 2, n. 6); and Nielsen, *The Golden Donors* (see Chap. 1, n. 2).

4. See Crutchfield, Kanna, and Kramer, *Do More than Give* (see Chap. 3, n. 2); Ellen Remmer, *What's a Donor to Do? The State of Donors Resources in America Today* (Boston: The Philanthropic Initiative, Inc., 2000).

5. These other organizations providing learning materials and programming include the Foundation Center/GrantCraft, the Giving Pledge, Rockefeller Philanthropy Advisors, Synergos, and The Philanthropy Workshop. Exponent Philanthropy, Resource Generation, Slingshot, many community foundations, and other organizations offer next gen peer networks and giving circles as well.

6. See L. A. Hill et al., *Collective Genius: The Art and Practice of Leading Innovation* (Brighton, MA: Harvard Business Review Press, 2014).

Chapter 8: Living Values Seamlessly

1. See *2016 U.S. Trust Study* (see Chap. 1, n. 10); Rosqueta, Noonan, and Shark, "I'm Not Rockefeller" (see Chap. 2, n. 6); Schervish, "Today's wealth" (see Chap. 2, n. 6); Ostrower, *Why the Wealthy* (see Chap. 2, n. 6).

2. "These 20 Heroes Under 40 Give Millennials a Good Name," *Observer*, March 30, 2016.

3. Jane Fonda is a well-known, award-winning actor, political activist, writer, former fashion model, and fitness guru. She is also a founder, along with Robin Morgan and Gloria Steinem, of the Women's Media Center.

4. Pat Mitchell is a veteran news producer, best known as the first woman to be president and CEO of PBS. She is the chair of the Women's Media Center and on numerous other boards.

5. Lynne C. Lancaster and David Stillman, *When Generations Collide: Who They Are. Why They Clash. How to Solve the Generational Puzzle at Work.* (New York: Harper Business, 2002).

6. See Bugg-Levine and Emerson, *Impact Investing* (see Chap. 4, n. 5); Jed Emerson, "The Blended Value Proposition: Integrating Social and Financial Returns," *California Management Review* 45(4) (2003): 35–51.

7. See Peter Singer, *The Life You Can Save: Acting Now to End World Poverty* (New York: Random House, 2009).

8. *Mind the Gaps: The 2015 Deloitte Millennial Survey* (Deloitte Touche Tohmatsu Limited, 2015).

9. Aaron Hurst, *The Purpose Economy: How Your Desire for Impact, Personal Growth and Community Is Changing the World* (Boise, ID: Elevate, 2014).

Chapter 9: On the Shoulders of Giants

1. This metaphor was originally used by Newton in a 1675 letter to Robert Hooke. On the origins of the aphorism, see Robert K. Merton, *On the Shoulders of Giants: A Shandean Postscript* (Chicago: University of Chicago Press, [1965] 1993).
2. As reported in Bruce Feiler, "The Stories that Bind Us," *New York Times*, March 15, 2013.
3. Ibid.
4. Tivadar Soros, *Masquerade: The Incredible True Story of How George Soros' Father Outsmarted the Gestapo.* trans. Humphrey Tonkin (New York: Arcade Publishing, [1965] 2011), p. 203.
5. Robert L. Payton and Michael Moody, "Stewardship," in *Philanthropy in America: A Comprehensive Historical Encyclopedia,* ed. Dwight F. Burlingame (Santa Barbara, CA: ABC-CLIO, Inc., 2004), pp. 457–460.
6. On ethical wills, see Susan B. Turnbull, *The Wealth of Your Life: A Step-by-Step Guide for Creating Your Ethical Will,* 3rd ed. (Charlotte, NC: St. Benedict Press, 2012); Eric Weiner, *Words from the HEART: A Practical Guide to Writing an Ethical Will* (Deutsch-Weiner Enterprises, Inc., and Family Legacy Advisor, 2010).
7. See U.S. Trust, *2016 U.S. Trust Insights on Wealth and Worth: Annual Survey on High-Net-Worth and Ultra-High-Net-Worth Americans* (Charlotte, NC: Bank of America Private Wealth Management, 2016).
8. Scott Fithian and Todd Fithian, *The Right Side of the Table: Where Do You Sit in the Minds of the Affluent?* (Denver, CO: FPA Press, 2007).

Chapter 10: Fielding a Multigenerational Team

1. Carnegie once noted how his approach was similar to the famous John Wesley sermon on money, which said it was a man's duty to make all the money he can, to save all he can, *and then* to give all he can. See Andrew Carnegie, "The Advantages of Poverty," in *The Gospel of Wealth and Other Timely Essays* (New York: The Century Co., 1900). See also Joseph Frazier Wall, *Andrew Carnegie* (Pittsburgh, PA: University of Pittsburgh Press, 1989).
2. See Peter M. Ascoli, *Julius Rosenwald: The Man Who Built Sears, Roebuck and Advanced the Cause of Black Education in the American South* (Bloomington, IN: Indiana University Press, 2006).
3. Elizabeth Arias, Melonie Heron, and Jiaquan Xu, "United States Life Tables, 2012," *National Vital Statistics Reports* 65:8 (2016), https://www.cdc.gov/nchs/data/nvsr/nvsr65/nvsr65_08.pdf. Wealthy individuals like Carnegie and Rosenwald had longer expected life spans than the average person of their time, for a variety of reasons. But their longevity is still

notable for the era, and the causes they supported in their unusual old age are better for it.

4. On "Gen Z," see Elizabeth Segran, "Your Guide to Gen Z: The Frugal, Brand-wary, Determined Anti-Millennials," *Fast Company,* September 8, 2016; and David Stillman and Jonah Stillman, *Gen Z @ Work: How the Next Generation Is Transforming the Workplace* (New York: HarperBusiness, 2017).

5. On the growing shift toward next generation control of family foundations, see Richard Nalley, "Family Foundations: Millennials Take Charge," *Barron's,* December 10, 2016.

6. See Steve Treat's TED Talk entitled "Becoming a Peer."

7. Much of the generational personalities work, and the definitions of each historical generation, has its origins in writings by William Strauss and Neil Howe, originally given in *Generations: The History of America's Future, 1584 to 2069* (New York: Quill, 1991). For how this plays out in the for-profit space, see Saratovsky and Feldmann, *Cause for Change* (see Chap. 5, n. 2); and Lancaster and Stillman, *When Generations Collide* (see Chap. 8, n. 5).

8. On the relative neglect of Gen X despite its major giving potential, see Heather Joslyn, "Generation X Comes of Age as Donor Group with Big Potential," *Chronicle of Philanthropy,* September 6, 2016.

9. Dan Schawbel, *The High School Careers Study* (Boston, MA: Millennial Branding, 2014).

10. See Stillman and Stillman, *Gen Z @ Work.*

11. This is a central finding of "group identity formation" theory. See Bruce W. Tuckman, "Developmental Sequence in Small Groups," *Psychological Bulletin* 63 (1965): 384–399.

12. On the complexities of various different models of multigenerational family foundations, see Kelin E. Gersick, *Generations of Giving: Leadership and Continuity in Family Foundations* (Lanham, MA: Lexington Books, 2004).

Chapter 11: Next Gen Philanthropic Identity

1. James Grubman, *Strangers in Paradise: How Families Adapt to Wealth Across Generations,* (San Jose, CA: Family Wealth Consulting, 2013).

2. This phrase "paralyzed by predecessors, prosperity, or possibilities" comes from Kristin Keffler, "Grace in the Cauldron of Chaos" (Illumination360, 2010), http://www.connect-gens.com/docs/Article-Grace-in-the-Cauldron -of-Chaos-Next-Gen.pdf.

3. Bryan Stevenson, *Just Mercy: A Story of Justice and Redemption,* reprint edition (New York: Spiegel & Grau, 2015).

4. Jeffrey Jensen Arnett, *Emerging Adulthood: The Winding Road from the Late Teens through the Twenties* (New York: Oxford University Press, 2014).

5. Meg Jay, *The Defining Decade: Why Your Twenties Matter—And How to Make the Most of Them Now* (New York: Grand Central Publishing, 2012), p. 6.

6. Erik H. Erikson, *Identity and the Lifecycle* (New York: W.W. Norton & Company, [1959] 1994).

7. See James E. Hughes, Jr., Susan E. Massenzio, and Keith Whitaker, *The Voice of the Rising Generation: Family Wealth and Wisdom* (Bloomberg Press, 2014). This book speaks to the next generation of wealth holders, encouraging them to individuate, develop resilience, and find their own voice despite the significant footprints of their successful predecessors.

8. For helpful books, see Charles Bronfman, and Jeffrey Solomon, *The Art of Doing Good: Where Passion Meets Action* (San Francisco: Jossey-Bass, 2012); and Paul Shoemaker, *Can't Not Do: The Compelling Social Drive That Changes Our World* (Hoboken, NJ: Wiley, 2015). Shoemaker writes extensively on the importance of identity formation, which he calls "finding your focus."

9. PricewaterhouseCooper, *Anticipating a New Age in Wealth Management: Global Private Banking and Wealth Management Survey* (PwC Private Banking and Wealth Management, 2011), https://www.pwc.com/gx/en /private-banking-wealth-mgmt-survey/pdf/global-private-banking-wealth -2011.pdf.

Chapter 12: Conclusion

1. Havens, O'Herlihy, and Schervish, "Charitable Giving" (see Chap. 1, n. 10).

2. For commentary on this democratic challenge, see Rob Reich, Chiara Cordelli, and Lucy Bernholz, eds., *Philanthropy in Democratic Societies: History, Institutions, Values.* (Chicago: University of Chicago Press, 2016); David Callahan, "Hollowed Out: Big Donors, Inequality, and the Threat to Civil Society," *Inside Philanthropy,* November 17, 2016; Joel L. Fleishman, *The Foundation: A Great American Secret: How Private Wealth is Changing the World* (New York: Public Affairs Books, 2007).

3. This research challenge is one of selection bias. See the Appendix for further explanation of this bias and why we feel it, in part, serves a positive research purpose.

4. See www.gatesnotes.com/2016-Annual-Letter.

Appendix

1. 21/64 and Dorothy A. Johnson Center for Philanthropy, *Next Gen Donors* (see Chap. 1, n. 15).

2. Note that interviewees were not selected from survey respondents because the survey was anonymous. We only identified the interviewees who took the survey if they volunteered this information during the interview.
3. The interviews were conducted in two intensive phases—the first in 2012 and the second in 2015–2016.
4. The survey instrument and interview guide are both available at nextgen donors.org.
5. For more extensive treatment of the survey, see the original report: 21/64 and Dorothy A. Johnson Center for Philanthropy, *Next Gen Donors* (see Chap. 1, n. 15).
6. Note that not all survey respondents answered every demographic question, and not all interviewees filled out the online questionnaire we used to gather this information. Specific "n" for each question is included in Table A.1.
7. We discovered after their interviews that two interviewees were slightly over 40 at the time of the interview. We kept them in the sample because this age variation was small and was outweighed by the need for sufficient interview data. However, in the survey, anyone over 40 who responded was eliminated from the sample.
8. For initial evidence that many of the qualities of U.S. next gen donors will be shared by similar donors around the world, see Clark et al., "What do the next . . ." (see Chap. 1, n. 15).
9. For data on this, see Taylor, *Next America* (see Chap. 1, n. 12).
10. See Lisa A. Keister, *Faith and Money: How Religion Contributes to Wealth and Poverty* (Cambridge: Cambridge University Press, 2011). For evidence that Jews have a higher average rate of giving, and higher median level of giving, than the general population, see Jim Gerstein, Steven M. Cohen, and J. Shawn Landres, *Connected to Give: Key Findings from the National Study of American Jewish Giving* (Los Angeles: Jumpstart, 2013).
11. See Urvashi Vaid and Ashindi Maxton, *The Apparitional Donor: Understanding and Engaging High Net Worth Donors of Color* (POC Donor Collaborative, 2017).

ABOUT THE AUTHORS

Sharna Goldseker is a speaker, writer, and consultant who engages multiple generations in the intersection of values and strategy to transform the ways in which they give. She is today's leading expert on multigenerational and next generation philanthropy and—as a next gen donor herself—offers a trusted insider's perspective. As executive director of 21/64, the nonprofit practice she founded to serve philanthropic and family enterprises, she has created the industry's gold-standard tools for transforming how philanthropic families define their values, collaborate, and govern.

Sharna is a recipient of the J.J. Greenberg Memorial Award for extraordinary leadership and the RayLign Foundation Family Well-Being Award. She was named one of 2016's Women of Influence by *New York Business Journal* and one of 2014's Women to Watch by *Jewish Women International*. She is editor of *The Grandparent Legacy Project*, a resource that helps philanthropic elders pass on their stories to future generations, and has written for such publications as *Forbes and Stanford Social Innovation Review*. She has been featured in others such as the *New York Times, Chronicle of Philanthropy,* and *The Huffington Post*.

She has been a consistent presence in the philanthropic field for two decades and is known for her quiet gravitas and insight. Today, prominent nonprofits, philanthropic networks, and foundations look to Sharna for training in next generation engagement and multigenerational advising. Sharna currently serves on the board of directors of the Goldseker Foundation, a foundation established by her great-uncle, and is a member of the Collaboration for Family Flourishing, a network of leading family wealth advisors. She is married, with two children, and lives in New York City.

Michael Moody helps people appreciate and navigate today's complex world of giving and social innovation. He holds the world's first-ever endowed chair for family philanthropy and is a well-known writer, speaker, and commentator on the vital role that the nonprofit and philanthropic sector plays in our lives. He has coauthored two books, *Understanding Philanthropy: Its Meaning and Mission* with Robert L. Payton (2008) and *The Philanthropy Reader* with Beth Breeze (2016), as well as many other publications on donors, ethical giving, and philanthropic trends.

As the Frey Foundation Chair at the Dorothy A. Johnson Center for Philanthropy at Grand Valley State University, Michael straddles the worlds of scholarship and practice, shining a light on the connections between giving and lived experience with both expertise and enthusiasm. A cultural sociologist with a master's in social science from the University of Chicago and a PhD from Princeton, he has strived for over 25 years to grow and spread knowledge of philanthropy. He started his career as one of the first employees of Indiana University's renowned Center on Philanthropy, and later held faculty positions at Boston University and the University of Southern California and ran a consulting practice based in Richmond, Virginia. Michael lives with his wife in Grand Rapids, Michigan, and balances a life of the mind by practicing kung fu and hitting golf balls and drums, though rarely at the same time.

INDEX